PTE ACADEMIC™

EXPERT

B1 COURSEBOOK

Clare Walsh and Lindsay Warwick

Contents

Module	Section	Reading 1 / Listening 1	Academic vocabulary 1	Language development 1	Speaking 1 / Writing 1
1 A good influence (p.7)	**A** Have you got what it takes?	**Reading** Multiple-choice, choose single answer (pp. 8–9) **Listening** Highlight correct summary (p. 12)	Education; Collocations related to education; Word patterns (p. 10)	Parts of speech; Word formation (p. 13)	**Speaking** Read aloud; Answer short question (p. 11) **Summary writing** Summarize written text (p. 14)
Module 1 review (p. 22)					
2 More than a feeling (p.23)	**A** Feeling emotional	**Reading** Reading: Fill in the blanks (pp. 24–25) **Listening** Multiple-choice, choose single answer (p. 28)	Adjectives and prepositions related to feelings; Academic collocations (p. 26)	Relative clauses (p. 29)	**Speaking** Repeat sentence; Answer short question (p. 27) **Writing** Write essay (p. 30)
Module 2 review (p. 38)					
3 Wild world (p. 39)	**A** Changing planet	**Reading** Multiple-choice, choose multiple answers (pp. 40–41) **Listening** Select missing word (p. 44)	Academic collocations list; Academic word list; The environment; Prepositional phrases related to the environment (p. 42)	Future forms; Predictions (p. 45)	**Speaking** Read aloud; Answer short question (p. 43) **Summary writing** Summarize spoken text (p. 46)
Module 3 review (p. 54)					
4 The global village (p. 55)	**A** A globalised world	**Reading** Re-order paragraphs (pp. 56–57) **Listening** Multiple-choice, choose multiple answers (p. 60)	Academic word list; Academic collocations list; Travel and transport (p. 58)	Past tenses (p. 61)	**Speaking** Repeat sentence; Answer short question (p. 59) **Writing** Write essay (p. 62)
Module 4 review (p. 70)					
5 Sensational (p. 71)	**A** Sound	**Reading** Reading & writing: Fill in the blanks (pp. 72–73) **Listening** Fill in the blanks (p. 76)	Academic collocations list; Academic word list; Entertainment; Word formation (p. 74)	Expressing quantity (p. 77)	**Speaking** Read aloud; Answer short question (p. 75) **Summary writing** Summarize spoken text (p. 78)
Module 5 review (p.86)					

Contents

Section	Reading 2 / Listening 2	Academic vocabulary 2	Language development 2	Speaking 2	Writing 2
B How you work	**Listening** Highlight correct summary; Write from dictation (p. 15) **Reading** Multiple-choice, choose single answer (p. 18)	Compound nouns related to work; Verb + noun collocations related to work; Easily confused words related to work (p. 17)	Present tenses (p. 16)	Describe image (p. 19)	Summarize written text (pp. 20–21)
B Attitudes to life	**Listening** Multiple choice, choose single answer; Write from dictation (p. 31) **Reading** Fill in the blanks (p. 34)	Easily confused words and collocations related to family, friends and people (p. 33)	Sentence structure and prepositional phrases (p. 32)	Re-tell lecture (p. 35)	Write essay (pp. 36–37)
B Animal magic	**Listening** Select missing word; Write from dictation (p. 47) **Reading** Multiple-choice, choose multiple answers (p. 50)	Collocations related to the natural world; Negative prefixes (p. 49)	Zero and first conditionals (p. 48)	Describe image (p. 51)	Summarize spoken text (pp. 52–53)
B A cultural world	**Listening** Multiple-choice, choose multiple answers; Write from dictation (p. 63) **Reading** Re-order paragraphs (p. 66)	Academic collocations list; Word formation with language and culture; Academic word list (p. 65)	Second conditional (p. 64)	Re-tell lecture (p. 67)	Write essay (pp. 68–69)
B Vision	**Listening** Highlight incorrect words (p. 79) **Reading** Reading & writing: Fill in the blanks (p. 82)	Academic word list; Adverbs; The arts (p. 81)	Comparative adjectives; Superlative adjectives; Adjectives and adverbs (p. 80)	Describe image (p. 83)	Summarize spoken text (pp. 84–85)

3

Module	Section	Reading 1 Listening 1	Academic vocabulary 1	Language development 1	Speaking 1 Writing 1
6 City intelligence (p. 87)	A Cities for today	**Reading** Multiple-choice, choose single answer (pp. 88–89) **Listening** Highlight correct summary (p. 92)	Cities and towns; Academic collocations list; Academic word list; Prefixes (p. 90)	Verb patterns (p. 93)	**Speaking** Repeat sentence; Answer short question (p. 91) **Writing** Write essay (p. 94)
Module 6 review (p. 102)					
7 The future of food (p. 103)	A The food we produce	**Reading** Reading: Fill in the blanks (pp. 104–105) **Listening** Multiple-choice, choose single answer (p. 108)	Academic word list; Academic collocations list; Food; Word categorisation (pp. 106–107)	The passive (p. 109)	**Speaking** Read aloud; Answer short question (p. 107) **Summary writing** Summarize written text (p. 110)
Module 7 review (p. 118)					
8 Being human (p. 119)	A Man and machine	**Reading** Reading & writing: Fill in the blanks (pp. 120–121) **Listening** Select missing word (p. 124)	Science; Phrasal verbs; Technology (p. 122)	Expressing obligation and permission (p. 125)	**Speaking** Repeat sentence; Answer short question (p. 123) **Writing** Write essay (p. 126)
Module 8 review (p. 134)					
9 Winning counts! (p. 135)	A A sporting chance	**Reading** Re-order paragraphs (p. 136–137) **Listening** Multiple-choice, choose multiple answers (p. 140)	Academic collocations list; Academic word list; Verb + preposition; Sports (p. 138)	Articles (p. 141)	**Speaking** Read aloud; Answer short question (p. 139) **Summary writing** Summarize spoken text (p. 142)
Module 9 review (p.150)					
10 Let's talk! (p. 151)	A Now you're talking!	**Reading** Multiple-choice, choose multiple answers (p. 152–153) **Listening** Fill in the blanks (p. 156)	Academic nouns; Academic collocations list; Research (p. 154)	Present perfect and past simple (p. 157)	**Speaking** Repeat sentence; Answer short question (p. 155) **Writing** Write essay (p. 158)
Module 10 review (p. 166)					

Exam overview (p. 6)   Reviews (p. 22) (p. 38) (p. 54) (p. 70) (p. 86) (p. 102) (p. 118) (p. 134) (p. 150) (p. 166)

Test reference (pp. 167–189)   Expert speaking (pp. 190–195)

Expert writing (pp. 196–202)   Expert grammar (pp. 203–214)

Contents

Section	Reading 2 Listening 2	Academic vocabulary 2	Language development 2	Speaking 2	Writing 2
B Homes of the future	**Listening** Highlight correct summary; Write from dictation (p. 95) **Reading** Multiple-choice, choose single answer (p. 98)	Academic collocations list; Academic word list; Social problems (p. 97)	Expressing probability; Expressing future probability (p. 96)	Re-tell lecture (p. 99)	Write essay (pp. 100–101)
B The food we eat	**Listening** Multiple choice, choose single answer; Write from dictation (p. 111) **Reading** Reading: Fill in the blanks (p. 114)	Prepositions; Business (p. 113)	Reduced relative clauses (p. 112)	Describe image (p. 115)	Summarize written text (pp. 116–117)
B Body and soul	**Listening** Select missing word; Write from dictation (p. 127) **Reading** Reading & writing: Fill in the blanks (p. 130)	Academic collocations list; Academic word list Health (129)	Academic language	Re-tell lecture (p. 131)	Write essay (pp. 132–133)
B Do your best!	**Listening** Multiple choice, choose single answer; Write from dictation (p. 143) **Reading** Re-order paragraphs (p. 146)	Academic collocations list; Money (p. 145)	Grammatical linkers	Describe image (p. 147)	Summarize spoken text (pp. 148–149)
B Reaching the masses	**Listening** Highlight incorrect words (p. 159) **Reading** Multiple-choice, choose multiple answers (p. 162)	Academic collocations list; Academic word list; Shops and advertising (p. 161)	Reported speech (p. 160)	Re-tell lecture (p. 163)	Write essay (pp. 164–165)

Exam overview

▶ See the Exam reference on page 167 for more detailed information and task strategies.

The PTEA is completed online in a Pearson test centre. It takes around three hours, including an optional ten-minute break. Score Reports are available within five working days of taking the test; they show your overall score on a scale from 10 to 90, as well as scores for communicative skills (reading, writing, speaking and listening) and enabling skills (grammar, oral fluency, pronunciation, spelling, vocabulary and written discourse). The overall score is mapped to the Common European Framework of Reference (CEFR).

Task type	Communicative skills assessed	Number of tasks	Time allowed
Part 1: Speaking and writing			
Personal introduction	n/a (unscored)	1	1 minute
Read aloud	reading and speaking	6–7	30–35 minutes
Repeat sentence	listening and speaking	10–12	
Describe image	speaking	6–7	
Re-tell lecture	listening and speaking	3–4	
Answer short question	listening and speaking	10–12	
Summarize written text	reading and writing	2–3	50–60 minutes
Write essay	writing	1–2	
Part 2: Reading			
Multiple-choice, choose single answer	reading	2–3	32–41 minutes
Multiple-choice, choose multiple answers	reading	2–3	
Re-order paragraphs	reading	2–3	
Reading: Fill in the blanks	reading	4–5	
Reading & writing: Fill in the blanks	reading and writing	5–6	
Part 3: Listening			
Summarize spoken text	listening and writing	2–3	20–30 minutes
Multiple-choice, choose multiple answers	listening	2–3	23–28 minutes
Fill in the blanks	listening and writing	2–3	
Highlight correct summary	listening and reading	2–3	
Multiple-choice, choose single answer	listening	2–3	
Select missing word	listening	2–3	
Highlight incorrect words	listening and reading	2–3	
Write from dictation	listening and writing	3–4	

1 A good influence

Overview

1A
- **Reading:** Multiple-choice, choose single answer
- **Academic vocabulary:** Education and learning
- **Speaking:** Read aloud; Answer short question
- **Listening:** Highlight correct summary
- **Language development:** Parts of speech
- **Summary writing:** Summarize written text

1B
- **Listening:** Highlight correct summary; Write from dictation
- **Language development:** Present tenses
- **Academic vocabulary:** Work and jobs
- **Reading:** Multiple-choice, choose single answer
- **Speaking:** Describe image
- **Summary writing:** Summarize written text

Lead-in

1 Discuss the questions in pairs.
1 Describe a person you admire. Why do you admire that person?
2 Read the quotes. Do you agree with what the people think?

'Students are influenced by television, video games, advertising, music, fashion, and their teachers. I'm looking to hire teachers that can reverse that order.'

'The key to successful leadership is influence, not authority.'
Kenneth H. Blanchard, author and management expert

'You don't have to be a person of influence to be influential. In fact, the most influential people in my life are probably not even aware of the things they've taught me.'
Scott Adams, cartoonist

2 Work in pairs. Look at the list of influences in our lives and discuss the questions.

| brothers and sisters | country of birth | famous people | friends | parents | teachers | television |

1 How do these people/things influence your life?
2 Which of these has the greatest influence on a person's life?
3 How might these sometimes have a negative influence?

1A Have you got what it takes?

Reading 1 (Multiple-choice, choose single answer)

Before you read   1   Discuss the questions in pairs. Check the meaning of the words in bold in a dictionary if you are unsure.
1 Do you think all students have the same amount of **motivation**?
2 Were you ever given a **reward** for doing well at school? What was it?
3 Do you think **punishment** works with children who behave badly?

Identifying main points and text development   In *Multiple-choice, choose single answer*, you will need to identify the difference between the main point and the supporting information in a text.

2a A topic sentence is a sentence which summarises the main idea in a paragraph. Look at the underlined topic sentence in paragraph 1 of the text and answer the questions.
1 Where do you usually find the topic sentence?
2 Does the paragraph continue with a general discussion or with examples?

There are two types of motivation. Students with intrinsic motivation are fascinated by a subject or its usefulness in life and will frequently use phrases such as 'Speaking English allows me to meet new people.' Extrinsic motivation comes from outside consequences of actions. Students with extrinsic motivation will use phrases such as 'My dad will give me €50 if I pass this exam.'

Extrinsic motivation can have an effect on intrinsic motivation. However, this is not always in ways we might expect. In one study, psychologists promised to give a group of children sweets if they completed a drawing. These children showed less intrinsic interest than the group who were invited to draw without the promise of rewards. In another study, children who were threatened with punishment if they played with a particular toy showed more intrinsic interest in that toy.

b Underline the topic sentence in paragraph 2. What information follows the topic sentence?

c The answer to multiple-choice questions often paraphrases a sentence in the text. Which two sentences (1–4) best paraphrase the topic sentences in paragraphs 1 and 2?
1 Intrinsic motivation is more common than extrinsic motivation.
2 People are motivated to work harder for two different kinds of reasons.
3 There may be surprising effects of extrinsic motivation on intrinsic motivation.
4 Children work better when they are offered something nice in the end.

Module 1
A good influence   1A

3a Look at the text in Exercise 4. Which sentence (1–3) best paraphrases the topic sentence?
  1 Students need to have goals to work towards.
  2 Students will always put more effort into their social activities.
  3 Students generally have something they are keen and willing to do.

b What information follows the topic sentence?
  1 comparison and contrast of different types of motivation
  2 examples of different kinds of motivation and reasons why they are important
  3 identifying a problem with motivation and explaining why it exists

Test practice
➤ EXPERT STRATEGIES page 177

4 Complete the task.

Read the text and answer the multiple-choice question by selecting the correct response. Only one response is correct.

Almost all students are motivated in one way or another. One student may be keenly interested in classroom subjects and purposely look for information and challenging coursework. Another student may be more concerned with the social side of school, socialising with classmates frequently and attending after-school activities almost every day. Motivation is important in education because it has several effects on students' learning and behaviour. It encourages students to work towards a particular goal, increases the amount of effort and energy the student invests, makes students more likely to begin and continue with activities, affects cognitive processes and decides which consequences are rewarding or punishing. Because of these issues just identified, motivation produces improved performance.

By writing this article, the writer wants to show that

A ○ students generally show less motivation than they should.
B ○ ways of increasing student motivation have been used well.
C ○ the effects of student motivation can be seen in positive results.
D ○ some students use their motivation in ways that waste time.

➤ **HELP**

• Which option suggests a moral question about student behaviour? Is this in the text?
• Which option suggests a judgement on how students use their time? Is this in the text?

Task analysis

5 Work in pairs. Compare and discuss how you approached the task.
  1 Which options were the opposite of what was said in the text?
  2 Which options were not mentioned?
  3 Did the correct option refer to one sentence or the general idea?

Discussion

6 Discuss the questions in pairs.
  1 What are your reasons for taking this course?
  2 Do you think that extrinsic motivation works?

7 Check the meaning of these key words from the text. Write them in your vocabulary notebook with an example sentence.

EXPERT WORD CHECK

cognitive processes   consequences   performance   psychologists
threaten

➤ See **Reading 2** for more practice of this task type.

1A Module 1
A good influence

Academic vocabulary 1

Education

1a Work in pairs. Discuss the meaning of the words in bold.
1 There are some **benefits** of **homeschooling** but there is also a **negative** side.
2 Many countries see **single-sex education** as a **positive** thing.
3 Large **institutions** offer better **support** for students.
4 It's more effective to **reward** good behaviour than to **punish** poor behaviour.
5 The main **aims** of **higher education** should be to **carry out** research, not to teach.

b Complete the article with words from Exercise 1a.

---

search News

THE MOST SUCCESSFUL EDUCATION IN THE WORLD?

Experts regularly ¹ _____ research to identify the best education system. Many institutions offering ² _____, particularly undergraduate programmes, compete internationally for students. So what system works the best? Many people believe that ³ _____ , where boys go to one school and girls go to another, is better and has more ⁴ _____ than problems. These schools often have very ⁵ _____ results in end-of-school tests. However, with the internet and better communications, more children don't go to school but learn through ⁶ _____ . There have always been worries that not mixing with other children would have a(n) ⁷ _____ effect on their social skills when they are older but there has not been much research recently in ⁸ _____ of this argument.
Educational ⁹ _____ in different countries may have very different views on how to ¹⁰ _____ good behaviour and ¹¹ _____ bad behaviour. There is one thing which all experts agree on: education systems in different countries, or even within different neighbourhoods, have different ¹² _____ to suit their social needs and there is no one ideal system.

---

c Discuss the questions in small groups.
1 What do you think of the different systems of education mentioned in the article?
2 Which system of education do you think works best in your country?

Collocations related to education

2 Choose the correct options in *italics* to complete the sentences.
1 It can be helpful for children to *attend / make* after-school classes.
2 Schools often don't *notice / identify* issues until it's too late.
3 It's a good thing to specialise in a *certain / particular* area at a young age.
4 Hard work is the only way to improve *academic / study* performance in the long term.
5 You need to *use / invest* time in your interests as well as your studies.
6 A *completely-educated / well-educated* population is important for the economy.

Word patterns

3a Complete the questions with prepositions. Then find the words in *italics* in the text on page 9 and check your answers.
1 What kind of people are *concerned* _____ children's education?
2 What are the good things about *socialising* _____ students outside of class?
3 How does the school you go to *have an effect* _____ your life later?
4 Are university graduates more *likely* _____ find a job than school-leavers?
5 Do you want to *continue* _____ education after finishing this course?

b Decide if the words (1–6) are verbs, nouns or adjectives. Then match them with their meanings (A–F).
1 challenging *adjective, C*   4 effort   _____
2 energy   _____   5 goal   _____
3 issue   _____   6 encourage _____

A physical and mental strength
B something you hope to do in the future
C difficult in an enjoyable way
D give someone the confidence to do something
E the hard work needed to do something
F a subject or problem that people often discuss

c Complete the sentences with the correct form of words from Exercises 3a and b. Then discuss the statements in pairs.
1 It's important that classes are _____ but not too difficult.
2 Teamwork is easier when students _____ with each other outside class.
3 Some people can learn a language without putting in much _____ .
4 Rewards are not enough to _____ students to work hard.
5 Family background has a major _____ on student results.

10

Module 1
1A A good influence

Speaking 1 (Read aloud; Answer short question)

Pronunciation: Dividing text into sense groups

In *Read aloud* you are scored on pronunciation and oral fluency. To improve in these areas, you will need to be able to divide a sentence into sense groups as you speak, pausing slightly between each.

1a 🎧 02 Listen to the sentence. The speaker makes a slight pause between sense groups. Slash marks (//) indicate the pauses. Work in pairs and take turns to read the sentence aloud.

> In most countries // education is not only a right // but an obligation. // Parents of children // who are found outside of school // can be punished under the law.

b 🎧 03 Listen and mark // between each sense group in the sentences.
  1 Education, in its modern form, appeared at the same time as the industrial revolution.
  2 The invention of the printing press, which was necessary for schools to exist, changed the way knowledge could be reproduced forever.

c Compare answers in pairs. Then practise reading the sentences aloud.

2a Mark // between each sense group in the sentences. Use the commas to help you decide.
  1 With industrialisation, factories needed a population that could read and count, skills which were unnecessary for an economy which was based on farming.
  2 Teaching the population to respect rules was also a key goal, and even learning knowledge was secondary to this. No lesson was ever considered so important that it could continue after the bell.

b 🎧 04 Listen and check your answers.

c Work in pairs. Practise reading the sentences aloud. Speak at natural speed, pausing slightly between sense groups.

Test practice 1: Read aloud

➤ **EXPERT STRATEGIES** page 170

3 Complete the task. Remember to think about sense groups as you read aloud.

> ⏱ 40 sec. *Look at the text below. In 40 seconds, you must read this text aloud as naturally and clearly as possible. You have 40 seconds to read aloud.*
>
> The idea of emotional intelligence has become more popular, particularly since the idea of 'emotional literacy' was developed, which, as the name suggests, is something that can be taught in schools. Many believe children can be taught the emotional skills to deal with difficulties and to come through experiences like failing, feeling strong and being able to cope.

Task analysis

4a 🎧 05 Listen to a model *Read aloud* answer. Did you pause in the same places in Exercise 3?

b Read the text in Exercise 3 again. Try reading in the same way as the model.

Test practice 2: Answer short question

➤ **EXPERT STRATEGIES** page 174

5 🎧 06 Complete the task in pairs. You will hear six questions.

> ⏱ 10 sec. *You will hear a question. Please give a simple and short answer. Often just one or a few words is enough.*

11

1A Module 1
A good influence

Listening 1 (Highlight correct summary)

Before you listen

1 Read the statements. Are they true or false, in your opinion?
   1 Young people today should study harder.
   2 Teachers need to think again about the way they teach.
   3 Young people need the same job skills as their parents.

Identifying the main idea

In *Highlight correct summary* you need to identify the main idea and the points that support that idea.

2a 🎧 07 Listen to a talk about an expert's view on education and take notes.

b What is Dr Wagner's main point? Choose from statements 1–3 in Exercise 1. Use your notes to help you.

Identifying supporting points

3a 🎧 07 Listen again and add to your notes.

b Tick (✓) the reasons Dr Wagner gives to support his main point. Use your notes to help you.
   1 Teams do not meet in one place any more.
   2 You need to be able to speak English.
   3 You need to understand that people live differently.
   4 Team leaders are usually managers.
   5 Young people do not have the skills to be leaders.

Test practice

➤ EXPERT STRATEGIES page 185

4 🎧 07 Underline the topic sentence in each paragraph. Then complete the task.

You will hear a recording. Choose the paragraph that best relates to the recording.

A ○ People who are involved in education need to think about the way they teach. It is important that young people leave school with the key skills they need to succeed in the workplace but they do not have these skills today.

B ○ Schools must work harder to train students to become good managers so that they can lead and influence other people. This is the most important skill that young people need if they want to get – and keep – their dream job.

C ○ Young people need to know how to talk to people around the world. Technology has changed the way business people meet; meetings are no longer held in one building but instead an international group of people meet online.

D ○ Young people are being taught just seven key workplace skills and one expert believes they will find it difficult to get work in the future as a result. He therefore suggests that schools need to change the skills that they teach in the future.

Task analysis

5 Why is each of the other three paragraphs incorrect? Match the incorrect paragraphs with reasons 1–3. There may be more than one reason for each paragraph.
   1 It gives information that is not on the recording.
   2 It talks about a minor supporting idea and not the main idea.
   3 It gives opposing information to the recording.

➤ See **Listening 2** for more practice of this task type.

Module 1
A good influence   1A

Language development 1

Parts of speech

▶ EXPERT GRAMMAR page 203

1a Write the words in the sentence next to the correct part of speech.

> Educators do not always teach useful skills for the workplace but this must change.

1 noun (e.g. *teacher*) _educators_ , _____ , _____
2 auxiliary verb (e.g. *is*) _____
3 modal verb (e.g. *can*) _____
4 verb (e.g. *create*) _____ , _____
5 adjective (e.g. *good*) _____
6 adverb (e.g. *carefully*) _____ , _____
7 preposition (e.g. *in*) _____
8 pronoun (e.g. *she*) _____
9 article (e.g. *a*) _____
10 conjunction (e.g. *and*) _____

b Find and correct the incorrect parts of speech in the sentences.

1 I work good first thing in the morning.
2 I try to write in English every daily.
3 I think I have a bad understand of English verb forms.
4 I enjoy meeting new people and speaking English with they.

Word formation

▶ EXPERT GRAMMAR page 203

2 Many words have different forms. Put the underlined words in the sentences in the correct place in the notes on the right. Then complete the rest of the notes.

1 Speaking fluently in English can be <u>challenging</u>.
2 Use an English–English dictionary to find the <u>definition</u> of this word.
3 I enjoy being <u>creative</u> with the English language.
4 I don't have a lot of <u>motivation</u> to write in English.
5 I want to be able to communicate in an English-speaking <u>society</u>.
6 It's a student's responsibility to <u>educate</u> themselves.
7 Vocabulary <u>development</u> is quite easy for me.
8 You need to be <u>intelligent</u> to learn a language.

	Noun	Verb	Adjective
1	_challenge_	_challenge_	_challenging_
2	____	____	____
3	____	____	____
4	____	____	____
5	____	____	____
6	____	____	____
7	____	____	____
8	____	-	____

3a Tick (✓) the words in the box that are both verbs and nouns. Use a dictionary to help you.

> affect   assess   benefit   challenge   comment
> design   focus   process   punish   repeat   reward
> solve   support   translate

b Write the noun forms of the words in Exercise 3a that you did not tick.

affect (v) – effect (n)

4a Choose the correct options in *italics* to complete the article.

How to learn vocabulary

English students are often [1] *challenge / challenged* by the number of words in the English language. So how can a student learn new words [2] *effect / effectively*? The first step is to record them in a notebook. Many students write down a word and then [3] *translate / translation* it into their own language. It is also important to write a [4] *define / definition* and example sentence so you can see it in context. Try to be [5] *creation / creative* and use pictures or diagrams. It is also [6] *beneficial / benefit* to write down common collocations as we often remember groups of words together.

After recording new words, you need to [7] *focus / focusing* on getting them into your long-term memory. You should also place [8] *importance / important* on [9] *repeat / repetition*. You need to see a word in context several times before you will remember it, so regular reading will have a big impact on your [10] *develop / development*. However, make sure you are [11] *motivate / motivated* by your reading material as this will [12] *affect / effect* how much attention you pay to it. If you are interested, you will remember more.

b How do you learn new vocabulary? Share your ideas with the class.

13

1A Module 1
A good influence

Summary writing 1 (Summarize written text)

Taking notes when reading a text

In *Summarize written text* it is important to recognise and note down key points in the reading text to help you understand it better. You can then use these points to form your summary.

1 Read paragraph 1 of the article. Then look at a student's notes and answer the questions.
   1 The words in the notes are key words. What are key words?
   2 Are there individual words or groups of words in the notes? Why?
   3 Are there any grammar words (e.g. articles, prepositions) in the notes? Why/Why not?
   4 Has the student copied words exactly from the text or has he/she re-organised them?

Online learning is becoming more popular but, according to a new study, students still believe it's easier to learn in a traditional classroom. Researchers recently asked 1,345 college students in the US about their views on the future of education. The study found that 53 percent of students agree that online colleges are reliable. However, only 43 percent think that online classrooms are better quality than traditional ones.

About 36 percent of students said that online learning gives you time to work and study and half of the students questioned think technology is necessary to education. However, almost 78 percent think it's easier to learn in a traditional classroom than through online courses.

Despite their preference for traditional classrooms, students still believe that education will become more virtual in the future. 19 percent predict that social media will be used to interest students in the classroom.

study: 1,345 college students, only 43% – online classroom better

2a Read paragraph 2 of the article and look at the underlined words. Which six words are not key words?

b Look at the notes for paragraph 2. Rewrite them to make them more effective.

*36% students online learning time to work study
half technology necessary education
78% easier learn traditional classroom*

3a Read paragraph 3 of the article. Find the key words and use them to help you write short, simple notes on the main point.

b Compare your notes in pairs. Have you included the same key information as your partner?

▶ See **Summary writing 2** for more practice of this task type.

1B How you work

Listening 2 (Highlight correct summary; Write from dictation)

Before you listen

1 Read the question and check the meaning of the words in bold in a dictionary. Then discuss the question.

> How does **social** media have a positive and negative impact on a company's **brand**, **recruitment**, **sales** and the amount of work produced?

Test practice 1: Highlight correct summary
➤ EXPERT STRATEGIES page 185

2 🎧 08 Complete the task. Remember to identify the main idea and supporting points.

> *You will hear a recording. Click on the paragraph that best relates to the recording.*
>
> A ○ There are both advantages and disadvantages of social media in the workplace. On one side, a company's brand can become stronger. On the other side, there is a chance that the company's brand will become weaker if an employee says something negative about the company.
>
> B ○ Because social media can stop employees working, some employers prevent them from using social media. However, these employers do not enjoy the benefits that social media can bring, such as an increase in customer demand for their product or a stronger brand.
>
> C ○ Social media can help employers to develop their businesses and find new staff. However, it is a problem when an employee criticises the company online or spends too much time using social media. To stop employees spending time on social media, employers must develop and challenge their staff.
>
> D ○ Employers only see the negative side of social media because they have too many problems with employees being rude or spending too much time using social media instead of working. Because this situation is challenging, it is easier for companies to stop the use of social media.

➤ **HELP**

Do any of the summaries
• include incorrect information or information not in the recording?
• fail to include the main idea and supporting points?

Test practice 2: Write from dictation
➤ EXPERT STRATEGIES page 189

3 🎧 09 Complete the task. You will hear three sentences. Then compare answers in pairs.

> *You will hear a sentence. Type the sentence in the box below exactly as you hear it. Write as much of the sentence as you can. You will hear the sentence only once.*

Task analysis

4 Answer the questions.
1 *Highlight correct summary*: Did you ignore summaries in Exercise 2 that gave incorrect information or information not in the recording?
2 *Write from dictation*: Did you guess words you could not remember in Exercise 3 by looking at the words around it?

1B Module 1
A good influence

Language development 2

Present tenses

> EXPERT GRAMMAR page 203

1a Choose the correct options in *italics* to complete the sentences from Listening 1.

> Employers [1] *currently experience / are currently experiencing* a love-hate relationship with social media. Some [2] *use / are using* it to their advantage: they [3] *reach / are reaching* more customers and [4] *improve / improving* their brand image through social networking sites. They [5] *also use / are also using* them for recruitment.

b Complete the sentences with the correct form of the verbs in brackets so they are true for you.
1 I _____ (study) in a language school at the moment.
2 I _____ (like) reading articles in other languages.
3 I _____ (feel) confident that I have the right answers.
4 I _____ (go) to work before I start studying.
5 I _____ (have) a lot of free time these days.

2a Read the article below and answer the questions.
1 What did the researchers look at in this study?
2 Which has a stronger influence on work: positive experiences or negative experiences?
3 What affects mood more: events at home or events in the workplace?

b Read the article again and underline the subject in each sentence. Then choose the correct options in *italics* to complete the article.

3a Look at the flowchart on the recruitment process and answer the questions.
1 Who writes the job description?
2 Who does the candidate send the CV to?
3 Who reviews the CVs?
4 Who does the department head interview?
5 Who checks the documents are correct?
6 Who sends the offer letter?

b Work in pairs and take it in turns to describe the recruitment process to your partner.

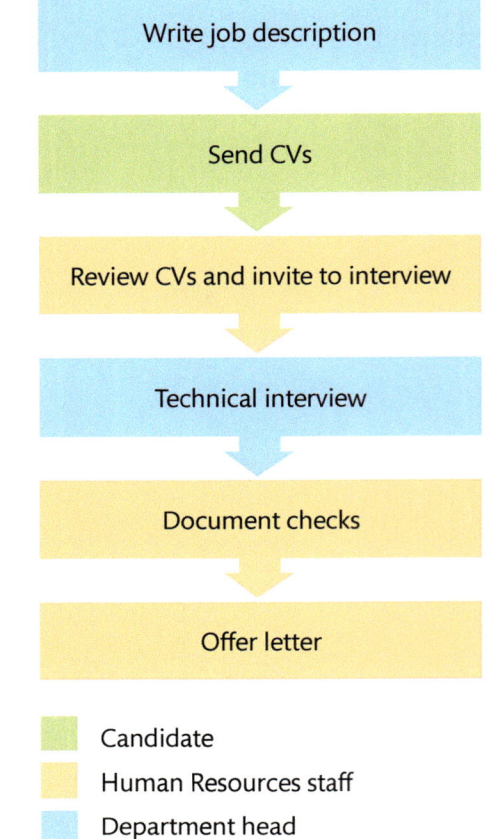

Waking up on the wrong side of the desk

You know how it goes. A traffic jam [1] *block / blocks* your way and you [2] *arrive / arrives* late in a bad mood. From there the day just [3] *go / goes* downhill.

Or does it? [4] *Do / Does* a bad mood really colour your whole day? A large amount of work from the past 20 years [5] *is / are* available on work-family conflicts but very few studies actually [6] *look / looks* at the effect of mood on performance in the workplace. Two scientists [7] *is / are* studying this at the moment. So far, the results of their research [8] *suggest / suggests* that positive and negative moods [9] *affect / affects* employees but that the effects of a positive mood [10] *is / are* more powerful. It seems that the mood people [11] *bring / brings* with them to work [12] *have / has* a stronger effect on the day's mood and on work performance than the mood changes which [13] *is / are* caused by events in the workplace. These findings [14] *mean / means* that performance might improve if businesses [15] *help / helps* employees to deal with mood-affecting influences in their private lives.

Module 1
1B A good influence

Academic vocabulary 2 AWL ACL

Compound nouns related to work

1a Match the beginnings of the sentences (1–6) with the endings (A–F). Then note the compound nouns in *italics*.

1 Normal *working*
2 Some companies use *social*
3 Many *development*
4 Employees use *networking*
5 Employers take an *active*
6 Negative comments may stop a *potential*

A *customer* from buying a company's products.
B *hours* for office workers are 9–5.
C *sites* to make new business contacts.
D *role* in making sure their staff are happy.
E *opportunities* are available for staff.
F *media* to recruit new staff.

b Which compound nouns in Exercise 1a are made up of adjective + noun? Which are made up of noun + noun?

adjective + noun: social media   noun + noun: working hours

Verb + noun collocations related to work

2a Complete the text with the words in the box.

address   affect   complete   establish   give   make
offer   providing   see   setting

Employers want to get the best work out of their employees, so they need to help them find some job satisfaction. Employers can challenge staff members by ¹_____ them new goals. They can also ²_____ development opportunities so staff can learn new skills. It's a good idea to ³_____ positive feedback to staff when they ⁴_____ tasks effectively. This will make them feel valued.

If a staff member is worried about an aspect of their job, the employer should ⁵_____ arrangements for that person to speak privately to a manager outside their team. This manager should try to ⁶_____ a good relationship with the staff member. Many employers ⁷_____ the positive side of this system: by listening to the employee's concerns and ⁸_____ support, they can quickly ⁹_____ an issue before it becomes too big and starts to ¹⁰_____ their work.

b 🎧 10 Listen and check your answers.

c Read the text again and underline the nouns that follow the verbs in the blanks.

d What do employers in your country do to help motivate employees to work hard? Think about the things in the box.

colleagues   facilities   other financial benefits
responsibility   salary   training
working environment   working hours

Easily confused words related to work

3 Complete the sentences with the words in *italics*.

1 *career, job, work*
   A When you start a new _____ , it's important to look motivated.
   B Many young people want to follow a _____ in the media.
   C It is difficult for young people to find _____ in some countries these days.

2 *hear, listen*
   A Employees should always _____ to their managers.
   B Employers don't want potential employees to _____ negative comments about them.

3 *salary, wages*
   A Some of the employees have asked for an increase in their annual _____ .
   B Staff receive _____ each Friday for the hours they worked during the week.

4 *raise, rise*
   A All employees expect their salaries to _____ each year.
   B If employers _____ their employees' salaries, the employees will only be more motivated for a short time.

17

1B Module 1
A good influence

Reading 2 (Multiple-choice, choose single answer)

ANY OTHER STRENGTHS?

Before you read

1 Look at the two interview questions that companies often ask candidates. Discuss the questions in pairs.
  1 How would you answer these interview questions?
  2 Why are they 'trick' questions?
  3 Do you think these questions have any value in a job interview?

'If you could be any superhero, who would it be?'

'What colour best represents your personality?'

Test practice

> EXPERT STRATEGIES page 177

2 Complete the task. Think about the difference between the main point and the supporting information in the text.

Read the text and answer the multiple-choice question by selecting the correct response. Only one response is correct.

| Trick interview questions are annoying. You would have to be a bit strange to feel comfortable with them. But ever since Microsoft decided to use 'brain teaser questions' in recruitment interviews back in the 1990s, they've been growing in popularity. They don't necessarily work though. They also actively discourage good candidates and have a long-term effect on a company's ability to attract talent, as reported in research that came out in October. After putting 360 participants through job interviews, the researchers found that the most qualified workers preferred not to attend interviews that use trick questions because they personally see them as unfair and are designed to make them fail. | According to the research, trick interview questions fail for which reason?

A ○ Modern companies are not using them.

B ○ Skilled people are not attracted to them.

C ○ Ordinary people are not able to answer them.

D ○ High levels of ability are needed to understand them. |

> HELP
> • Read the first sentence. What is the writer's view of this topic?
> • Read the task question. Whose view do you need to identify?
> • Where in the text is this view reported?

Task analysis

3 Work in pairs. Compare and discuss how you approached the task.
  1 Which options were the easiest to locate in the text?
  2 Where was the correct option paraphrased in the text?

Discussion

4 Discuss the questions in pairs.
  1 Do you think that interviews are a good way of choosing new employees?
  2 How do people find a new job in your country?

Module 1
A good influence — 1B

Speaking 2 (Describe image)

Organising your description

To score well on *Describe image*, you need to be able to organise your description of a chart.

1 a Look at the chart in Exercise 4 and complete the topic sentence.

The chart _____ the percentage of people who _____ in four countries in the year _____ .

b An overview sentence summarises the results of the research. Which is the correct overview sentence for the chart?
1. There was a large difference in the percentage of people working in these countries.
2. The country with the largest percentage of the population working was Qatar.
3. Some countries have a higher level of unemployment than others.

c What is the difference between a topic sentence and an overview sentence?

2 a Complete the sentences with the words in the box.

| clear | gap | highest | illustrates | much lower |
| over half | possible | 70 percent |

A The _____ percentage can be seen in Qatar, where around _____ of the population is in employment.
B It's _____ that some of these countries have high unemployment.
C China is the only other country with _____ the population in work. However, in Turkey and Iraq the numbers are _____ – around 25 percent and 35 percent respectively.
D It's _____ that there's quite a large _____ in the size of working populations.
E The chart _____ how many people are in the labour force in four countries.

b Match the stages of describing a chart (1–5) with the sentences in Exercise 2a (A–E). Then compare answers in pairs.

Stages of a description
1. *a topic sentence of what the chart shows*
2. *an overview sentence about the results*
3. *the country with the highest %*
4. *the other statistics*
5. *providing a conclusion*

Sample response

3 🎧 11 Listen to a student describing the chart and check your answers in Exercise 4. Then listen again. Does she finish within 40 seconds?

Test practice

➤ EXPERT STRATEGIES page 172

4 Complete the task in pairs. Take turns to describe the chart.

> **40 sec.** *Look at the chart below. In 25 seconds, please speak into the microphone and describe in detail what the chart is showing. You will have 40 seconds to give your response.*

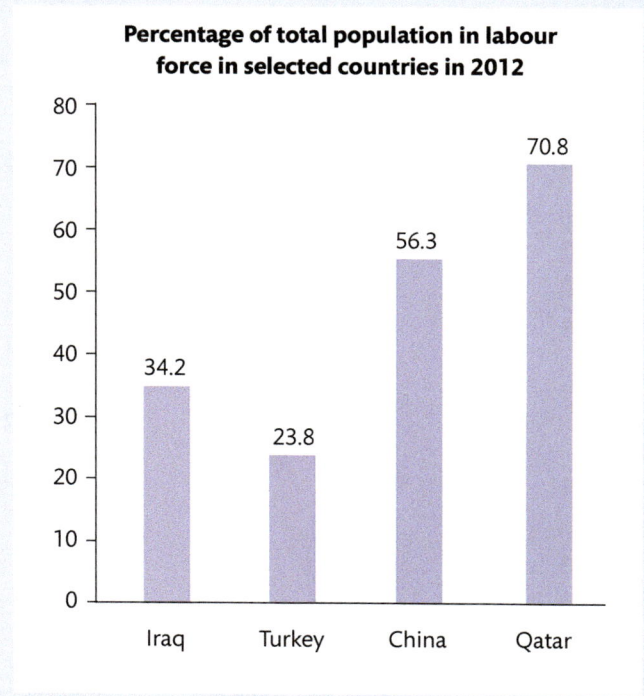

Percentage of total population in labour force in selected countries in 2012

➤ HELP

Look at the numbers in the chart. Where do they start and end?

5 Turn to page 190 and complete another timed test practice.

➤ EXPERT SPEAKING page 190

Task analysis

6 Did you:
1. finish in the 40-second time limit?
2. include all five stages of the descriptions?

1B Module 1
A good influence

Summary writing 2 (Summarize written text)

Lead-in 1 Discuss the questions in pairs.
1 What job would you like to do in the future? What has influenced your decision?
2 What job do you think the identical twins in the photo do? Do you think their job choice was influenced by childhood experiences or by their genes (DNA)?

Understand the task
> EXPERT STRATEGIES page 175

2a Read the instructions for *Summarize written text* and answer the questions.
1 How many sentences should your summary have?
2 In the test, where do you type your summary?
3 How much time do you have to complete the task?
4 How is your summary scored?

b Read the text quickly. Look at the first and last line of the text and the first line of each paragraph. What is the topic of the text?

> ⏱ 10 min. *Read the passage below and summarize it using one sentence. Type your response in the box at the bottom of the screen. You have 10 minutes to finish this task. Your response will be judged on the quality of your writing and on how well your response presents the key points in the passage.*

Twin studies have been very useful in giving us information about whether our genes or our environment makes us who we are. A surprising result is the way that genes influence our work. At a basic level, our genes affect how we look and so they influence whether we can become a basketball player or a supermodel, for example. However, there is evidence that genes influence our job choice in much greater ways.

Research shows that identical twins choose more similar jobs than non-identical twins. In fact, identical twins who have grown up apart choose more similar jobs than non-identical twins who have grown up together. Studies also show that identical twins are more likely to find the same kind of work satisfying. The research suggests that our genes affect both the satisfaction that comes from doing a job and the satisfaction that comes from working conditions such as a person's pay or their manager.

So what does this mean? It means that from birth, you are more likely to prefer one occupation to another and find certain jobs more satisfying than others. However, genes are not the only factor. Other things in your life, such as family background and education, will also be influential in your career choices.

Plan your summary sentence

3a Read the text more carefully. Find the key words and use them to help you write notes on the key information.

b Compare your notes in pairs. Has your partner included any information that you haven't?

c Look at the underlined sentences in paragraphs 1 and 2 of the text. Which one is the topic sentence of each paragraph? Can you find the topic sentence of paragraph 3?

Module 1
A good influence — 1B

d Look at your notes again. What is the main point of the text? Use these questions to help you.
1 What have twin studies shown?
2 What are the results of this?

Language and content

4a In a summary, a writer has to connect ideas within a text. Look at the summaries and underline the words or phrases that express cause (why something happens) and effect (the result of something).
1 Studies have shown that people decide on a job <u>because</u> their genes influence what they want to do.
2 Scientists have discovered that identical twins have the same genes, so they choose similar jobs.
3 A person gets their genes from their parents, with the result that they choose the same job as their mother or father.
4 Research suggests that genes decide how happy we are in our jobs, as we choose jobs based on our skills.
5 Scientists believe that we do not have a choice over our job for the reason that genes decide it for us.
6 Twins choose quite similar jobs and, therefore, it is likely that genes affect the work we choose.

b Write the words and phrases you underlined in Exercise 4a in the correct column.

Cause	Effect
because	_____
_____	_____
_____	_____

c Join each pair of sentences in two different ways using the words in brackets.
1 Non-identical twins do not have the same genes. They are less likely to choose the same job. (therefore, because)
2 Genes determine our height. They determine whether we can become basketball players or not. (as, so)
3 Identical twins choose more similar jobs than non-identical twins. They have the same genes. (reason, result)

d Look at the example phrases in the table. Choose one phrase to begin your summary sentence. Then choose one word or phrase to express cause or one to express effect to use in your summary sentence.

Beginning the summary	Twin studies show that … Research suggests that … Researchers believe that …
Cause	… **as** our genes affect these decisions … … **because** twins choose similar jobs … … **for the reason that** it affects job satisfaction …
Effect	… **therefore** our genes influence our job choice … … **are a result/consequence** of our genes … … **so** our genes help to decide on our career …

Write your summary sentence

5 Write your summary sentence. Use your notes from Exercise 3 and the language in Exercise 4 to help you.

Check your summary sentence

▶ EXPERT WRITING page 196

6 Check your summary sentence using the checklist on page 196.

1B Module 1
A good influence

Review

1 Complete the sentences with words formed from the words in brackets.
1. Single-sex schools _____ (education) boys and girls separately.
2. If teens _____ (social) too much, it can affect their grades.
3. Different schools _____ (punishment) bad behaviour in different ways.
4. A teacher's job is to give _____ (supportive) to their students.
5. A good night's sleep is _____ (benefit) for learning.
6. There are different types of _____ (intelligent).
7. A teenager's body clock is _____ (influence) in the way they learn.
8. It is good to set yourself _____ (challenge) goals when learning.

2 Complete the text with the words in the box.

active   affect   complete   effect   likely   media
negative   potential

With the increased popularity of social ¹_____, employers today are taking a more ²_____ role in checking whether ³_____ employees are suitable for a company or not. More and more employers are looking at applicants' online profiles to find out what kind of person they are and what they do in their free time as this can ⁴_____ the work they do and their ability to ⁵_____ tasks. They also look for any ⁶_____ comments made about previous employers as this type of behaviour can have a significant ⁷_____ on a company's brand. So, employees who are careful about what they say online are more ⁸_____ to receive a job offer than those who are not.

3a Choose the correct options in *italics* to complete the sentences about creativity.
1. Boredom *encourages / rewards* children to be creative.
2. Children who are busy all the time are less *worried / likely* to use their imagination.
3. We should be more *concerned / interested* with reducing the amount of technology children use.
4. Parents who want to *raise / rise* their children's level of intelligence should turn off the TV.
5. Children should spend time alone for the simple *reason / result* that they need thinking time.
6. Young people who want a *career / work* in the arts need to develop their creativity.
7. Children who *know / socialise* with each other online are less likely to play creatively.
8. *As / Therefore* children use their imagination more, they often find unusual solutions to things.

b Tick (✓) the sentences in Exercise 3a that you agree with.

4 Complete the article with the present simple or present continuous form of the verbs in brackets.

According to traditional stereotypes, men ¹_____ (make) things and women ²_____ (clean) or ³_____ (take) care of people. Men were traditionally expected to become engineers, doctors and mechanics, whereas women were sent to work as cooks, cleaners and carers. These days, both men and women should ⁴_____ (have) the opportunity to do any job they desire. But do they?

It is still true that very few women ⁵_____ (be) engineers but in the UK the number of male and female doctors is the same and currently more women ⁶_____ (study) medicine at university. In addition, because of the high unemployment that ⁷_____ (exist) in many countries right now, more men ⁸_____ (choose) jobs that are traditionally female. They ⁹_____ (work) in kindergartens or primary schools, and more ¹⁰_____ (train) to be nurses. Of course, women traditionally ¹¹_____ (stay) at home and look after the children but these days men ¹²_____ (do) it too, either because they ¹³_____ (want) to or because their wives have more secure jobs.

2 More than a feeling

2A
- **Reading:** Reading: Fill in the blanks
- **Academic vocabulary:** Feelings and emotions
- **Speaking:** Repeat sentence; Answer short question
- **Listening:** Multiple-choice, choose single answer
- **Language development:** Relative clauses
- **Writing:** Write essay

2B
- **Listening:** Multiple-choice, choose single answer; Write from dictation
- **Language development:** Sentence structure and prepositional phrases
- **Academic vocabulary:** Family, friends and people
- **Reading:** Reading: Fill in the blanks
- **Speaking:** Re-tell lecture
- **Writing:** Write essay

Lead-in

1 Scientists believe there are six emotions that all people show in the same way. Look at the photos. What do you think the six emotions are?

2 Look at the emotions in the box and discuss the questions in pairs.

| anxiety | envy | guilt | hate | hope | interest | patience | pity | pleasure | pride | respect | wonder |

1 Which of the emotions are positive? Which are negative?
2 Which three emotions do you think are the most important for life?
3 Choose five emotions. When did you last feel each of them?

2A Feeling emotional

Reading 1 (Reading: Fill in the blanks)

Before you read

1 Discuss the questions in pairs.
1 Why do people cry?
2 Why does our body produce tears?
3 Is it men or women who cry more?

Understanding the meaning of unknown words

In all reading tasks you will need to try to understand the meaning of unknown words. In *Reading: Fill in the blanks* you will need to recognise the meaning of missing words in a text.

2 a Read the text quickly. Which question from Exercise 1 does it answer?

> The human eye [1] <u>generates</u> three types of tears. The first type protects the eye and keeps it wet. The second type cleans the eye when it becomes [2] <u>irritated</u> by dirt. The third kind, emotional tears, [3] <u>flow</u> in response to sadness, worry or physical pain. Studies show that an emotional tear contains chemicals which are [4] <u>related</u> to stress. When we cry, we [5] <u>get rid of</u> these chemicals. This helps to [6] <u>balance</u> our body's stress level and makes us feel better.

b Read the text more carefully. Look at the underlined words and answer the questions.
1 What part of speech is each one?
2 Is the word similar to one you already know? Does this help you to understand the meaning?
3 Can the words around it help you to understand its meaning? Is it positive, negative or neutral? Are there any words in the sentence which go with it?

c Choose the correct meanings for the underlined words in Exercise 2a. Use your answers in Exercise 2b to help you.

1 A produces   B gets
2 A weak   B painful
3 A stop quickly   B move continuously
4 A connected   B unconnected
5 A take in   B make something leave
6 A cause an increase B keep in control

24

Module 2
More than a feeling
2A

Test practice
> EXPERT STRATEGIES page 180

3 a Read the text quickly. Which question from Exercise 1 does it answer?

b Complete the task. Think about the meaning of the missing words in context.

In the text below some words are missing. Drag words from the box below to the appropriate place in the text. To undo an answer choice, drag the word back to the box below the text.

One possible explanation for the production of emotional tears is that it's a [1]_____ of communication. Before babies can speak, the only way for them to express frustration, pain, [2]_____ and need is to cry. Adults may use crying to connect with other humans, as showing sadness can prompt comfort and [3]_____ from peers. There are also culturally acceptable [4]_____ for crying that bring people together, such as at funerals or weddings.

caring	fear	form	miserable
reasons	support	ways	

> HELP

- What part of speech is each word in the box?
- Do the words in the box have neutral, positive or negative meanings?
- Do any of the words collocate with other words around the blanks?

Task analysis
4 Why were the three extra words wrong for each blank?
A The meaning did not match the sentence.
B The part of speech was not correct.
C The word did not fit the sentence grammatically.
D The word did not collocate with other words in the sentence (e.g. adjective + preposition).

Discussion
5 Discuss the questions in pairs.
1 In your culture, is it acceptable for people to cry in public? Why/Why not?
2 Is crying a sign of weakness? Why/Why not?

EXPERT WORD CHECK
chemical   comfort   express   peer   prompt

> See **Reading 2** for more practice of this task type.

25

2A Module 2
More than a feeling

Academic vocabulary 1 AWL ACL

Adjectives and prepositions related to feelings

1a Complete the sentences with the prepositions in the box.

about (x3)   by (x2)   of (x2)   to   with (x2)

1 A recent survey showed that 47 percent of students are irritated _____ their roommates.
2 46 percent of students are anxious _____ receiving final grades.
3 Three quarters are excited _____ going home to see their parents.
4 12 percent are proud _____ the hard work they put into their studies.
5 A fifth of students are frustrated _____ their lack of typing skills.
6 More than 50 percent of students are pleased _____ their academic progress.
7 44 percent of students are concerned _____ getting a job after they graduate.
8 28 percent were disappointed _____ their last grade.
9 Almost two-thirds of students are afraid _____ not being successful.
10 Over 90 percent are opposed _____ higher fees for students.

b Underline the verbs which follow a preposition in Exercise 1a. What form are they in? Make a note of this pattern in your vocabulary notebook.

c Complete the sentences so they are true for you.

1 I get irritated _____ .
2 I'm anxious _____ .
3 I'm really excited _____ .
4 I'm proud _____ .
5 I'm sometimes frustrated _____ .
6 I'm pleased _____ .
7 I'm concerned _____ .
8 I was disappointed _____ .
9 I'm afraid _____ .
10 I'm opposed _____ .

d Work in pairs. Discuss your answers in Exercise 1c and find out what you and your partner have in common.

Academic verbs

2a Choose the correct options in *italics* to complete the text about stress at work. Check the meaning of any unknown words in a dictionary.

A group of scientists is planning to [1] *involve / research* the topic of stress at work. Their study, which will [2] *interpret / involve* 500 people who work in business, is likely to [3] *analyse / generate* a lot of interest in the business world. The research will [4] *investigate / generate* how our working lives are affected when we are stressed. The scientists carrying out the research will first collect and then [5] *analyse / identify* data. They will then [6] *interpret / investigate* the results and come to a conclusion. The results will hopefully [7] *identify / release* ways that stress chemicals affect our working lives.

b The underlined words in Exercise 2a are words that often follow the (correct) verbs. Make a note of these collocations in your vocabulary notebook.

c Have you ever felt stressed? How did it feel?

Academic collocations

3a Match the beginnings of the sentences (1–8) with the endings (A–H). Then note the collocations in *italics*.

1 Crying is a *form*
2 Tears can fall *in*
3 Anxiety can cause *physical*
4 High *stress*
5 Envy is one *possible*
6 In my country, it is not *culturally*
7 Guilt is *related*
8 Stress chemicals are *released*

A *acceptable* to show anger at work.
B *to* something you did wrong in the past.
C *of communication*.
D *response* to dirt in your eye.
E *pain*, for example, a headache.
F *by* your body because it thinks it is in danger.
G *explanation* for disliking someone.
H *levels* are bad for you.

b Cross out the word in *italics* that does not collocate with the word in bold.

1 **physical** *activity / appearance / figure / health*
2 *direct / effective / personal / speaking* **communication**
3 *individual / high / emotional / appropriate* **response**
4 *give / hear / provide / say* **an explanation**

26

Module 2
More than a feeling   2A

Speaking 1 (Repeat sentence; Answer short question)

Pronunciation: Using sentence stress

In English not every word in a sentence has the same stress. In *Repeat sentence* you will need to stress the correct words in the sentence you hear.

1a Read the sentences (1–2) and answer the questions (A–B).
  1 Disgust _____ basic emotion _____ people often experience.
  2 We are _____ by _____ which are _____ to the _____ .

  A Can you guess the meaning of the sentences? Why/Why not?
  B Which parts of speech can you see in each sentence? Choose from the words in the box.

  adjective   adverb   article   auxiliary verb   main verb
  noun   preposition   pronoun

b 🎧 12 Listen and complete the sentences in Exercise 1a. Did you guess correctly?

c 🎧 12 Listen again and underline the stressed words.

2a 🎧 13 Underline the stressed words in the sentences about disgust. Then listen and check your answers.
  1 It's difficult for us to control our feelings of disgust.
  2 The feeling of disgust is related to the stomach.
  3 Disgust helps us to avoid diseases and viruses.
  4 We acquire disgust through our genes and culture.

b 🎧 13 Listen again and repeat the sentences. Remember to stress the correct words.

Test practice 1: Repeat sentence

▶ EXPERT STRATEGIES page 171

3 🎧 14 Complete the task. You will hear ten sentences. Remember to stress the correct words.

> ⏱ 15 sec. *You will hear a sentence. Please repeat the sentence exactly as you hear it. You will hear the sentence only once.*

Task analysis

4 🎧 14 Listen again and repeat the task. This time try each technique (1–4) with two sentences. Which is the most/least helpful?
  1 Write down all or some of the words as you hear them.
  2 Listen to the sentence stress and rhythm as well as the words.
  3 Think about the meaning of the sentence as you listen.
  4 Imagine you are speaking to someone else in the room so you speak clearly.

Test practice 2: Answer short question

▶ EXPERT STRATEGIES page 174

5 🎧 15 Complete the task in pairs. You will hear five questions.

> ⏱ 10 sec. *You will hear a question. Please give a simple and short answer. Often just one or a few words is enough.*

27

2A Module 2
More than a feeling

Listening 1 (Multiple-choice, choose single answer)

Before you listen

1 Write definitions for the words in bold. Use a dictionary to help you if you are unsure.

> Emotional shock happens after a [1] **deep** shock. An irregular heart rate can make people feel [2] **dizzy**. Their hands might [3] **go** cold because of the low blood pressure. It can be worrying to experience emotional shock [4] **first-hand**.

Understanding gist

Some questions in *Multiple-choice, choose single answer* test the main idea or the theme of the recording. This is called the *gist* of a talk.

2a 🎧 16 Listen to three experts talking about the importance of surprise or shock in their area of study. Match the speakers (1–3) with the general themes (A–C).
 A possible stages of surprise
 B emotional effect of new products
 C long-term effects of emotional shock

b 🎧 16 Listen again and decide which sentence (A or B) most closely matches the main point of each speaker.
 1 A People may become angry after a surprise.
   B It is important to treat emotional shock seriously.
 2 A After surprise passes, people react either positively or negatively.
   B The physical signs of emotions have only recently been studied.
 3 A Products create a variety of emotions in their users.
   B Designers do not think about the emotions their products create.

c Look at the incorrect sentences in Exercise 2b. Which sentence:
 1 states the opposite of what was said?
 2 is a detail that was mentioned but not the main point?
 3 is not mentioned in the recording?

3 🎧 17 Listen to a lecture on surprise and take notes. What is the general theme?
 1 what the physical reactions to surprise are
 2 why people feel different types of surprise
 3 how we can control surprise in daily life

Test practice
> EXPERT STRATEGIES page 186

4 🎧 17 Listen again and complete the task. Use your notes from Exercise 3 to help you.

> HELP

- Is option A about the cause or effects of surprise?
- Is the whole talk about first-hand surprise or is this a detail?
- What does *proved* mean in option C: 'shown to be' or 'understood'?
- What makes the events sudden in option D?

Listen to the recording and answer the multiple-choice question by selecting the correct response. Only one response is correct.

What is the speaker's main point?

A ○ The cause of the physical effects of surprise is unknown.
B ○ First-hand surprise is only experienced as events happen.
C ○ Surprise happens when past beliefs are proved wrong.
D ○ Surprise is stronger when events happen suddenly.

Task analysis
> See **Listening 2** for more practice of this task type.

5 Discuss the questions in pairs.
 1 Did your notes help you to find the answer? If not, why not?
 2 Which options were clearly wrong according to the recording?

28

Language development 1

Relative clauses

▶ EXPERT GRAMMAR page 204

Relative clauses are very common in academic English. Read about them on page 204, then complete the exercises below.

1a Read a summary of the lecture on surprise from Listening 1. Match the underlined relative pronouns with what they refer to (A–E).

> Surprise occurs in two different situations. The first happens in situations <u>when</u> you receive new information <u>which</u> is different to your previous knowledge. For example, you are surprised by a friend <u>whose</u> actions are unexpected: you thought he was in Berlin but he arrives at your door. The second situation happens when an event is very different to your long-term knowledge. For example, you believe your home is a place <u>where</u> you are safe. You also believe the police never arrest people <u>who</u> are honest. However, one day a police officer comes to your home and arrests you for a crime you did not do. This is a failure in our knowledge.

A a person   C a thing   E possession
B a place   D a time

b We can also use *that* to talk about people and things. Replace two relative pronouns in the summary in Exercise 1a with *that*.

c We use *whose* to talk about possession. *Who's* means 'who is'. Choose the correct options in *italics* to complete the sentences.
1 A person *whose / who's* test results are better than expected feels surprise.
2 Someone *whose / who's* experiencing a surprise feels dizzy.
3 A person *whose / who's* surprised gets cold hands.
4 Someone *whose / who's* expectation is correct is unsurprised.

d Complete the text about fear with *who*, *which*, *whose* or *where*.

> Fear is an emotion ¹_____ we hope we will not experience too often but it is not always negative. A child ² _____ is scared of the dark will learn how to deal with fear better when they are older. A person ³ _____ watches a horror film in a place ⁴ _____ they are safe benefits from the excitement that fear brings. However, a person ⁵ _____ fear causes them to avoid certain things may have a phobia. This is a kind of fear ⁶ _____ can stop them from living a normal life.

2a Join the sentences using relative clauses. Replace the underlined words with relative pronouns.
1 Fear is a healthy emotion. Everybody experiences <u>it</u>.
   Fear is a healthy emotion which everybody experiences.
2 Fear is a high level of stress. <u>It</u> is caused by danger.
3 People turn white. <u>They</u> are frightened.
4 A person might scream. <u>The person's</u> fear is strong.
5 Dark houses are scary places. People feel frightened <u>there</u>.

b Complete the sentences using relative clauses. Use your own ideas.
1 Surprise is an emotion _____.
2 Fear happens _____.
3 A study is something _____.
4 A scientist is a person _____.
5 A person _____ eye produces tears _____.
6 A psychologist's office is a place _____.
7 A person _____ has a phobia _____.
8 An extreme sport is a sport _____.

3a Read the article and take notes. What is an extreme adventure break?

Holidaymakers seek excitement

Extreme adventure breaks are becoming increasingly popular as more and more people seek fear during their time away from work. No longer are people happy to relax on a hot beach for seven days while people serve them cold drinks; they want to experience the fear and excitement that activities such as mountain biking and skydiving can bring.

These kinds of holidays are growing faster than any other type in the travel industry and seem to offer more than just excitement. Holidaymakers say they are able to completely forget about work and focus on something completely different. They also say they meet more local people and learn more about the local environment.

b Complete the sentence to make a brief summary of the article. Include a relative clause. Use your notes from Exercise 3a to help you.
An extreme adventure break is a holiday ...

c Would you like to go on this kind of holiday? Why/Why not?

2A Module 2 — More than a feeling

Writing 1 (Write essay)

Understanding the task and making the content relevant

To score well in *Write essay*, it is essential to understand the prompt and make sure the content of your essay is relevant.

1 Read the essay prompt and look at the underlined words. Then discuss the questions in pairs.

> <u>Teaching values and behaviour</u> should be part of the <u>school curriculum</u> in <u>every school</u>. Discuss the arguments for and against this view.
> 1 How were you taught values and behaviour?
> 2 What else should be part of the school curriculum?
> 3 Should every school teach values? Do we need different rules for different age groups?

→ EXPERT WRITING page 197

2 In this test task you have to write an argumentative essay. Which words in the prompt tell you this? Read about argumentative essays on page 197. Then answer the questions.
   1 What are the advantages of teaching values in schools?
   2 What are the disadvantages of teaching values in schools?

3 Look at a student's ideas for topic sentences for this essay. Write the notes as complete sentences in paragraphs 1–3 in the essay plan below.

> 1 not all children receive / correct values / home / so it / important / teach values in schools
> 2 there / large number / subjects which children need / study / school curriculum these days
> 3 children of different ages need / different approach / learning values

Plan
- Introduction
- Para 1 _____
  A _____
  B _____
- Para 2 _____
  C _____
  D _____
- Para 3 _____
  E _____
- Conclusion

4 Look at the arguments to support the opinions in the topic sentences in the essay plan. Write them in the correct place (A–E) in the plan.
   1 values = important in primary schools, by secondary = preparation for work = important
   2 maths / computer technology / languages = important and take time
   3 people who commit crime / use drugs or alcohol / still have children
   4 universities ask for higher grades + many children already work into the night
   5 television = poor values + in many countries religion is falling in importance

→ See **Writing 2** for more practice of this task type.

5 Now write your own essay plan for this prompt.

30

2B Attitudes to life

Listening 2 (Multiple-choice, choose single answer; Write from dictation)

Before you listen

Test practice 1: Multiple-choice, choose single answer
➤ EXPERT STRATEGIES page 186

1 Complete the sentences with the words in *italics*.
  1 *opportunities, possibilities*
    A At present few _____ exist for students to get help with difficult subjects.
    B The college is looking at the _____ of offering extra classes.
  2 *behaviour, attitude*
    A Some people have a negative _____ towards certain subjects.
    B Few teachers will allow bad _____ in their lessons.
  3 *prevent, protect*
    A Teachers need to _____ a fear of certain subjects.
    B All adults need to _____ children from harm.
  4 *optimistic, pessimistic*
    A The most _____ people look forward to test results.
    B The most _____ people learn to be afraid of getting results.

2 🎧 18 Complete the task. Remember to take notes and identify the gist of the text.

> Listen to the recording and answer the multiple-choice question by selecting the correct response. Only one response is correct.
>
> According to the speaker, 'learned helplessness'
>
> A ○ makes people work even harder at difficult tasks.
> B ○ stops people repeating positive experiences.
> C ○ causes people to lose hope in their abilities.
> D ○ affects people in many unpredictable ways.

➤ HELP
  • Is 'learned helplessness' good or bad, according to the speaker? Cross out the option that says it has a positive effect.
  • Which other option is definitely wrong because the information isn't mentioned?

Test practice 2: Write from dictation
➤ EXPERT STRATEGIES page 189

3 🎧 19 Complete the task. You will hear three sentences.

> You will hear a sentence. Type the sentence in the box below exactly as you hear it. Write as much of the sentence as you can. You will hear the sentence only once.

Task analysis

4 Discuss the questions in pairs.
  1 How did you reach your answer in Exercise 2?
  2 How did you remember the sentences in Exercise 3? Did you try to remember them in your head, did you write down key words or did you use another method?

31

2B Module 2
More than a feeling

Language development 2

Sentence structure and prepositional phrases

▶ EXPERT GRAMMAR page 205

A prepositional phrase is used to add information to a subject, verb or object of a sentence. They are very common in academic English.

1a Read the sentences about 'learned helplessness' and underline the subject, verb and direct object in each sentence.

1 The animal might have opportunities to escape _____ .
2 Nothing will have an effect _____ .
3 That child will experience that same feeling of helplessness _____ .

b Now complete the sentences with the prepositional phrases in the box.

from this environment   on another occasion
on the child's maths performance

c Match the prepositional phrases in Exercise 1b with what they express (1–3). Where do these appear in a sentence?

1 time (when?)   2 place (where?)   3 manner (how?)

2 Complete the sentences about teenagers and risky behaviour with the phrases in *italics*.

1 *in the developing brain, of teenagers*
   The risky behaviour _____ may come from a difference _____ .
2 *as adults, at understanding*
   Scientists have found that teenagers are as good _____ the risks of dangerous behaviour _____ .
3 *of possible actions, in our brain, from a number*
   Teams _____ of universities have identified a special area _____ that weighs the costs and benefits _____ .
4 *in unusual ways, in teen brains*
   Their research shows the main difference _____ is that they weigh those costs and benefits _____ .

Changing verbs to noun + preposition phrases

3a Look at the sentences. What part of speech or type of clause do the different colours represent? Then look at the chart and write two sentences for each item in the survey using *decrease* or *increase* as a verb, then as a noun.

1 The number of 10–24-year-olds who had driven a car increased from 1991 to 2011.
2 There was an increase in the number of 10–24-year-olds who had driven a car from 1991 to 2011.

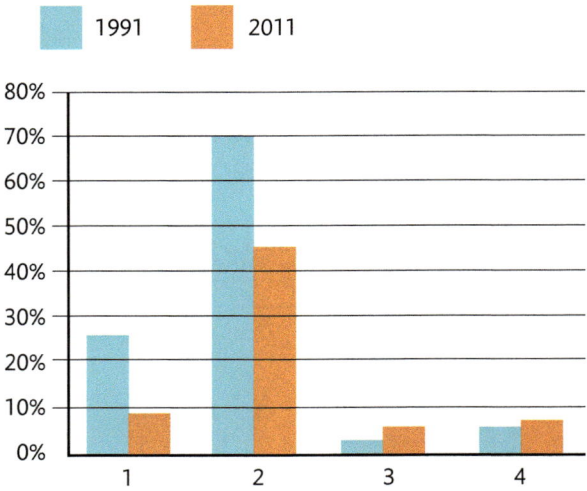

Risk habits among 10–24-year-olds in the USA
■ 1991   ■ 2011

1 rarely or never wore a seat belt)
2 had tried a cigarette
3 had not eaten any fruit
4 had not eaten any vegetables

1 A The number of 10–24-year-olds who rarely or never wore a seat belt decreased from 1991 to 2011.
  B There was a decrease in the number of 10–24-year-olds who rarely or never wore a seat belt from 1991 to 2011.

b Work in pairs and create a survey.

1 Think of three questions to ask about changes in lifestyle/habits in the last five to ten years.
2 Find ten people to complete your survey.
3 Report back to the class on the results, using *decrease* and *increase*.

Essay editing skills

4 Find and correct four word order errors and four spelling errors in the text.

Sientists from Stanford carried out fascinating research on the social causes in 2010 of emotion. They studied femail undergraduates aged between 18 and 20 from different social backgrounds. Half were paired of the undergraduates with actors who had similar likes and dislikes to them. The actors were trained to answer questions about giving speeches by acting in front of their partner stressed. They found that the undergraduates in the test group showed to their partner similar facical reactions.

32

Module 2
More than a feeling
2B

Academic vocabulary 2 [AWL] [ACL]

Easily confused words related to family, friends and people

1a Complete the sentences with the words in *italics*.

1 *bring up, grow up*
   A I think it's better for children to _____ in the city.
   B It's important that grandparents help to _____ children.

2 *relative, relationship*
   A The _____ between family background and success is well-known.
   B It's good to have one _____ that you can talk to about anything.

3 *community, society*
   A There are some really effective _____ groups for young people in my area.
   B Modern _____ is a better place to raise children.

4 *accept, except*
   A Families can take a while to _____ new members.
   B Children shouldn't have to do any work, _____ homework.

5 *sensible, sensitive*
   A Keeping the same friends throughout life is a _____ decision.
   B Older people tend to be more _____ to other people's needs.

6 *first generation, younger generation*
   A Life's going to be easier for the _____ .
   B _____ computers were very basic.

b Discuss the sentences in Exercise 1a in pairs. Do you agree?

Collocations related to family, friends and people

2 Match the beginnings of the sentences (1–6) with the endings (A–F). Then note the collocations in *italics*.

1 It's hard to question the *cultural*
2 There are some similarities between the *human*
3 You would expect people from similar *cultural*
4 We are social creatures and *human*
5 Grandparents need to pass on *cultural*
6 You can learn a lot about *human*

A *behaviour* by looking at young babies.
B *norms* of society.
C *interaction* is a necessary part of life.
D *values* to the younger generation.
E *species* and other animals.
F *backgrounds* to have a lot in common.

Academic word list

3 Read the article and complete it with the words in the box.

analysis   area   construct   despite   identify   injury   physical   project

Meet the family

Cheddar, UK. After a 23-year-old man was killed by a(n) ¹_____ to the face, members of his family laid his body in a cave in southwest England, where he remained undiscovered for years.
Now, some 90 centuries and 300 generations later, scientists from Oxford University are discovering some unexpected secrets about the young man. They have been using DNA ²_____ to learn more about his life. ³_____ the age of the skeleton, the team were able to ⁴_____ a particular gene which is passed directly down the mother's family line. At the end of a major ⁵_____ involving months of work, one of the scientists decided to test a group of people born and raised in the local ⁶_____ , just for the fun of it. He never imagined that one of those people, history teacher Adrian Targett, would be directly related to the 9,000-year-old man.
Targett admitted he was shocked to learn of his family connection to the body in the caves. The bones have since been studied by a police artist, who was able to ⁷_____ a picture of the caveman's face from the bones. Any similarities in ⁸_____ appearance between Mr Targett and his relative were harder to find.

2B Module 2
More than a feeling

Reading 2 (Reading: Fill in the blanks)

Before you read

1 Discuss the questions in pairs. Check the meaning of the words in bold in a dictionary if you are unsure.
  1 How often do you get angry? What causes this **anger**?
  2 Do **insignificant** things sometimes make you angry?
  3 What is a good way for a person to **reduce** their level of anger?
  4 What are your **expectations** of the future? Do you expect things to end well or badly?

Test practice
> EXPERT STRATEGIES page 180

2 Complete the task. Remember to think about the meaning of the missing words in context.

In the text below some words are missing. Drag words from the box below to the appropriate place in the text. To undo an answer choice, drag the word back to the box below the text.

Roman philosopher Seneca was worried about the high levels of anger that [1]_____ during his lifetime. It was common for a person to be killed after doing or saying something insignificant to someone in [2]_____. He believed anger was caused by [3]_____ expectations that everything would always end well. When they ended badly, people became angry. He believed they could reduce this anger by changing their view of the world and becoming more [4]_____ about life.

existed	happened	negative	patient
power	top	unrealistic	

> HELP

- What part of speech fits each blank? What parts of speech are the words in the box?
- Blank 1: Do we use *existed* or *happened* to describe a state?
- Blank 3: Things do not always end well in life, so what kind of expectations did people have?

Task analysis

3 Discuss the questions in pairs.
  1 Why is each of the three incorrect words wrong for each blank?
  2 How confident did you feel about your answers?
  3 What can you do to feel more confident next time?

Discussion

4a Work in small groups. Do you think Seneca's suggestion was useful?

b Read the quotes. Do you agree or disagree with each one?

'You'll never find a rainbow if you're looking down.'
Charles Chaplin, actor

'If you expect the worst, you'll never be disappointed.'
Sarah Dessen, author

34

Module 2
More than a feeling
2B

Speaking 2 (Re-tell lecture)

Taking notes on the main point

In *Re-tell lecture* you will need to identify the main point of the lecture and take notes on it.

1 a 🎧 20 Look at the photo in Exercise 3. What do you think is a gratitude journal? Listen and check your answer.

  b 🎧 20 Look at the notes a student has made on the speaker's main point and listen again. Find and correct five mistakes in the notes.

> • appreciate happiness only after something good
> • but habit of grateful = decrease happiness
> • gratitude journal = less successful, less healthy, less generous

  c What type of words has the student included in the notes? Why? Choose from the words in the box.

  adjectives   adverbs   articles   auxiliary verbs   linking words   nouns
  prepositions   verbs

Sample response

2 🎧 21 Listen to two students re-telling the lecture. Which student is more effective? Why?
  1 She uses her notes to help her.
  2 She presents the main idea accurately.
  3 She links her ideas, so they make sense.

Test practice
➤ EXPERT STRATEGIES page 173

3 🎧 20 Complete the task in pairs. Take notes, then present the information to your partner.

⏱ 40 sec. You will hear a lecture. After listening to the lecture, in 10 seconds, please speak into the microphone and re-tell what you have just heard from the lecture in your own words. You will have 40 seconds to give your response.

➤ **HELP**

Look at the photo. What is the topic of the lecture? What vocabulary do you think you might hear?

➤ EXPERT SPEAKING page 193

4 🎧 22 Turn to page 193 and complete another timed test practice.

Task analysis

5 Work in pairs. Discuss what you can do to improve your re-telling skills. Think about the areas in the box.

organising your ideas as you speak   taking notes as you listen
understanding the lecture   understanding your notes

35

2B Module 2
More than a feeling

Writing 2 (Write essay)

Lead-in 1 Discuss the questions in pairs. Check the meaning of any unknown words in a dictionary.
1 Who have you inherited your looks from? Are you similar to them in other ways?
2 How do parents, schooling and country of birth affect a child's opportunities in life?
3 Which do you think is more important: your genes or the environment you live in?

Understand the task
> EXPERT STRATEGIES page 176

2a Read the essay prompt. Which question in Exercise 1 is most similar to the prompt?

> ⏱ 20 min. You will have 20 minutes to plan, write and revise an essay about the topic below. Your response will be judged on how well you develop a position, organise your ideas, present supporting details and control the elements of standard written English. You should write 200–300 words.

> Many scientists these days argue that genetic inheritance has more influence on our lives than the environment which we grow up in. Are humans influenced by their DNA or are their surroundings responsible for the lives we lead? Discuss both views.

> **HELP**
> • Find two words in the second sentence that mean the same as *genetic inheritance* and *the environment* from the first sentence.
> • Do you need to give one side of the argument or both sides?

b Work in pairs. Share ideas on this topic. Think of three things you could discuss for each question.
1 How do genetics affect people?
2 How does the environment affect people?

Plan your essay
To score well in *Write essay*, you need to consider what an educated reader already knows about a subject and make sure all the content is directly relevant to all parts of the prompt.

3a Look at the ideas for supporting points in the essay. Write them in the correct place (A–D) in the essay plan on page 37.
1 hard work + education = success = opportunities
2 Some jobs (e.g. model) need certain genes.
3 Money buys opportunities.
4 Some illnesses affect people and they can't work.

Module 2
2B More than a feeling

> **Plan**
> - Introduction: People have discussed the influence of biology and the environment on children's lives for years.
> - Para 1:
>   1 Some genes stop you having choices in life.
>   A _____
>   B _____
> - Para 2:
>   2 However, your lifestyle and environment will have a bigger effect over a lifetime.
>   C _____
>   D _____
> - Conclusion:
>   3 Both genes and the environment affect our lives in complex ways.

b Now write your own essay plan. What ideas from your experience could you use?

Language and content When you write in academic English, you need to use complex noun phrases and show clearly when you are giving your opinion or the opinion of others.

4a Complete the noun phrases with prepositions or relative pronouns.
1 the effect __of__ genes _____ someone's personality
2 the role _____ the environment plays _____ creating personal qualities
3 a number _____ different influences _____ a person's life
4 the opportunities _____ money can bring _____ a child
5 a mixture _____ both genes and the environment _____ a child grows up

b Write complete sentences using the noun phrases in Exercise 4a. Where can you use these in your essay?

5a Look at the phrases in bold in the table. Which ones could you use at the beginning of sentences 1–3 in the essay plan in Exercise 3a?

b Choose some expressions to use in your own plan.

Expressing opinions of others	**It is generally believed that** both genes and the environment are important.
	Recently, scientists have shown that genes are more important than we thought before.
	Some scientists have claimed that they have found genes for things such as overeating.
	Research suggests that even when we get illnesses from our parents, the right diet helps …
Giving examples	**For instance**, if someone eats badly, their health will be poor.
	There are many examples of this. Take, **for instance**, the kind of jobs people do.
	This is particularly true in my country, where …
Expressing your own view	**It seems to me that** both genes and the environment are important …
	In my opinion, our genes still have a bigger influence in our lives …

Write your essay

6 Write your essay. Use your plan from Exercise 3b and the language in Exercise 5 to help you. Remember to write 200–300 words.

Check your essay
▶ EXPERT WRITING page 196

7 Check your essay using the checklist on page 196.

2B Module 2
More than a feeling

Review

1 Complete the sentences with the words in the box.

> data   identified   interested   interpret
> investigating   involve   research   results

1 _____ suggests that all kinds of things cause people to feel embarrassed but they all _____ the same basic problem: doing something that is socially unacceptable.
2 Many people worry that others will _____ a mistake as a challenge to the other person's importance.
3 Interestingly, everyone in one particular survey correctly _____ the symptoms of embarrassment: increased heart rate, lowered head and a need to get away.
4 Researchers _____ behaviour in other species have recorded similar _____ in the animal world.
5 Scientists are now _____ in collecting _____ to understand if making a mistake socially does, in fact, make someone less popular.

2 Choose the correct options in *italics* to complete the article.

What is face?

One ¹ *possible / big* explanation of face is 'taking action to avoid embarrassment at all costs'. Although it is central to life in many countries, particularly in Asia, the idea is totally foreign for anyone growing ² *to / up* in western culture. The Chinese use the word 'guanxi' to refer to the complicated social ³ *relations / relationships* in their society, where everyone has a clearly defined role to play. The success of everyone in a ⁴ *population / community* depends on an understanding of this. It may, for example, be perfectly culturally ⁵ *reasonable / acceptable* for a worker in the United States to point out his manager's errors but that would not be true in China. The pressure to 'give face' to others is so strong that even close family and friends may cut off contact in ⁶ *answer / response* to actions which show disrespect.

How do you show face?
- Be ⁷ *sensitive / sensible* to relationships and keep opinions to yourself unless you are asked.
- Be polite in all ⁸ *designs / forms* of communication.
- Hide your technical skills and knowledge to bridge the gap between you and others.

3 Put the words in *italics* in the correct order to complete the sentences.

1 *of happiness / measuring / people's experience*
_____ is easier than you think.
2 *results / accurate / surprisingly*
Just asking people how they feel produces _____ .
3 *asked / the world's / question / most frequently*
'How are you?' is probably _____ and nobody minds answering it.
4 *the brain / to / blood flow*
Alternatively, it is possible to use MRI scans to measure _____ .
5 *of the smile muscles / the activity / in the face*
Other machines measure _____ .
6 *naturally / something / in a laboratory / which people experience*
But happiness is not _____ .
7 *one person's 'five' / the possibility that / is another person's 'six'*
There is _____ .
8 *in / the differences / their measurements*
However, when you ask a large number of people, _____ even out, making it possible to understand a nation's general happiness.

4 Complete the second sentence so that it has a similar meaning to the first sentence.

1 The number of people who own a car in my country has increased in recent years.
There _____
_____ .
2 There has been a decrease in the number of people who own their own home in my country in the last 50 years.
The number _____
_____ .
3 The number of people who eat a good diet has risen in my country in the last ten years.
There _____
_____ .
4 There has been a fall in the number of people who get enough exercise all over the world in the last 30 years.
The number _____
_____ .

3 Wild world

Overview

3A
- **Reading:** Multiple-choice, choose multiple answers
- **Academic vocabulary:** The environment and environmental problems
- **Speaking:** Read aloud; Answer short question
- **Listening:** Select missing word
- **Language development:** Future forms
- **Summary writing:** Summarize spoken text

3B
- **Listening:** Select missing word; Write from dictation
- **Language development:** Zero and first conditionals
- **Academic vocabulary:** The natural world
- **Reading:** Multiple-choice, choose multiple answers
- **Speaking:** Describe image
- **Summary writing:** Summarize spoken text

Lead-in

'We have not inherited this world from our parents. We have been loaned it by our children.'
Native American tradition

1 Look at the photos and discuss the questions.
　1 What's your favourite animal? Why?
　2 Do you think the animals in the photos are worth saving? Why/Why not? Use the ideas in the box to help you.

benefits to humans　　chances of succeeding　　costs of saving them　　importance to other species　　tourism

2 Discuss the quote in pairs. What do you think it means? What does it say about how we live our daily lives?

39

3A Changing planet

Reading 1 (Multiple-choice, choose multiple answers)

Identifying facts and opinions

Multiple-choice, choose multiple answers often tests your understanding of the difference between a fact and an opinion.

2a What is the difference between a fact and an opinion?

b Read the statements and decide if they are expressed as facts or opinions.
1 Research has shown that CO_2 levels have been high for decades.
2 In 2011 Arctic sea ice was at the lowest level ever recorded.
3 As far as I'm concerned, people don't want to change their habits.
4 Scientists have proven that CO_2 can be removed from the air artificially.
5 Environmental workers claim the average tree can remove 300 kg of CO_2 per year.
6 Some scientists have suggested that the best solution is planting more trees.
7 Many are of the opinion that planting trees means taking land away from farming.
8 Some scientists have argued that it's time to take extreme action.

c Underline the words or phrases in Exercise 2b which are used to express facts or opinions.

3a Read the text in Exercise 4 quickly and answer the questions.
1 What has Klaus Lackner invented?
2 Match the numbers in the box with the things they refer to (A–E).

1,000 times   3.6 billion tons   10% $30–$600
$100

A the percentage of world CO_2 production that ten million trees take away
B the amount of CO_2 ten million of these trees take out of the air
C the costs of taking a ton of CO_2 from the air with these trees
D the value of the fuel produced by a ton of CO_2
E a comparison of the CO_2 removed by Lackner's trees and normal trees

b Read the text again and answer the questions.
1 Which of the numbers in Exercise 3a are facts and which are opinions?
2 What language helps you to decide this?

c Find one more fact and one more opinion in the text which is not related to the numbers.

Before you read

1 Work in pairs and look at the table. Which activity do you think uses the least amount of carbon dioxide (CO_2)? Which uses the most? Number them 1–6 (1 = least, 6 = most). Then discuss your ideas with another pair.

Activity	
breathing (one adult, one year)	
flying from New York to Mumbai (12,570 km per passenger)	
watching TV (one year)	
heating a home (Europe, one year)	
driving (medium-sized car in Europe, approximately 15,000 km per year)	
using the computer and phone (one year)	

Module 3
Wild world — 3A

Test practice

> EXPERT STRATEGIES page 178

4 Complete the task. Think about language for expressing facts and opinions.

Read the text and answer the question by selecting all the correct responses. More than one response is correct.

Klaus Lackner has designed an artificial tree to remove carbon dioxide (CO_2) from the air using 'leaves' that have proved to be 1,000 times more efficient than the real thing. In addition, real leaves need sunlight but research has shown that the artificial leaves do not. The surface of the papery leaves is coated with plastic that contains a chemical which takes CO_2 out of the air and stores it. To remove the CO_2, the leaves are washed with water once a month or as needed. They can then dry naturally in the wind, taking in more CO_2.

Lackner calculates that his tree can remove one ton of CO_2 a day. Ten million of these trees could remove 3.6 billion tons of CO_2 a year – equal to about 10% of our global annual CO_2 production.

He suggests that the stores of CO_2 could be turned into liquid fuels to power vehicles. And indeed, past research has shown that this is possible. Whether it is economical or not is a different question. Lackner has argued that his trees would cost around $200 for each ton of CO_2 removed from the atmosphere and this could drop to $30 a ton as the project becomes bigger. While other people claim this figure is unrealistic (some calculate it at $600 per ton), it is clear that the project will only be economically possible at $30 if oil companies buy the liquid fuels for around $100 per ton, which has yet to be decided.

According to the writer, which of the following are true of Klaus Lackner's man-made trees?

A ☐ They do not depend on weather conditions to work.
B ☐ Their leaves have a similar appearance to real leaves.
C ☐ The CO_2 is cleaned off their leaves by rain.
D ☐ They remove more CO_2 than real trees.
E ☐ CO_2 collected from them has no identified uses.
F ☐ Nobody knows accurately how much they will cost.
G ☐ Oil companies have expressed an interest in them.

> HELP
> • What do the pronouns *they* and *their* in options A, B, D and F refer to?
> • Underline the key words in each option and find the section of the text which deals with that topic.

Task analysis **5** Work in pairs. Compare and discuss how you approached the task.
1 Which options were easiest to find paraphrased in the text?
2 Which options were not mentioned in the text?

Discussion **6** Discuss the questions in pairs.
1 Do you think artificial trees are a good solution?
2 Do you think the trees are worth the cost?

EXPERT WORD CHECK
artificial   atmosphere   indeed   store   surface   ton

> See **Reading 2** for more practice of this task type.

3A Module 3
Wild world

Academic vocabulary 1 AWL ACL

Academic collocations list

1a Complete the sentences with the words in the box. You will need to use each word twice. Then note the collocations in *italics*.

change   environmental   natural   widely

1. Do you think governments should spend time working on _____ *protection* policies?
2. Is using recyclable materials _____ *accepted* in your country?
3. Do you think the world will continue to _____ *rapidly* over the next 50 years?
4. Do you think dinosaurs were killed by a(n) _____ *disaster*?
5. What causes the most _____ *damage* in your country?
6. Do you think public transport will be _____ *used* in the future?
7. Are all endangered animals and plants in *the _____ world* equally important?
8. What could be done to _____ *people's attitudes* towards renewable energy?

b Write the collocations in Exercise 1a in your vocabulary notebook with an example sentence.

Academic word list

2a Complete the sentences with a word formed from the word in capitals.

1. A lot of problems have been caused by *intensive* farming methods. INTENSE
2. It is hard to _____ count how many species have died out. ACCURATE
3. The Siberian Tiger will be one of the _____ , thanks to science. SURVIVE
4. Environmental problems will _____ correct themselves. EVENTUAL
5. _____ will invest in renewable forms of energy for their homes in the future. INDIVIDUAL
6. The _____ of recyclable waste to Asia for processing is common. TRANSPORT
7. We need more _____ answers to the problems of the environment. CREATE
8. Thanks to technology, earthquakes will be more _____ in the future. PREDICT

b Choose two statements you agree with and two you disagree with from Exercise 2a. Discuss your ideas in pairs. Then carry out a class survey to compare ideas.

The environment

3a Work in pairs and read the article. What have the scientists at MIT created?

In the near future bacteria could be used to turn CO_2 gas into fuel!

Biologists at the Massachusetts Institute of Technology (MIT) have succeeded in using genetic [1] _____ to produce a new kind of bacteria which might turn the pollution into an alcohol that can power cars in the next few years. It is hoped that this technology could help reduce our dependence on [2] _____ like coal or petrol and lessen the amount of CO_2 which is [3] _____ into the air.

Unlike many other alternatives to oil like [4] _____ (which use plants like corn or palm to produce oil), this product can be used immediately and it doesn't need any further [5] _____ . At the moment the bacteria which the biologists have created in their research [6] _____ at MIT get their carbon from fruit sugars but with a few more genetic changes, they should be able to [7] _____ on carbon from almost any source, including agricultural or city [8] _____ .

b Complete the article with the words in the box.

biofuels   engineering   feed   fossil fuels   laboratory   processing   released   waste

c Do you think it is better to create new fuels or to reduce the amount of oil we use? How can people reduce the amount of oil they use at the moment?

Prepositional phrases related to the environment

4 Complete the sentences with the prepositions in the box.

at   from   into   to (x2)   with

1. The new trees were designed _____ take CO_2 out of the atmosphere.
2. The CO_2 is removed _____ the air by the plastic layer on the leaves.
3. The trees are coated _____ plastic.
4. Scientists can turn the CO_2 _____ liquid fuel.
5. Scientists calculate the cost _____ different levels.
6. The costs could drop _____ $30 per ton.

Module 3
Wild world — 3A

Speaking 1 (Read aloud; Answer short question)

Pronunciation: Word stress 1

In *Read aloud* you are scored on pronunciation and oral fluency. To improve in these areas, you will need to be able to use the correct stress on words.

1a 🎧 23 A syllable is a word or part of a word which contains a single vowel sound. Listen and look at the stressed syllables in sentence 1. Then underline the stressed syllables in the words in bold in sentence 2.
  1 **Oceans** cover two thirds of the earth's **surface**.
  2 **Oceans regulate** the earth's **climate** and **weather** systems.

b In words of more than one syllable, with no prefixes and suffixes, which syllable is stressed more often in English?

2a Work in pairs. Write the words in the box in the correct group. Then practise saying the words.

<del>analyse</del> <del>approach</del> benefit chemical <del>colleague</del> <del>community</del> damage design discovery environment event focus global justify participate percent

1 ●●	2 ●●	3 ●●●	4 ●●●●
colleague	approach	analyse	community
____	____	____	____
____	____	____	____
____	____	____	____

b 🎧 24 Listen and check your answers.

Test practice 1: Read aloud

➤ EXPERT STRATEGIES page 170

3 Complete the task. Remember to think about word stress before you read.

> ⏱ **40 sec.** *Look at the text below. In 40 seconds, you must read this text aloud as naturally and clearly as possible. You have 40 seconds to read aloud.*
>
> Deep-water marine environments have been a relatively unexplored area until now. Hardly any drug discovery research has targeted the deep-water reef communities in this habitat and, in particular, the bacteria living in these communities. Early studies by a new research group, as well as a thorough review of published reports, strongly supports the theory that these areas could produce new medicines.

➤ **HELP**
- Try saying the phrase *relatively unexplored area*. Make sure you stress the correct syllable in each word: *rel**a**tively un**ex**plored **a**rea*.
- Think about the word stress of other multi-syllable words: *com**mu**nities, **par**ticular, bac**te**ria*.

Task analysis

4 🎧 25 Listen to a model answer. Did the speaker use the same stress as you? Try the task again.

Test practice 2: Answer short question

➤ EXPERT STRATEGIES page 174

5 🎧 26 Complete the task in pairs. You will hear six questions.

> ⏱ **10 sec.** *You will hear a question. Please give a simple and short answer. Often just one or a few words is enough.*

43

3A Module 3
Wild world

Listening 1 (Select missing word)

Before you listen

1 Which of the places in the box have we fully explored? Why?

the African deserts   the Amazon rainforest
the Antarctic   Australia   the Himalayas
the oceans   the Sahara desert

Following a sequence of ideas

In *Select missing word*, you will need to follow the speaker's ideas in order to predict the missing word(s).

2a 🎧 27 Listen to a lecture and take notes. What is the topic?

b Discourse markers are words and phrases we use to introduce new information and link ideas. Match the discourse markers in the box with their uses (1–6).

anyway   however   in fact   so   well   you know

1 to introduce true information
2 to introduce contrasting information
3 to change the subject
4 to give information the listener probably knows
5 to give the speaker time to pause and think
6 to talk about the result of something

3a 🎧 28 Listen to the first half of five sentences (1–5) and take notes. Then match them with the second half (A–E). Use the discourse marker at the end of the first half to help you decide what information comes next.

A ... the wealthy businessman, is sending several vehicles to underwater locations around the world. ___
B ... many of them have bodies that you can see through. _1_
C ... in the future this cost will probably decrease. ___
D ... pressure equipment. ___
E ... many scientists think we will. ___

b 🎧 29 Listen and check your answers.

Test practice

> EXPERT STRATEGIES page 187

4 🎧 30 Complete the task. Remember to take notes as you listen.

You will hear a recording about our oceans. At the end of the recording the last word or group of words has been replaced by a beep. Select the correct option to complete the recording.

A ○ the surface of the ocean
B ○ the quality of the air
C ○ the creatures that exist there
D ○ the light which is produced

> HELP

What is the topic of the final part (i.e. the last two sentences) of the recording? The missing words must match that topic.

Task analysis

5 Why is each of the other three options in Exercise 4 incorrect?

1 The meaning does not fit the final sentence.
2 The meaning matches the final sentence but not the previous sentence.
3 The meaning matches the final sentence but not the whole recording.

> See **Listening 2** for more practice of this task type.

Module 3
Wild world 3A

Language development 1

Future forms

➤ EXPERT GRAMMAR page 205

1a Speakers use different future forms for different purposes. Choose the correct future form in *italics* based on the speaker's purpose in brackets.
1. In the future scientists *are going to try / are trying* to find out more about the creatures that exist under the ocean. (intention)
2. Richard Branson *is sending / will send* several vehicles to underwater locations around the world next year. (arrangement)
3. Many scientists think that we *are going to know / will know* more about the deep sea in the future. (prediction based on opinion)
4. Deep sea exploration *is going to be / will be* better in the future because of the new technologies that are being made now. (prediction based on present evidence)

b Complete the sentences with the correct future form of the verbs in brackets.
1. Business people _____ (spend) more money on exploration than governments due to the weak world economy. (prediction based on present evidence)
2. Sir Richard Branson _____ (travel) to the ocean floor in one of his vehicles. (intention)
3. China and India are investing in deep-sea mining, so other governments _____ (do) the same. (prediction based on opinion)
4. The company _____ (start) to mine for new resources next month. (arrangement)
5. Geologists _____ (learn) about earthquakes from James Cameron's underwater film. (intention)
6. Scientists _____ (meet) next month to discuss the results of the project. (arrangement)

Predictions

2a Complete the predictions about the next 20 years. Use *will/won't* to give your opinion. Use *(not) going to* if you have present evidence.
1. We _____ farm our oceans for minerals.
2. Climate change _____ make it harder to grow food.
3. Food shortages _____ cause social problems and public protests.
4. We _____ have days without access to energy in our homes.
5. We _____ be able to control the weather.
6. Our bodies _____ change shape because we spend so much time sitting down.
7. People _____ be able to travel to space cheaply and easily.

b Read the sentences. Which speaker is very sure? Which speaker is quite sure? Which speaker is not sure?
1. World population is definitely not going to increase further.
2. African countries will possibly become wealthier.
3. We probably won't farm our oceans for minerals.

c How sure are you about your predictions in Exercise 2a? Add *definitely* (very sure), *probably* (quite sure) or *possibly* (not sure) to each sentence.

d Compare your predictions in Exercise 2a in pairs.

3a We can use *be likely/unlikely to* when we make predictions. Put the words in the correct order to see some predictions engineer John Elfreth Watkins, Jr made in 1900.
1. become / much / likely to / people / taller / are
2. less than / per hour / trains / unlikely to / 150 miles / are / travel
3. ready-cooked meals delivered to / eat / we / likely to / our homes / are
4. disappear / C, X and Q / likely to / from the alphabet / are / the letters

b Work in pairs. Which of Watkins' predictions in Exercise 3a came true?

4a Choose five topics from the box and write one prediction for each that you believe will come true in the next 20 years. Think about why.

education   families   food   friendships   homes
sport   work

Families will get smaller because people cannot afford to have many children.

b Work in small groups. Find out how many people agree or disagree with each of your predictions from Exercise 4a.

> I definitely think that families will get smaller. Do you agree?

> No, I think it's unlikely. Just look at the world population growth.

> Well, I think they probably will. It'll become too expensive to have large families.

45

3A Module 3 Wild world

Summary writing 1 (Summarize spoken text)

Taking notes on the main idea

In *Summarize spoken text* you must identify the main point of the recording and take notes before you can summarise it well.

1a 🎧 31 Listen to a lecture. What is the topic?

b When taking notes, we often shorten some words. Match the words in the box with the shortened words (1–8) in the notes.

about	because	negative	people	positive	results in	talk	to

> ¹ ppl tired of global warming ² b/c _____
> ³ neg. _____ ⁴ = ppl feel _____
> suggest _____ stories; ⁵ tlk ⁶ abt ⁷ pos. effect of
> actions ⁸ 2 motivate ppl

c How is each shortened word in the notes formed?

d 🎧 31 Listen again and complete the notes in Exercise 1b. What is the main idea?

2a Shorten the words in the box so that you can write them quickly and remember them later.

but	environment	especially	for example	great	increase	problem
research	smaller than	twice	very	with		

b 🎧 32 Listen to another lecture. What is the topic?

c 🎧 32 Listen again and take notes. Use shortened words. What is the main idea?

Writing a topic sentence

A topic sentence summarises the main idea of a text. *Summarize spoken text* should start with a topic sentence.

3 Choose the best topic sentence (1–3) for the lecture in Exercise 1a.
  1 Journalists like writing stories about the negative impact of global warming.
  2 Global warming campaigners should talk about the positive effects of their actions.
  3 Global warming is causing people to feel depressed about their economic situation.

4 Look at your notes from the lecture in Exercise 2b and complete the topic sentence.

   A new report suggests that …

➤ See **Summary writing 2** for more practice of this task type.

3B Animal magic

Listening 2 (Select missing word; Write from dictation)

Before you listen

1 a Match the words in bold in the quiz (1–6) with their meanings (A–F).

Quick quiz

Name a ¹ **species** of animal which:
- is ² **wild**.
- is ³ **domestic**.
- does not ⁴ **breed** easily in zoos.
- has a ⁵ **leader** in the group.
- ⁶ **feeds** its babies for several months.

A have babies
B an animal or person who controls a group
C a group of animals or plants of the same kind
D give food to a person or animal
E not controlled by humans
F that can be trained to live with humans

b Work in pairs. Do the quiz in Exercise 1a.

Test practice 1: Select missing word
➤ EXPERT STRATEGIES page 187

2 🎧 33 Complete the task. Remember to take notes.

You will hear a recording about animal domestication. At the end of the recording the last word has been replaced by a beep. Select the correct option to complete the recording.

A ○ accept
B ○ follow
C ○ repeat
D ○ continue

➤ **HELP**

- Before you listen: what do you think animal domestication is?
- After you listen: what do people or animals do when they have a leader?

Test practice 2: Write from dictation
➤ EXPERT STRATEGIES page 189

3 🎧 34 Complete the task. You will hear three sentences. Then compare answers in pairs.

You will hear a sentence. Type the sentence in the box below exactly as you hear it. Write as much of the sentence as you can. You will hear the sentence only once.

Task analysis

4 Discuss the questions in pairs.
1 In *Select missing word*, did you try to guess the missing word(s) before reading the options? Did this help?
2 In *Write from dictation*, did you keep saying the sentences in your head as you wrote them? Was this easy or difficult?

3B Module 3
Wild world

Language development 2

Zero and first conditionals

▶ EXPERT GRAMMAR page 206

1a 🎧 35 Listen to the talk on animal domestication from Listening 2 again. As you listen, take notes next to the sentences.
1 Scientists consider six important things
2 <u>Unless</u> the animal eats cheap food,
3 <u>If</u> the animal doesn't grow quickly,
4 An animal will soon disappear
5 If the animal gets frightened in small spaces,
6 <u>Provided that</u> the animal is naturally sociable,

b Match the beginnings of sentences in Exercise 1a (1–6) with the endings (A–F). Use your notes to help you.
A farmers won't want to pay to feed it.
B if it doesn't breed easily on farms.
C it might be dangerous to humans.
D it will be unhelpful to humans.
E when they decide to domesticate an animal.
F it will probably see the farmer as its leader.

c Work in pairs. Look at the sentences in Exercises 1a and 1b and discuss the questions.
1 What tense follows *if*, *unless* and *provided that*? What tenses are used in the second part?
2 Which sentences refer to a general truth? Which refer to future possibilities?
3 When do we use a comma?
4 What is the difference in meaning between the underlined words?

2a Re-write the sentences using the sentence patterns in Exercise 1.
1 Temperatures go up. Then plants and trees die.
When <u>*temperatures go up, plants and trees die*</u>.
2 Mountains covered in ice will break up because we won't protect them.
Unless <u>*we protect mountains covered in ice, they'll break up*</u>.
3 Plants might die out. Then, as a result, small animals will find it hard to live.
If _____.
4 Large animals have a smaller area to hunt in because people build roads through forests.
When _____.
5 Large animals do not have enough space to find food, so they will die out.
Unless _____.
6 Roads should be carefully planned. Then the environment will be easier to manage.
Provided that _____.
7 Large animals aren't always protected, so tourism will suffer.
Unless _____.

b Complete the sentences using your own ideas.
1 If summers start to get hotter, …
2 If sea levels rise, …
3 The climate will improve provided that …
4 My country will have water shortages unless …

3a Read the article quickly. What is it about?

When to hunt the rare

Humans have been hunting wildlife for thousands of years. Today wildlife is hunted for food, clothes or medicine. Unless these activities [1] _____ (be) carefully controlled, the hunted species [2] _____ (quickly / become) at risk. In fact, there are many examples where species have disappeared because of over-hunting.

But evidence suggests hunting non-endangered animals [3] _____ (result) in a large number of economic benefits for communities, provided that local people carefully [4] _____ (control) it. However, it's possible there [5] _____ (be) much greater risks if the species [6] _____ (be) endangered. Unless the number of animals that are born and live to adulthood [7] _____ (be) higher than the number which are killed, future populations [8] _____ (die out). And this is not an easy thing to measure – counting animal numbers is expensive and takes time.

Communities [9] _____ (need) to consider all the social, cultural, environmental and economic effects if they [10] _____ (decide) to allow hunting, and make decisions using facts, not opinions.

b Complete the article with the correct form of the verbs in brackets.

48

Module 3
Wild world
3B

Academic vocabulary 2 AWL ACL

Collocations related to the natural world

1a Find and underline eight collocations in sentences 1–6 that match definitions A–H.
1 To become domestic, a <u>wild animal</u> must eat food that's readily available.
2 It helps if the animal lives in a group in its natural environment.
3 If the group has a social structure, the human can become its leader.
4 Service animals have become a common feature of modern society.
5 Dogs are able to provide assistance to people with disabilities.
6 Pets offer emotional support to sick and elderly people.

A creatures which live in a natural state (Sentence 1)
B quickly and easily found (Sentence 1)
C land that is not controlled by man (Sentence 2)
D the way people/animals live together (Sentence 3)
E something important that happens often (Sentence 4)
F the organisation of people today (Sentence 4)
G give help (Sentence 5)
H help related to feelings (Sentence 6)

b Match the collocations in Exercise 1a with their patterns.
1 adjective + noun
2 adverb + adjective
3 verb + noun

c Complete the sentences with collocations from Exercise 1a.
1 The plants that pandas eat aren't _____ in the wild.
2 Bees follow a(n) _____ where they all have different roles.
3 Floods are a(n) _____ of a kangaroo's life.
4 Working animals are used less in _____ compared to the past.
5 Forests are a koala's _____ .
6 A parrot in the USA provides _____ to its anxious owner by talking to him to keep him calm.
7 The WWF is one of many organisations which _____ to injured pets.

d Work in pairs. Which two sentences in Exercise 1c are false?

Negative prefixes

2a Read the sentences from Listening 2. How do the underlined prefixes change the meaning of the words?
1 Without these six things, it's <u>im</u>possible for an animal to become domestic.
2 The animal must eat <u>in</u>expensive food.
3 Slow-growing animals are <u>un</u>helpful to humans.
4 Dogs are able to provide assistance to people with <u>dis</u>abilities.

b Are all the words adjectives? Are there any verbs or nouns?

c Read the blog and add negative prefixes (*dis-*, *im-*, *in-* or *un-*) where necessary.

Insects and their effect on the economy

Insects may seem small and ¹ ___important but, in fact, our economy needs them. While it's ² ___common for insects to kill crops, which is ³ ___expensive and a huge ⁴ ___advantage to both farmers and the economy, insects provide several benefits. Firstly, the thought of eating them might be ⁵ ___pleasant to me but for many people insects provide an important food source and a food industry. Secondly, without insects, a fishing industry is ⁶ ___likely to survive because so many fish eat insects. Farmers may ⁷ ___like insects eating their crops but they like them keeping their land in good condition. And finally, without insects, pollen is ⁸ ___able to travel from one plant to another, which is necessary for life. So, insects might seem small to us humans but they affect our lives ⁹ ___directly every day.

3 Read the blog again and underline the key words. Then write a one-sentence summary. Identify the topic sentence to help you.

4 How do insects affect your country's economy?

3B Module 3: Wild world

Reading 2 (Multiple-choice, choose multiple answers)

Before you read

1 Match the words in bold in the sentences (1–3) with their meanings (A–C).
  1 Scientists are looking to see if an animal that receives help ever **returns the favour**.
  2 Unlike humans, animals don't have **empathy** for each other's emotions.
  3 Only humans have a **natural instinct** to help each other.

  A understanding other people's feelings or problems
  B a natural ability to know something
  C help someone because they helped you

Test practice

▶ EXPERT STRATEGIES page 178

2 Complete the task. Remember to consider facts and opinions.

▶ HELP

 • Underline the key words in option A. Then look for these key words or synonyms in the first paragraph. What is the conclusion of that paragraph?
 • Read option B. Can you find anything in the text about the different parts of the brain?

Read the text and answer the question by selecting all the correct responses. More than one response is correct.

After Hurricane Katrina hit the Gulf Coast of America in 2005, researchers questioned individuals who were able to leave the city but chose to stay. Around 18 percent said they stayed because they did not want to leave family members but nearly 50 percent of them would not leave their dogs and cats. 1,400 people died that day; some of them surely died because they loved their pets too much.

Evolutionary psychologists argue that caring is a technique present from birth, designed to keep us alive by helping relatives or others who will someday help us. Why, then, should we invest time, money and love in animals, who are unlikely to ever return the favour?

I believe our love for pets comes from three features of human nature: natural instincts, culture and empathy. The human brain makes us feel warm and happy when we see baby cheeks and big eyes. This developed to persuade us to take care of our own young. But it makes kittens and puppies seem attractive too. It also explains why we feel strongly about an animal such as a baby seal, yet care so little about one like the much rarer – but rather ugly – Chinese salamander.

But if this theory is true, we would expect that pet-keeping would, like music, be found in all human societies. This is not the case. In the Kenyan village where anthropologist Nyaga Mwaniki was born, people use dogs to guard against strangers and chase away wild animals. The dogs, however, are never touched or allowed to sleep in a human's bed. Indeed, Nyaga's native language does not even contain a word for 'pet'.

According to the text, which of the following statements is true about the human connection with pets?

A ☐ Evidence suggests that people were prepared to die in Hurricane Katrina to save their pets.
B ☐ Different parts of the brain recognise the need to care for different species.
C ☐ Humans are born with natural caring behaviours.
D ☐ The decision to care for animals offers some benefits to humans.
E ☐ Animals have never shown kindness to humans in return.
F ☐ People have a stronger emotional response to some animals more than others.
G ☐ The need to treat animals as pets is a universal one.

Task analysis

3 Work in pairs. Compare and discuss how you approached the task.
  1 What did you find most difficult about this task?
  2 How important do you think it is to move to the next option quickly if you cannot find paraphrases in the text?

Discussion

4 Discuss the questions in pairs.
  1 Why are children's books and films about pets so popular?
  2 What animals are popular as pets in your country? Why?

Module 3
Wild world
3B

Speaking 2 (Describe image)

Describing the stages of a process

To score well on *Describe image*, you need to be able to show how ideas are connected in your description.

1 Look at the diagram in Exercise 4 and answer the questions.
   1 What is an eel and where is it born?
   2 What kind of changes occur during the eel's life?
   3 Complete this topic sentence: *The diagram shows the _____ of a(n) _____ , in terms of the changes to its _____ and the _____ where it lives.*

2 Complete the article with the words in the box.

   after that   also   during   finally   the second stage   when   where

EELS

There are five key stages in the eel life cycle. The cycle begins in the ocean, [1]_____ the eel starts life as an egg. During [2]_____ , the eel is born, leaf-shaped. [3]_____ it grows, it enters the glass eel stage. [4]_____ this time it starts its journey, migrating to a fresh water environment. It [5]_____ changes shape, taking the more traditional snake-shape of an eel. [6]_____ the colour changes again and the young eel turns yellow and grows in size. It spends its life in fresh water until, [7]_____ , when the colour turns silver, it makes its way back to the ocean, where it reproduces and the cycle starts again.

Sample response

3 🎧 36 Listen to a student describing the diagram and answer the questions.
   1 Does he start in the best place?
   2 Does he cover all the stages?
   3 Does he use time connectors?
   4 Does he finish within the time limit?

Test practice

▶ EXPERT STRATEGIES page 172

4 Complete the task in pairs. Take turns to describe the diagram.

⏱ 40 sec. *Look at the diagram below. In 25 seconds, please speak into the microphone and describe in detail what the diagram is showing. You will have 40 seconds to give your response.*

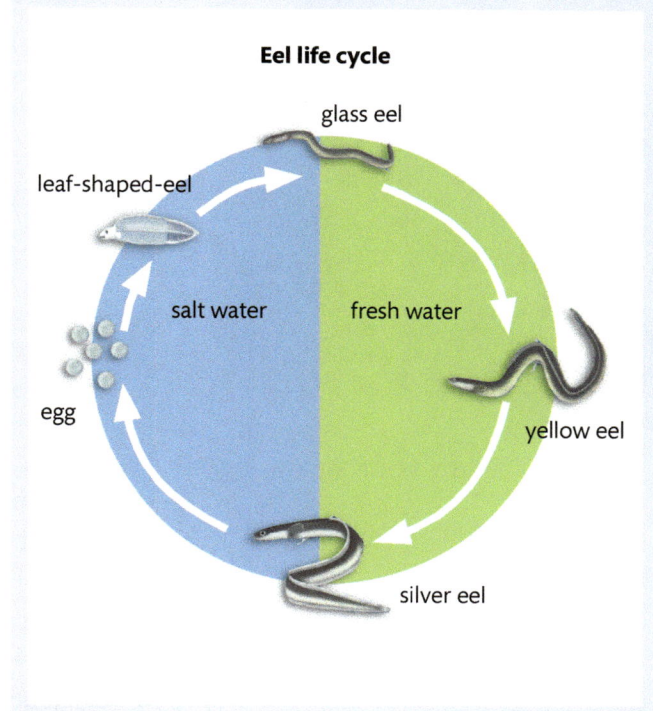

Eel life cycle

(Diagram labels: glass eel, leaf-shaped-eel, salt water, fresh water, egg, yellow eel, silver eel)

5 Turn to page 191 and complete another timed test practice.

▶ EXPERT SPEAKING page 191

Task analysis

6 Discuss the questions in pairs.
   1 Did you use time connectors and organise your work?
   2 Were you able to continue speaking without pausing?
   3 If you answered *no* to questions 1 and 2, try the activity again to see if you can improve.

3B Module 3: Wild world

Summary writing 2 (Summarize spoken text)

Lead-in 1 Discuss the questions in pairs.
1 Why do people have friends? Think of at least three reasons.
2 Do you think animals socialise for the same or different reasons? Why?

Understand the task 2 Read the instructions and answer the questions.
➤ EXPERT STRATEGIES page 182

> **10 min.** You will hear a short interview. Write a summary for a fellow student who was not present at the interview. You should write 50–70 words.
>
> You will have 10 minutes to finish this task. Your response will be judged on the quality of your writing and on how well your response presents the key points presented in the interview.

1 What are you going to hear?
2 What do you have to write?
3 How many words should you write?
4 How long do you have to write your summary?
5 How is your summary assessed?

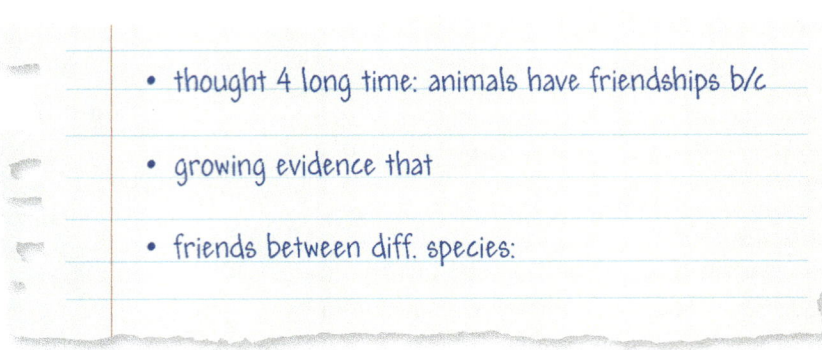

3 🎧 37 Listen to the interview and complete the notes.

- thought 4 long time: animals have friendships b/c
- growing evidence that
- friends between diff. species:

Plan your summary 4a Look at your notes from Exercise 3 and answer the questions about the speaker's main point.
1 What did scientists believe about animals and friendships?
2 Do they still believe this today?

b Write a topic sentence that summarises the speaker's main point. Use your answers to Exercise 4a to help you.

5a What points did the speaker make to support her main point? Answer the questions.
1 What exactly do scientists know about animal friendships today?
2 What do scientists know about friendships between animals of different species?

b The supporting points in Exercise 5a should follow your topic sentence. Organise them into a logical order (A–C).

c Compare your plans in pairs. Explain your decisions.

Module 3
Wild world
3B

Language and content

6a Match the beginnings of the sentences (1–6) with the endings (A–F).

1 Humans walk on two legs, whereas
2 Animals do not question their place on earth. However,
3 Arithmetic is a very human ability, although
4 Humans have a sense of humour, while
5 Empathy seems to be a very human emotion and yet
6 Some animals are able to use tools. On the other hand,

A they are unable to use them in different ways as humans do.
B humans do.
C elephants also show this feeling.
D only apes do in the animal world.
E other mammals usually walk on four.
F chimpanzees show some skill in adding up.

b Underline the linking words that show contrast in Exercise 6a. Which of them link two sentences? Which start a new sentence?

c Rewrite the sentences using the linking word in brackets. Replace the underlined words with the words in the box.

| are   do it   he   one   them   they (x3) |

1 Animals communicate through sound. Humans communicate through language. (whereas)
Animals communicate through sound whereas humans do it through language.
2 Scientists believed that only humans had real friendships. Scientists now believe this is not true. (however)
3 Scientists believed that animals have friends to protect their genes. Humans have friends for emotional purposes. (while)
4 Scientists believed that animals are not generous. Humans are generous. (whereas)
5 Some animals do a favour for a friend. The animals do not expect a favour in return. (and yet)
6 One chimpanzee helped another. The chimpanzee did not expect a favour in return. (although)
7 Scientists are learning about friendships between animals of the same species. Scientists know very little about friendships between animals from different species. (On the other hand)

7 Study the table.

Introduction	The speaker said that … The speaker suggested that … The speaker believes that … The speaker claims that …
Weak contrast	while, whereas, but, although, though (less formal/spoken English), and yet
Strong contrast	however, on the other hand, on the contrary, in contrast

Write your summary

8 Write your summary. Remember to begin with a topic sentence. Then include supporting points. Pay attention to the number of words you write.

Check your summary

➤ EXPERT WRITING page 196

9 Check your summary sentence using the checklist on page 196.

53

3B Module 3
Wild world

Review

1a Make the words in the box negative by adding prefixes.

appeared   directly   expensive   like   likely
pleasant   possible   usual

b Complete the sentences about bees with the negative words from Exercise 1a.

1 Until recently, scientists believed it was _____ for bees to fly because of the structure of their wings.
2 Bees are _____ to hurt you unless you disturb them or their home.
3 Most bees _____ living alone and prefer to live in families.
4 It is _____ for a queen bee to do any work except lay eggs.
5 The part of a hive that a queen bee lives in can be untidy and _____ .
6 It is _____ to keep bees in your garden as you do not need a lot of equipment.
7 In recent years the honey bee has _____ in large numbers.
8 Experts agree that the diet we enjoy _____ depends on bees.

2 Choose the correct options in *italics* to complete the article.

---

search News

Bees are a common ¹ *feature / thing* of gardens and woodlands all over the world but during the last decade their numbers have ² *dropped / lost* so much that scientists are worried. It is difficult to ³ *accurately / rightly* count numbers but if bees do not pollinate our plants, it is likely that our crops and food supply ⁴ *are going to / will* be in danger and we will be unable to ⁵ *eat / feed* ourselves.

Three new reports suggest that the cause may be certain chemicals which farmers use on their crops. When pollen is ⁶ *changed / removed* from a plant by a bee, the chemical goes with it. This causes the bee to become confused and ⁷ *disabled / unable* to find its way home. Because honey bees live within ⁸ *environmental / social* structures, they cannot survive on their own and soon die.

Scientists believe there may be other causes that can affect bee numbers, such as a decrease in woodland. As a result, next month our university department ⁹ *is starting / will start* a research project into the effects of building on green land. A report about the ¹⁰ *discoveries / events* we make will be available next year.

---

3 Complete the article with the words in the box.

attitudes   community   environmental   focus
leaders   modern   natural   policies   reduce
widely

Global warming is one of today's biggest issues but the importance of this problem is still not ¹ ____ accepted. This is because scientists have spent many years in the past disagreeing about why global warming exists. Some people in the science ² ____ argued that the changes are caused by the ³ ____ environment but others said it was caused by us and our ⁴ ____ society. Today the majority of scientists agree that the ⁵ ____ damage we have caused is the reason why global warming exists. We must therefore ⁶ ____ our attention on educating people and changing their ⁷ ____ to the problem. Then we may be able to encourage world ⁸ ____ , governments and organisations to introduce effective environmental ⁹ ____ which help to ¹⁰ ____ the effects of global warming in the future.

4 Complete the conditional sentences about the article in Exercise 3 with the correct form of the verbs in brackets.

1 When people _____ (think) about global warming, many _____ (believe) it does not actually exist.
2 When people _____ (hear) that scientists disagree, they _____ (not understand) why.
3 Unless people _____ (be) educated about global warming, they _____ (change) their attitudes in future.
4 Provided that people _____ (understand) global warming, more governments _____ (introduce) environmental policies.
5 We _____ (reduce) the effects of global warming if governments _____ (introduce) policies.
6 Unless we _____ (reduce) the effects of global warming, our climate _____ (continue) to change.

4 The global village

Overview

4A
- **Reading:** Re-order paragraphs
- **Academic vocabulary:** Travel and transport
- **Speaking:** Repeat sentence; Answer short question
- **Listening:** Multiple-choice, choose multiple answers
- **Language development:** Past tenses
- **Writing:** Write essay

4B
- **Listening:** Multiple-choice, choose multiple answers; Write from dictation
- **Language development:** Second conditional
- **Academic vocabulary:** Politics, history, language and culture
- **Reading:** Re-order paragraphs
- **Speaking:** Re-tell lecture
- **Writing:** Write essay

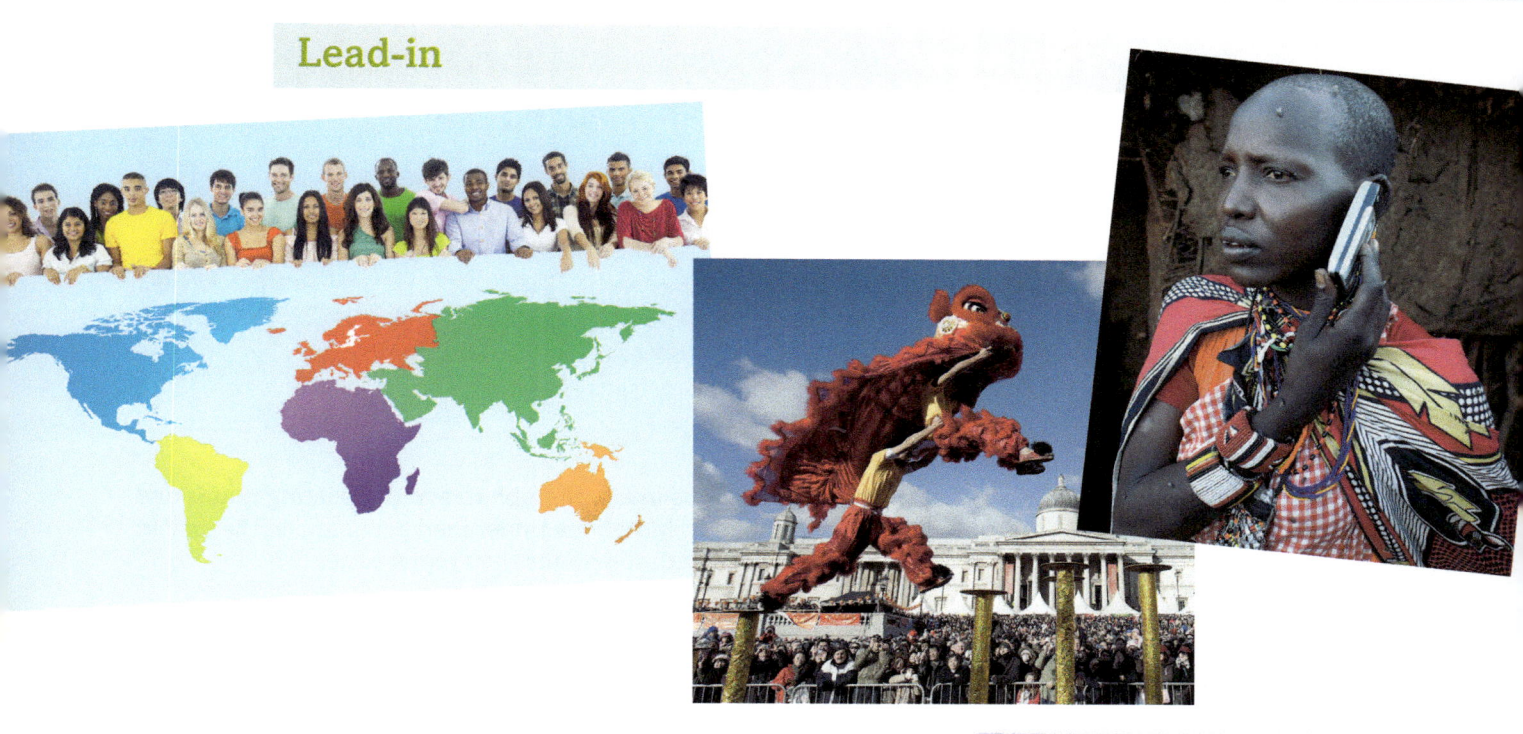

Lead-in

'It's a small world.'
common saying

'One day there will be no borders, no boundaries, no flags and no countries and the only passport will be the heart.'
Carlos Santana, musician

'Globalisation has changed us into a company that searches the world, not just to sell or source but to find the world's best talents and the greatest ideas.'
Jack Welch, former CEO of General Electric

1   Read the quotes and discuss the questions.
   1   How is the first quote true? Think about business, food and travel. How do the photos show this?
   2   Do you agree with the second quote? Why/Why not?
   3   What does the third quote mean?
       A   Today companies can operate in a lot of different countries and employ the best staff from around the world.
       B   Today there is greater communication between businesses and their employees in countries around the world.

2   How has globalisation affected each of the areas in the box? Think of both positive and negative effects.

   business   language   shopping   sport   travel   work

4A A globalised world

Reading 1 (Re-order paragraphs)

Before you read

1 Work in pairs and discuss the questions.
   1 What was your favourite toy during your childhood?
   2 Where do you think that toy was made?

Identifying relationships between sentences in a paragraph

Re-order paragraphs tests your understanding of how a text is organised.

2a Read the first part of an article. Match each sentence in the article with the descriptions.
   A topic sentence (a general statement to introduce the main idea)
   B supporting point (information and examples to support the main idea)
   C concluding sentence (a sentence that gives a conclusion)

A GLOBAL TOY

The manufacturing of Barbie dolls is a great example of globalisation. While ¹ they were originally made cheaply in post-World War II Japan, wages there started to rise and the local economy began to grow again. Consequently, Mattel had to look elsewhere to keep ² its manufacturing costs low. These days the label says the doll is made in China but Saudi Arabia, Malaysia, Indonesia, Japan, the USA, Taiwan, Hong Kong and mainland China all contribute to ³ its manufacture and distribution. ⁴ This makes ⁵ it a truly global product.

b We use pronouns in a paragraph to avoid repeating nouns and link ideas better. Match the underlined pronouns in the article in Exercise 2a with the nouns they replace.
   A the doll ___
   B the dolls __1__
   C Mattel's ___
   D the contribution of different countries ___
   E the doll's ___

3a Read the second part of the article. What noun does each of the underlined pronouns replace?
   1 *Barbie doll*

When we look at how a Barbie doll is made, we can see just how global ¹ it is. Firstly, a petrol company in mainland China buys a chemical from Saudi Arabia and then sells ² it to a company in Taiwan. ³ They turn ⁴ it into plastic, which is then shipped to Indonesia, Malaysia or mainland China. There, ⁵ it is used to make the bodies of the dolls. ⁶ These are sent to Hong Kong, where ⁷ they are put in trucks and driven to factories in southern China. At the same time, nylon hair is imported from Japan and cotton dresses arrive from other parts of China. All of ⁸ these are put together in the factories to create the doll. So, while the label says that Barbie dolls are made in China, this is not completely correct.

b Read the article in Exercise 3a again and identify the topic sentence, supporting points and concluding sentence.

Module 4
The global village
4A

Test practice
➤ EXPERT STRATEGIES page 179

4 Complete the task. Remember to think about the relationship between sentences in a paragraph.

The text boxes in the left panel have been placed in a random order. Restore the original order by dragging the text boxes from the left panel to the right panel.

Source | Target

A The shipping system required many changes and other technical innovations before the containers could be used.

B This situation caused delays and created opportunities for damage that were only reduced when the shipping container was invented.

C 60 years ago, when businesses did not think of the distribution of goods as a single process, someone had to physically transfer every box each time goods were moved from one transport to another.

D It was also necessary to build new roads and rail lines, requiring companies to invest millions.

E While this invention promised companies a lot of benefits, there were many difficulties at first.

➤ HELP
- What does *This situation* refer to in box B?
- What does *also* refer to in box D? What other thing was built or made?
- What does *this invention* refer to in box E?

Task analysis

5 Discuss the questions in pairs.
1 Does the paragraph start with a topic sentence and end with a concluding sentence?
2 Does the topic sentence start with a pronoun? Is it possible?

Discussion

6a Work in pairs. What inventions do you think have changed the world in the past? Make a list.

b Choose one invention on your list and give a short presentation to the class explaining why it changed the world. Which invention had the most impact?

EXPERT WORD CHECK
invent/invention   label   manufacture   originally   passenger

➤ See **Reading 2** for more practice of this task type.

57

4A Module 4
The global village

Academic vocabulary 1 AWL ACL

Travel and transport

Academic word list

1a Look at the map of the Panama Canal. How do you think this canal helps businesses today?

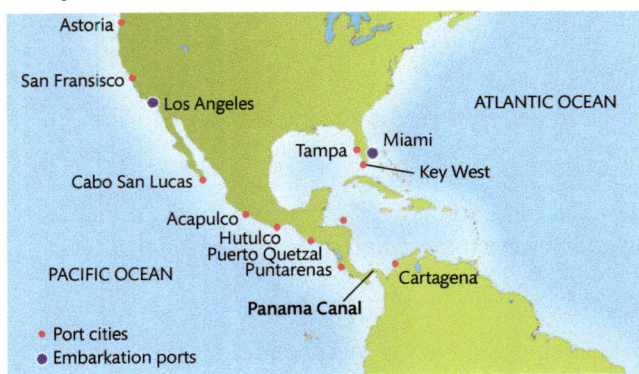

b Complete the article about the Panama Canal with the words in the box.

contribute   distribution   equipment   innovation
invest   required

The Panama Canal was built over 100 years ago to reduce the time ships spent travelling around South America. It was not a(n) ¹ _____ because the Suez Canal had been built ten years earlier but it was a difficult process which ² _____ several countries to ³ _____ large amounts of money. This money was used to buy ⁴ _____ and employ workers.
The possibility of easier ⁵ _____ of gold to Europe persuaded the USA to ⁶ _____ to the project. They bought and owned the land around the Panama Canal, which divided Panama in two for many decades, but ownership returned to the Panamanians in 1999.

Academic collocations list

2 Match the beginnings of the sentences (1–7) with the endings (A–G). Then note the collocations in *italics*.

1 The building of the Panama Canal *required*
2 A large amount of *foreign*
3 *Technological*
4 The building of the canal was a *slow*
5 The French and the Americans *contributed to*
6 Today the Panama Canal is important for the *local*
7 The Canal *creates*

A the development of the *project*.
B *economy*.
C *process*, taking over 30 years.
D *resources* such as machinery, workers and housing.
E *innovations* were also needed.
F *opportunities* for 14,000 workers.
G *investment* was needed.

Travel and transport

3a Read the article quickly. What is it about?

During the late 1800s the invention of steamships made it possible for people to travel ¹ *abroad / foreign*, sailing along ² *routes / ways* such as Liverpool to New York. Most passengers set off on a one-way ³ *journey / travel* to find work in a different country but wealthy people used to make the ⁴ *crossing / flight* for business or to see the ⁵ *sights / tourism*. The journeys were slow and it took several days for passengers to reach their ⁶ *arrival / destination*. When the jet engine was invented, people began to ⁷ *board / depart* planes because they were a much faster way to ⁸ *transport / travel* people and things from one place to another. So the ship industry focused on tourists who wanted to visit several countries during one holiday and the cruise ship was born.

b Choose the correct options in *italics* to complete the article in Exercise 3a.

c Complete the article with the correct form of the underlined verbs in Exercise 3a.

Although these days people regularly ¹ _____ abroad for business or to ² _____ local sights, such journeys were not always pleasurable. During the first half of the 19th century two million Irish people ³ _____ the Atlantic crossing to start a new life in the USA. Political problems and a lack of food in Ireland in the 1840s meant these people were sick and hungry. Some chose to ⁴ _____ along the New York route, while others went to Canada. These journeys were long and difficult and not everyone who ⁵ _____ a ship ⁶ _____ North America safely. Those who arrived in Canada had to ⁷ _____ on another difficult journey across land to the USA. But when people finally arrived in the USA, they often succeeded in finding a better life.

d Why do people choose to travel by ship today?

Module 4 4A
The global village

Speaking 1 (Repeat sentence; Answer short question)

Pronunciation: Intonation The level of an English speaker's voice changes when they speak. This is called intonation. In *Repeat sentence* you will need to use appropriate intonation.

1 a 🎧 38 Listen to the sentence. Which option, 1 or 2, best illustrates the speaker's intonation? Does the voice go up or down at the end?

   1 In 2011 the population of the world reached seven billion.

   2 In 2011 the population of the world reached seven billion.

   b 🎧 39 Listen to a second sentence. Does the speaker use the same or different intonation? Draw the intonation pattern.

   There are several reasons for population growth, such as better education.

   c 🎧 40 Listen and repeat both sentences. Copy the speaker's intonation.

2 🎧 41 Listen and repeat the sentences. Notice the same intonation each time.

Test practice 1: Repeat sentence
➤ EXPERT STRATEGIES page 171

3 🎧 42 Complete the task in pairs. You will hear ten sentences. Remember to use the correct intonation.

> ⏱ 15 sec. You will hear a sentence. Please repeat the sentence exactly as you hear it. You will hear the sentence only once.

Task analysis

4 🎧 43 Listen to a student repeating four of the sentences in Exercise 3. What is the problem with each sentence? Did you have any of these problems?

Test practice 2: Answer short question
➤ EXPERT STRATEGIES page 174

5 🎧 44 Complete the task in pairs. You will hear six questions.

> ⏱ 10 sec. You will hear a question. Please give a simple and short answer. Often just one or a few words is enough.

59

4A Module 4
The global village

Listening 1 (Multiple-choice, choose multiple answers)

Before you listen

1 a Read the text about modern society. Check the meaning of the words in bold in a dictionary.

> One of the **key features** of the modern world is speed. People want things that will help them to **organise** their time effectively. They don't want to sit down in a restaurant, so they go to **drive-through** restaurants. They don't want to wait for furniture to be built and then delivered, so they buy it **flat-pack** and take it home in the back of the car that day. And they prefer the **predictable** content of a series of films rather than something completely new.

b What do you do to save time?

Identifying speaker attitude and purpose

In *Multiple-choice, choose multiple answers* you may need to identify the attitude and purpose of a talk.

2 a Look at the words in the box. How do people with these attitudes behave or talk?

| annoyed | enthusiastic | surprised | worried |

b 🎧 45 Listen and match the speakers (1–4) with the attitudes in Exercise 2a.

c 🎧 45 Listen again. What helped you to decide?
1. The speaker used specific phrases (e.g. *that's why …, it's not that …*).
2. The level of the speaker's voice went up or down.
3. The speaker repeated surprising information.

Test practice

▶ EXPERT STRATEGIES page 183

3 a 🎧 46 Listen to a talk about 'McDonaldisation'. What is the speaker's purpose?
1. to praise how a system has developed
2. to criticise how a system works
3. to explain how a system can be used

b 🎧 46 Complete the task. Think about the speaker's attitude.

Listen to the recording and answer the question by selecting all the correct responses. You will need to select more than one response.

The speaker is

A ☐ enthusiastic about the name chosen for this business style.

B ☐ happy about the appearance of 'McDonaldisation' in education.

C ☐ worried that furniture delivery companies would lose business.

D ☐ surprised that customers quickly agreed to take on some tasks.

E ☐ annoyed that pasta companies misrepresent their products.

F ☐ pleased that standards of restaurants are the same around the world.

G ☐ unsure that the customer receives a better deal from this system.

▶ HELP

Underline both the words that show the speaker's attitude and the key words in the options.

Task analysis

4 Compare and discuss your answers. Did you listen for the speaker's attitude as well as the facts?

▶ See **Listening 2** for more practice of this task type.

Module 4
4A The global village

Language development 1

Past tenses

> EXPERT GRAMMAR page 206

1a Choose the correct options in *italics* to complete the sentences about 'McDonaldisation'.
1 Ritzer *described / used to describe* how it *seemed / was seeming* that the methods of running a fast food restaurant *used to spread / were spreading* to other areas of our life.
2 After drive-through restaurants *appeared / were appearing*, customers *used to do / were doing* the work for the company.
3 They *was / were* even led to the mistaken belief that it *was / were* for their benefit.
4 Companies *used to advertise / were advertising* a pasta that *cooked / was cooking* in five minutes instead of ten as a benefit, when few people really *needed / were needing* the five minutes they *used to save / were saving*.
5 When a man *went / was going* into a McDonald's restaurant anywhere in the world, he *could / used to be able to* expect the experience to be the same.

b 🎧 47 Listen and check your answers.

c Can you name the different tenses you used in Exercise 1a?

2a Complete the questions with the past simple or past continuous form of the verbs in brackets.
1 What _____ (you / do) at half past eight yesterday morning?
2 When you _____ (get) home last night, what _____ (the others in your house / do)?
3 Just before the teacher _____ (arrive), what _____ (you / talk) about?
4 What sport _____ (you / like) best when you _____ (be) in primary school?
5 What _____ (you / dream) about before you _____ (wake up) this morning?
6 What _____ (you / think) about while you _____ (travel) to work/school this morning?
7 _____ (you / get) to sleep quickly last night?
8 Can you remember what your best friend _____ (wear) the last time you _____ (see) him/her?

b Work in pairs. Choose three questions from Exercise 2a to ask your partner.

3a Complete the sentences with the inventions in the box.

| car | computer | steam engine | telephone | television |

1 Before the _____ , people used to take messages in person.
2 Before the _____ , everything used to be done on paper by hand.
3 Before the _____ , people didn't use to get news until much later.
4 Before the _____ , the train used to be an option for travelling a long way.
5 Before the _____ , travelling by ship used to be dependent on the wind.

b Work in pairs. Choose three other inventions and write sentences like the ones in Exercise 3a. Then ask other students in the class to complete your sentences.

4a Read the article and answer the questions.
1 What is a risk society?
2 How did things change after 1986?

RISK SOCIETIES

Until the late 20th century, we [1] _____ (can) plan for risks. We [2] _____ (invent) the emergency services to deal with fires and accidents and when an accident [3] _____ (happen), the insurance company [4] _____ (pay) to fix it. Risks [5] _____ (stop) being something that nations could control themselves around the end of the last century. In the 1970s, Swedish scientists [6] _____ (begin) to realise that factories in the north of England [7] _____ (cause) the damage to their forests. Then, in 1986, the Chernobyl accident completely [8] _____ (change) the way we think about international risks. The accident [9] _____ (affect) countries all over Western Europe. Now, it's not the case that life [10] _____ (be) safer in the past. After all, people [11] _____ (experience) hunger, illness and natural disasters on a regular basis. But the risks we face today are basically different. This is because we [12] _____ (not have) nuclear, chemical or genetic technologies at that time – technologies that don't respect national borders.

b Read the article again and complete it with the correct past form of the verbs in brackets.

c Do you think that we live in a risk society?

61

4A Module 4
The global village

Writing 1 (Write essay)

Building a paragraph

To score well in *Write essay*, you will need to show that you can organise and write a good paragraph.

1 Read the essay prompt and look at the underlined words. Then discuss the questions in pairs.

> Do you think tourism is good for a country? Argue either for or against this view.

1 What are the different kinds of tourism?
2 Are all types of tourism good?
3 Does everyone in a country benefit from tourism?

2a In this test task you have to write a persuasive essay. Which words in the prompt tell you this? Read about persuasive essays on page 198. Then list the advantages and disadvantages of tourism, using the ideas in the box to help you.

▶ EXPERT WRITING page 198

crime and policing   culture and traditions   economy
natural environments   roads and transport

b Which position can you argue best: for or against tourism?

3a Look at the paragraph. What idea in Exercise 2 does it develop?

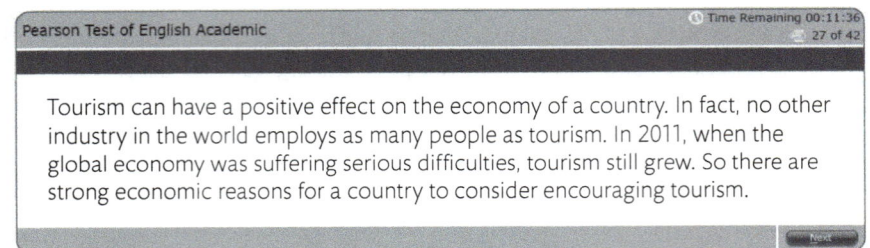

> Pearson Test of English Academic   Time Remaining 00:11:36
> 27 of 42
>
> Tourism can have a positive effect on the economy of a country. In fact, no other industry in the world employs as many people as tourism. In 2011, when the global economy was suffering serious difficulties, tourism still grew. So there are strong economic reasons for a country to consider encouraging tourism.

b Read about the PIE method of organising a paragraph. Then underline the *P*, *I* and *E* sections in the paragraph in Exercise 3a.

The PIE paragraph method
P – Make a point. (Write your topic sentence introducing the main idea.)
I – Illustrate it. (Give support in the form of examples or more details.)
E – Explain. (Write a concluding sentence, saying why this matters or how this relates back to the prompt.)

4 Now write your own paragraph for this prompt. Follow the steps below.
1 Choose an idea from the box in Exercise 2a.
2 Decide whether to argue for or against the statement.
3 Use the PIE paragraph method to organise your content.

▶ See **Writing 2** for more practice of this task type.

4B A cultural world

Listening 2 (Multiple-choice, choose multiple answers; Write from dictation)

Before you listen

1a Complete the questions with the words in the box.

century	classical	disappearing	endangered	legend	secrets

1 Do you think it's worth studying _____ languages like Latin these days?
2 Should we try to stop cultures and languages _____ ?
3 Should we be worried about looking after _____ cultures?
4 Do you think there are _____ written in some ancient languages?
5 There are around 6,500 languages currently spoken in the world. Do you think this number will increase or decrease in the next _____ ?
6 Can you describe an ancient _____ from your culture?

b How many different words are there for *rainy*, *windy*, *sunny* and *snowy* in your language? Why do some words have more synonyms than others?

Test practice 1: Multiple-choice, choose multiple answers
➤ EXPERT STRATEGIES page 183

2 🎧 48 Complete the task. Remember to take notes. You will not have time to read the options before the recording begins.

Listen to the recording and answer the question by selecting all the correct responses. You will need to select more than one response.

When talking about the Inuit language, the speaker is

A ☐ interested in how the number of words for *snow* has attracted attention.
B ☐ surprised that the different kinds of snow make so many words necessary.
C ☐ annoyed that foreigners find it hard to learn the difficult vocabulary.
D ☐ aware that several words may describe the same physical thing.
E ☐ confident that people who speak it understand life in a different way.

➤ **HELP**
- Underline the key words in the options.
- Look at option A. Is the speaker interested in the attention this topic has received? What words tell you this?
- Look at option B. Does the speaker think the words are necessary?

Test practice 2 Write from dictation
➤ EXPERT STRATEGIES page 189

3 🎧 49 Complete the task. You will hear three sentences. Then compare answers in pairs.

You will hear a sentence. Type the sentence in the box below exactly as you hear it. Write as much of the sentence as you can. You will hear the sentence only once.

Task analysis

4a Look at your notes from Exercise 2. Did you take notes on the attitude of the speaker as well as the content? How could you improve your notes?

b 🎧 49 Listen again and check your answers in Exercise 3.

4B Module 4
The global village

Language development 2

Second conditional

> EXPERT GRAMMAR page 207

1 Match the beginnings of the sentences (1–4) with the endings (A–D).
   1 Could you think of something new
   2 If we allowed a minority language like Inuit to die,
   3 If we had the language to understand the Inuit world,
   4 Whether you *ate* food or *consumed* food,

   A would we be able to access new experiences?
   B we'd lose the secrets they held forever.
   C your experience would be the same.
   D if you didn't have a name for it?

2a Complete the sentences with *would* and the verbs in the box.

   be   drive   eat   have   live   own

   If the world were a village of 100 people,
   1 80 of them _____ in poor quality housing.
   2 33 of them _____ unable to read or write.
   3 half _____ enough food to keep healthy.
   4 a third _____ access to clean drinking water.
   5 five of them _____ 32 percent of the village's wealth.
   6 seven of them _____ a car, perhaps more than one.

b Complete the sentences with the correct form of the verbs in brackets.
   1 If you _____ (speak) English to a person in the village, only seven of them _____ (understand) what you were saying.
   2 You _____ (need) to learn over 200 languages if you _____ (want) to understand everyone in the village.
   3 If you _____ (have) a computer, you _____ (can) email the seven other people with computers.
   4 If you _____ (be) from Australia, you _____ (be) the only person from that country.
   5 You _____ (be) one of 76 people if you _____ (have) electricity.
   6 If you _____ (be) one of the 76 people with electricity, you _____ (probably / use) it only for light at night.
   7 There _____ (be) 19 other children to play with if you _____ (be) a child.
   8 If you _____ (own) a telephone, you _____ (can) call 13 other numbers.

c Which statistic from Exercise 2a or b surprises you the most? Why?

3a Choose the correct options in *italics* to complete the article.

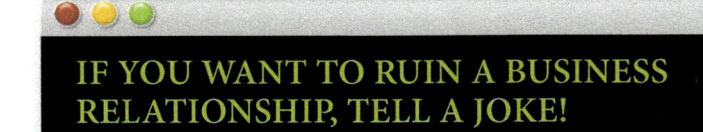

IF YOU WANT TO RUIN A BUSINESS RELATIONSHIP, TELL A JOKE!

Imagine you're at an international business meeting. The first barrier to humour would be language. For example, if the Japanese businessman [1] *told / would tell* an 'old man' joke or the American a 'doctor' joke, other business people [2] *didn't / wouldn't* understand it because the words [3] *didn't / wouldn't* translate with the same comic meaning.

The second barrier [4] *was / would be* shared culture. Humour takes our norms and changes them so they become funny. People at the meeting [5] *couldn't / wouldn't* be able to share a joke if they [6] *didn't / wouldn't* share those norms. Even if two people from different countries [7] *spoke / would speak* the same language, they [8] *didn't / wouldn't* always understand the joke. Topic [9] *was / would be* another issue. If the Brit [10] *told / would tell* a small joke about their royal family, it [11] *was / would be* funny to the Australian. But for the Thai businesswoman this [12] *was / would be* offensive. These are the reasons why interpreters often ignore jokes when translating during business meetings.

b Read the text about a project called *LaughLab*. Find three second conditional errors, three spelling errors and two punctuation errors.

One day Profesor Richard Wiseman had an idea. If he created a project called *LaughLab* he'd be able to search for the funiest international joke. If he create a website, he'd attract interest from people all over the world. If he attracted interest from people all over the world, he'll have the opportunity to collect thousands of jokes. And if he published those jokes, other people can rate them? So that's exactly what he did and the result was a winning joke by a 31-year-old psychiatrist from Manchester, UK.

c How would you feel if someone asked you to tell a joke in front of a group of people? Why?

Academic vocabulary 2 AWL ACL

Academic collocations list

1a Choose the correct options in *italics* to complete the sentences. Then write the collocations in bold in your vocabulary notebook.
1. There are always *personal / individual* **differences** within social groups.
2. My favourite *historical / past* **period** is the early 19th century.
3. Australian *population / national* **identity** is an interesting subject.
4. There are two main *political / voting* **parties** in the USA.
5. Everyone has *social / community* **responsibility**.
6. Life was more dangerous in *earlier / previous* **times**.
7. People with disabilities were legally given *same / equal* **opportunities** in 1995.
8. *World / International* **organisations** like the UN carry out a lot or research.

b Work in pairs. Underline the stressed syllables in the collocations in Exercise 1a. Then practise saying the collocations.

c Complete the facts with the collocations in Exercise 1a.
1. Studies of _____ in ability led to IQ tests.
2. Songs and food help make a country's _____ .
3. The word *class* meant 'a group of soldiers' in _____ .
4. The Conservatives and the New Democrats are the two largest _____ in Canada.
5. Many feel that _____ is the duty of every individual and organisation.
6. The WHO is one of the biggest _____ .
7. In the US Martin Luther King fought for _____ in the 1960s.
8. The oldest recorded _____ was 5,000 years ago.

Word formation with language and culture

2a Complete the sentences with a word formed from the word in capitals.
1. What is your __national__ language? NATION
2. Are there any regional _____ in accents in your country? DIFFER
3. Is eye contact important to communicate _____ in your culture? EFFECT
4. Has social media changed your methods of _____ ? COMMUNICATE
5. How many Chinese _____ are there in the world? SPEAK
6. Have you ever given a _____ ? SPEAK
7. Do certain flowers _____ anything special, like romance or peace? SYMBOL
8. Does your college _____ with any others on special projects? OPERATE
9. Do people use _____ language when they send text messages? STANDARD

b Work in pairs. Choose three questions from Exercise 2a to ask your partner.

Academic word list

3a Read the article quickly and answer the questions.
1. What is the greying of society?
2. Who does it affect these days?

b Complete the article with the words in the box.

diverse   immigration   individuals   located   majority
medical   range   relevant   revolution   roles

c When do you think is the best age to retire?

THE GREYING OF SOCIETY

Ever since the industrial [1] _____ , improvements in [2] _____ technology, changes in education and women's [3] _____ in and out of the home, and a wide [4] _____ of other causes have meant that populations around the world are getting older. United Nations data suggests that it now affects rich and poor countries alike. All around the world populations are changing. But why is this issue of ageing populations [5] _____ ? There's one main reason: the [6] _____ of pension systems were not designed for a large, older, non-working population. Many countries are starting to ask if [7] _____ need to keep working longer before retirement. But the effects of ageing populations are as [8] _____ as countries themselves. Although Scandinavia and France are [9] _____ in Europe, they currently have more youthful populations, while some Asian countries are already getting older. The USA has avoided the problem through high [10] _____ rates, with young people coming into the country.

4B Module 4
The global village

Reading 2 (Re-order paragraphs)

Before you read

1 Work in pairs. Think about three brands from your country and discuss the questions. Check the meaning of the words in bold in a dictionary if you are unsure.
  1 Does the brand name have a particular meaning or is it **made-up**?
  2 Does the brand name **reflect** the service the company provides?
  3 Is the brand name easy to **pronounce**?
  4 Do you think the word can be **translated** into other languages easily? Why/Why not?

Test practice
> EXPERT STRATEGIES page 179

2 Complete the task. Remember to think about how sentences are linked to create a paragraph.

The text boxes in the left panel have been placed in a random order. Restore the original order by dragging the text boxes from the left panel to the right panel.

Source | Target

A So a made-up word or compound word can be a good idea.

B However, if your brand name reflects a key benefit of your service, such as 'Budget Car Rental', then you may want to consider translating it for other markets.

C In other words, one that's simple, easy to pronounce and has no particular meaning.

D Ideally, the brand name you choose should be one that doesn't require translation.

> HELP

• Which sentence introduces the topic? This probably comes first.
• In box C, *In other words* introduces a different way of saying what?

Task analysis

3 Why is it important to read the sentences carefully in the correct order before you move on to the next task?

Discussion

4a Work in small groups. Which is the most popular brand in the industries in the box in your country? Are they global brands?

car   drink   fashion   footwear   technology

b How do global brands affect local companies? What is your opinion of this?

Module 4
The global village 4B

Speaking 2 (Re-tell lecture)

Taking notes on the main point and supporting points

In *Re-tell lecture* you will need to take good notes on all the points in the lecture so that you can re-tell it more easily.

1 a You are going to hear a lecture. Look at the presentation slide in Exercise 3. What is the topic of the lecture?

b 🎧 50 Listen to the lecture and look at the notes two students made. Which student has correctly noted down the main point of the speaker?

1   English most successful world lang but less use in future

2   English language of science = more translation tech needed

c 🎧 51 Listen to the first half of the lecture again and correct the mistakes in the notes on the supporting points.

1 spoken every country; learnt by adults
2 language of sci, music and popular culture
3 few people think Eng. spread more

d 🎧 52 Now listen to the second half of the lecture and complete the notes on the supporting points.

1 academic says 330 m 1st language speakers; this population not _____
2 non-Eng-speaking countries won't make English a _____
3 so English will _____; replaced by technology, e.g. _____

Sample response

2 🎧 53 Listen to a student re-telling the lecture. Do you think he took good notes?

Test practice
▶ EXPERT STRATEGIES page 173

3 🎧 50 Complete the task in pairs. Take notes, then present the information to your partner.

⏱ 40 sec. You will hear a lecture. After listening to the lecture, in 10 seconds, please speak into the microphone and re-tell what you have just heard from the lecture in your own words. You will have 40 seconds to give your response.

English as a world language

- 330 million speakers of English as a first language
- 1 billion speakers of English as a second language

NCSU

▶ EXPERT SPEAKING page 193

4 🎧 54 Turn to page 193 and complete another timed test practice.

Task analysis

5 Did your partner re-tell the main point and supporting points from the lecture? Do you think he/she took good notes?

4B Module 4
The global village

Writing 2 (Write essay)

Lead-in 1 Work in pairs. Describe some of the old traditions in your country. Use the ideas in the box to help you. Do you think these traditions will still be alive in 50 years' time?

art and crafts   clothing   dance   music and instruments

Understand the task
➤ EXPERT STRATEGIES page 176

2 Read the essay prompt and underline the key words. Then work in pairs and share ideas on the topic.

> **20 min.** You will have 20 minutes to plan, write and revise an essay about the topic below. Your response will be judged on how well you develop a position, organise your ideas, present supporting details and control the elements of standard written English. You should write 200–300 words.
>
> Languages and the cultures with them are disappearing every week. When they go, we lose knowledge, heritage and different ways of viewing the world, so we should try to save minority languages, cultures and traditions. Argue either in support of this view or against it.

➤ HELP
- Do you think *heritage* here means 'physical environment' or 'traditions'?
- What type of essay do you need to write? What words tell you this?

Plan your essay
To score well in *Write essay*, you need to support your opinions with evidence. Decide which side of this persuasive essay you can support more strongly: for or against.

3a Think of ways to use these ideas to argue for or against the view in the essay prompt. Add some more ideas of your own.
1 why these cultures are disappearing
2 how national and international languages can be useful
3 whether it is possible to save these cultures
4 what the cost of saving languages might be

b Decide which side of the argument you have more evidence for. Then write your ideas in the PIE plan.

Values in the classroom
Introduction: _____
Para 1:   P _____
          I _____
          E _____

Para 2:   P _____
          I _____
          E _____
Conclusion: _____

68

Module 4
The global village   4B

Language and content

When you write in academic English, you need to make sure that each idea within a paragraph is introduced and that you end your paragraph with an explanation of why this information is important.

4   Look at possible ways of beginning paragraphs and decide which of these expressions you could use in your essay. Match them with the paragraphs in your plan.

Introduce an idea	*Many people argue that* cultures need to be saved.
	It has been suggested that all cultures should be saved.
Link to a previous paragraph	*However*, it is important to also consider the costs.
	This leads us to the question of cost.
Reject an idea	*Experts continue to disagree about* the value of cultures.
	It is not true that children benefit from speaking minority languages.

5a Paragraphs often end with a prediction or a warning and conditional sentences are ideal for this. Complete the sentences using your own ideas. Then compare your ideas in pairs.
   1 If languages and minority cultures disappeared, …
   2 Unless governments offer media and education in these languages, …
   3 Provided that there are enough qualified teachers who speak the language, …
   4 Unless children speak the main national language of business, …
   5 If employees speak international languages, …
   6 If governments send scientists to record and translate the language, …

b Look at possible ways of ending paragraphs and decide which of these expressions you could use in your essay. Match them with the paragraphs in your plan.

Make a prediction	*If* we do something now, *we can* change this.
	Provided that we record these languages immediately, they will still exist.
Give a warning	*Unless* we do something now, this situation will only become worse.
	We must save these languages now. *If we do not*, it may soon be too late.
Explain why this is important	*This means that* young people can get better jobs.
	So, it is only natural for languages to die.
Point out a weakness in an idea (which you will discuss in the next paragraph)	*However, this does not take into account* the cost.
	While this is true, it does not address the problem of sending researchers to record the languages.

Write your essay

6   Write your essay. Use your plan from Exercise 3b and the language in Exercises 4 and 5 to help you. Remember to write 200–300 words.

Check your essay

➤ EXPERT WRITING page 196

7   Check your essay using the checklist on page 196.

4B Module 4
The global village

Review

1 Complete the article with the correct past form of the verbs in brackets.

Does your language change the way you think?

In the 1980s, a theory called Neurolinguistic Programming ¹ _____ (argue) that changing the words you use daily would make you more successful. This ² _____ (never / be) proven to work before, though scientists ³ _____ (since / find) that using positive language in daily conversation improves mood that particular day.

In the 1990s people working in the media in countries like the US and UK ⁴ _____ (realise) that the population ⁵ _____ (become) increasingly mixed. To avoid upsetting members of the audience, they ⁶ _____ (decide) to change the words they ⁷ _____ (use). They ⁸ _____ (drop) words like 'firemen' in favour of 'fire-fighters', to respect the fact that women ⁹ _____ (work) in these jobs at that time. 'Christmas' ¹⁰ _____ (turn) into 'the holidays', to avoid excluding people from other religions.

Whether the change in language ¹¹ _____ (cause) a positive change in social attitudes around that time or simply ¹² _____ (reflect) attitudes which ¹³ _____ (already / change) is hard to say.

2 Complete the sentences about business culture with the correct form of the verbs in the boxes. Make any verbs negative, if necessary.

be   go   need   offer   speak   try   understand   want

1 If you _____ to do business in a different country, you _____ to know about its laws, economy and culture.
2 If you _____ to a business meeting, it _____ quite a formal experience.
3 People _____ you easily if you _____ English.
4 If you _____ a fair price, business people _____ hard to reduce the price.

be   do   get   have to   import   spend   try   want

5 You _____ a lot of time filling in paperwork if you _____ products.
6 If you _____ business in my country, you _____ wear the local dress.
7 If you _____ to be rude, it _____ important to eat anything you are offered.
8 You _____ a good response if you _____ to talk about family during a business lunch.

3 Complete the article with the words in the box.

contribute   creates   distribution   equipment
foreign   innovations   process   require

What are the problems with international coffee chains?

We asked people for their opinions.

'They're only popular because they're cheap to set up and ¹ _____ few resources. They don't ² _____ anything to the locals, though, because they pay such low wages.'

'I don't think there are any problems. The ³ _____ investment which these companies bring is good for the local economy and ⁴ _____ opportunities through jobs.'

'Cafés have only become popular thanks to technological ⁵ _____ like wi-fi connections and portable computer ⁶ _____ , so people can sit and work in a café.'

'As the manager of a coffee shop, I know it's always a slow ⁷ _____ finding good locations. We need somewhere central, so people will stop but then ⁸ _____ , you know, getting fresh ingredients to the stores, becomes hard.'

4 Do the puzzle. What is the mystery word?

¹ e _ _ _ _ - t i m e s
² i
³ r
⁴ s o _ _ - r _ p _
⁵ i n
⁶ m
⁷ r a
⁸ i n

1 a period in the past
2 a country's culture, languages and traditions: national _____
3 the job or the thing you do in an organisation
4 the idea that an organisation should take decisions which benefit a community
5 one person, considered separately from the rest
6 most of the people or things in a group
7 a group of things that are different but belong to the same type
8 a group of people with members from around the world: _____ organisations

70

5 Sensational

Overview

5A
- **Reading:** Reading & writing: Fill in the blanks
- **Academic vocabulary:** Entertainment
- **Speaking:** Read aloud; Answer short question
- **Listening:** Fill in the blanks
- **Language development:** Expressing quantity
- **Summary writing:** Summarize spoken text

5B
- **Listening:** Highlight incorrect words
- **Language development:** Comparatives and superlatives
- **Academic vocabulary:** The arts
- **Reading:** Reading & writing: Fill in the blanks
- **Speaking:** Describe image
- **Summary writing:** Summarize spoken text

Lead-in

1 Discuss the questions in pairs.
   1 What do you think of the three sounds represented in the photos?
   2 What are your favourite sounds? Why?
   3 Are there any sounds you dislike?

2 🎧 55 Work in pairs. Listen and try to guess the sounds.

71

5A Sound

Reading 1 (Reading & writing: Fill in the blanks)

Before you read

1a Match the words in bold in the sentences (1–5) with their meanings (A–E).
1 Do you think good **pitch** is something people can learn?
2 Do you think listening to music can be a **productive** task?
3 How does your country **classify** types of music? Which are your favourites?
4 Have you ever tried to **compose** your own music?
5 What kind of thing **distracts** you from work?

A producing or achieving something useful
B write a piece of music
C the ability of a musician to play or sing a note at exactly the correct level
D decide what group something belongs to
E take someone's attention away from something

b Discuss the questions in Exercise 1a in pairs.

Recognising academic tone

Reading & writing: Fill in the blanks tests your overall understanding of a text. The correct choice of word might be decided by the correct tone for the context a word appears in.

2a Read the texts quickly. Which do you think is formal? Which is informal? Why?

1

Guys who can really play the guitar or the drums [1] **know absolutely loads** about music and sounds. And one or two can say the name of a note as soon as they hear it. [2] **Anyway**, this means that having to listen to other noises around them every day really starts to suck and stops them getting on with other stuff like working or sleeping.

2

Musicians [3] **are aware of** sounds in general and, in fact, some even have the ability to [4] **recognise pitch**, identifying a note without comparing it to any other sound. [5] **However**, for those who notice sounds, any form of noise can be emotionally upsetting and distract them from doing more productive tasks such as relaxation and sleep.

b Read the texts again and match the words in bold (1–5) with the features of formal and informal language (A–E).
A informal linkers (e.g. *besides, well*)
B formal linkers (e.g. *although, provided that, otherwise*)
C informal vocabulary (e.g. *mates, hang out, awesome*)
D formal vocabulary (e.g. *benefit, negative, cause*)
E technical words (e.g. *productive tasks*)

c Underline any other examples of formal and informal language you can find in the texts in Exercise 2a.

Module 5
5A Sensational

Test practice
➤ EXPERT STRATEGIES page 181

3 Complete the task. Remember to consider the tone of the text.

Below is a text with blanks. Click on each blank, a list of choices will appear. Select the appropriate answer choice for each blank.

When people describe themselves as 'tone deaf', 'having no rhythm' or 'no ear for music', they generally think of these things as defining characteristics. They are talents you are ¹ [____] born with or not. However, there is a variety of research on skill development which questions this. Carol Dweck's research shows that people who believe that skill can be developed will be far more successful, ² [____] supporting the old saying, 'Whether you believe you can or can't, you're right.' Along similar lines, Anders Ericsson found that what ³ [____] the experts from the amateurs in any field is about 10,000 hours of deliberate practice. The most important lesson, of course, is that change *is* possible. People can become something they aren't and change who they are. Talent, even one like music, can be cultivated. However, this is not to say that natural talent does not exist. One often overlooked study by Edwin Gordon showed that talent ⁴ [____] for about half the differences in musical skill development in a group of students after three years of studying. So ⁵ [____] anyone can become a musician, not everyone can become the best musician.

1	2	3	4	5
whether	clues	disconnects	showed	when
both	certification	separates	accounted	anyway
alternatively	evidence	groups	explained	although
either	document	identifies	predicted	therefore

➤ **HELP**
- Read the whole sentence before and after blank 1. What word collocates with *or not*?
- Look at the options in 2. Which word is more informal? Which word do we usually use with something that *research shows*?

Task analysis   **4** What helped you to decide which answers were wrong (e.g. the tone, singular/plural words, prepositions)?

Discussion   **5** Discuss the questions in pairs.
1 What talent would you like to develop?
2 Do you have the patience to learn new talents?

> What talent would you like to develop?

> I've always wished I could play the guitar.

> So what's stopping you?

> I think I'm too lazy!

➤ See **Reading 2** for more practice of this task type.

EXPERT WORD CHECK
along similar lines   defining characteristics   deliberate   note   overlooked

5A Module 5
Sensational

Academic vocabulary 1 AWL ACL

Academic collocations list

1a Discuss the questions in pairs. Check the meaning of the words in bold in a dictionary if you are unsure.
1. Is music in your country influenced by **western society**?
2. Did you enjoy studying **literary texts** at school?
3. Do you like reading books with **factual information**?
4. Where can you get **free access** to the internet?
5. Do you belong to any **virtual communities**?
6. What are the most **popular media** in your country?
7. What TV shows reach a **wider audience**?
8. Which has a more **powerful influence** in your country, television or newspapers?

b Discuss two questions from Exercise 1a.

Academic word list

2a Complete the sentences with the words in the box.

acquire   alternatives   beneficial   category   specific

1. Everyone should have a(n) _____ place where they can go to relax.
2. Spending time on a hobby is _____ .
3. It takes six months to _____ a new language.
4. The most popular _____ of music among young people is rock.
5. There are not enough _____ to reality TV.

b Write the words from Exercise 2a in your vocabulary notebook with an example sentence.

Entertainment

3a Complete the article with the words in the box.

advance   album   broadcast   commission   hit
illegal downloads   media   on tour   produce
promotion   recording artist   released

THE WAY THE MUSIC DIED

¹_____ are not the only threat to the music industry. A recent report suggests that for every $1,000 sold, the average ²_____ receives $23.40 – if they're lucky.
It starts with a new band getting a $1 million ³_____ . They spend half of that recording songs for their first ⁴_____ . They pay $100,000 to their manager, to cover his ⁵_____ and $50,000 to their lawyer. That leaves $350,000 for the four band members to share. After $170,000 in taxes, that leaves $45,000 per member to live on for a year until the CD gets ⁶_____ . The record is a big ⁷_____ and sells a million copies, so they need a video to go with it, which costs a million dollars to ⁸_____ and half those costs come from the band's royalties. The band is then advanced another $200,000 to go ⁹_____ around the country, which will need to be returned. Also, the $300,000 cost of ¹⁰_____ , such as getting the song ¹¹_____ on radio stations, comes out of the band's money. By that point, the band owes two million dollars to the record company, which is just covered by the two million dollars they made in royalties. How much did the ¹²_____ companies make? 11 million dollars!

b Work in pairs. Do you think being a musician is still a good career?

Word formation

4a Complete the sentences with the words in *italics*. Check the meaning of any unknown words in a dictionary.

1. *create, creative, creativity*
   A Have you ever tried _____ writing?
   B If you could _____ a work of music or art, which would you choose?
   C Do you think that schools do enough to encourage _____ ?

2. *entertain, entertaining, entertainment*
   A Do you have a wide choice of _____ in your country?
   B Do you think children's TV is more _____ today than in the past?
   C What could you do to _____ a small group of people?

3. *literacy, literate, literature*
   A What do you think is the best work of _____ your country has produced?
   B Is everybody in your country computer-_____ ?
   C What is the _____ rate in your country?

b Write the suffixes from Exercise 4a in 1–6 in the spidergram. Then write two examples for each suffix.

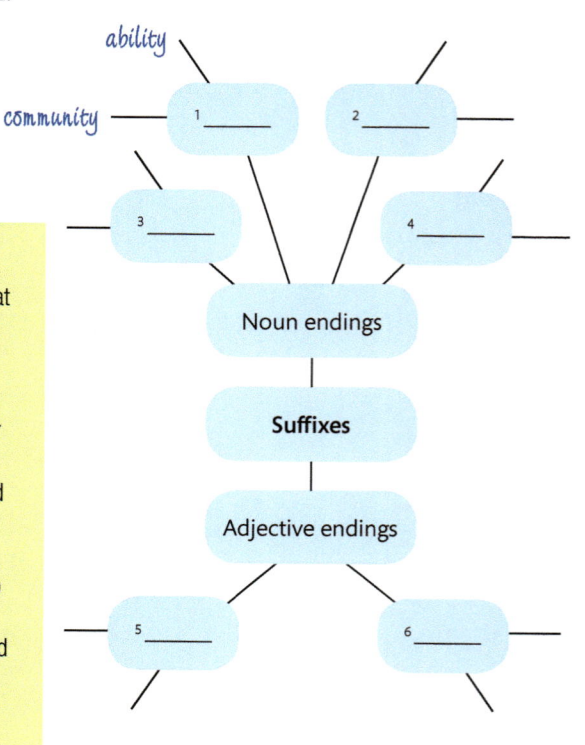

ability
community

Noun endings
Suffixes
Adjective endings

Module 5 Sensational — 5A

Speaking 1 (Read aloud; Answer short question)

Pronunciation: Word stress

To score well in *Read aloud*, you will need to use the correct word stress.

1a Look at the words with suffixes in the table and underline the stressed syllables. Then complete the third column. Compare answers in pairs.

b 🎧 56 Work in pairs. Practise saying the words in the table. Then listen and check.

Noun endings	Nouns	Stressed syllable
-ology	a<u>po</u>logy, so<u>cio</u>logy, psy<u>cho</u>logy	third from the end
-cy	frequency, accountancy, emergency	
-ity	university, nationality, celebrity	
-ment	document, instrument, government	
-tion/-sion	nation, promotion, commission	
Adjective endings	**Adjectives**	**Stressed syllable**
-ive	active, creative, interactive	
-able	lovable, available, microwavable	
-tional	national, emotional, professional	

2 Underline the stressed syllables in the words in bold. Then practise saying the sentences.
1 The best way to describe the advantages of digital sound **technology** is **quality**.
2 The **improvements** are clearer in **action** films.
3 There is often an **intentional decision** to make objects sound as though they are flying around the room.

Test practice 1: Read aloud

▶ EXPERT STRATEGIES page 170

3 Complete the task. Think about word stress before reading aloud.

> ⏱ 40 sec. *Look at the text below. In 40 seconds, you must read this text aloud as naturally and clearly as possible. You have 40 seconds to read aloud.*
>
> When recording instruments or vocals, not every place in a room is equal. Generally, for vocals, the singer should never sing directly into a hard surface and should always be pointed towards the middle of the room and the microphone. A quality microphone, located in front of the singer, will best record both the placement and the performance.

▶ **HELP**

- Say the word *instrument*. Stress the third syllable from the end: *instrument*.
- Say the phrase *quality microphone*. Stress the third syllable from the end: *quality microphone*.

Task analysis

4a 🎧 57 Listen to a student doing the task. Did she stress the same words as you? What would you change about how you read the text?

b Use your answers to Exercise 4a to make any necessary improvements and try the task again.

Test practice 2: Answer short question

▶ EXPERT STRATEGIES page 174

5 🎧 58 Complete the task in pairs. You will hear six questions.

> ⏱ 10 sec. *You will hear a question. Please give a simple and short answer. Often just one or a few words is enough.*

5A Module 5
Sensational

Listening 1 (Fill in the blanks)

Before you listen

1 Discuss the questions in pairs. Check the meaning of the words in bold in a dictionary if you are unsure.
   1 How do **soundtracks** try to create excitement, **comedy**, **panic**, sadness and **tension** in film **scenes**? Think about **pitch** and **volume**.
   2 Do you ever **download** soundtracks? Is it OK to **share** these music files **illegally**?

Identifying words and phrases appropriate to the context

In *Fill in the blanks*, you will need to listen for missing words and check they are appropriate to the context of the text.

2a Look at the words in the box. Can you think of words that sound the same as these words but have a different spelling?

| aloud | guessed | here | hire | peace | sail | scene |
| week | whether | worn | | | | |

aloud / allowed

b 🎧 59 Read and listen to the sentences. As you listen, note down the missing words next to the sentences.
   1 A composer knows that when audiences _____ light and gentle notes, they feel sad.
   2 _____ notes that jump to lower notes are good for comedy.
   3 Short, restricted high notes can add tension to a(n) _____ .
   4 Deep, heavy sounds _____ us of danger, whereas higher notes suggest panic.
   5 And music that increases in pitch can build excitement, _____ it's in an action film or a romantic comedy.

c Check the words you wrote down in Exercise 2b. Does the meaning and form of each word fit the sentence? Write the correct words in the blanks.

Test practice

▶ EXPERT STRATEGIES page 184

3 🎧 60 Complete the task. Remember to note down the words as you listen.

> *You will hear a recording. Type the missing words in each blank.*
>
> It's been a challenging decade for the music industry, with a significant decrease in ¹ [_____] . For years, little ² [_____] was taken against illegal downloads, with few effects for downloaders. However, two new approaches are seeing ³ [_____] results. Firstly, the industry's working with internet service providers to slow an illegal downloader's connection. Secondly, it's working ⁴ [_____] with digital music websites. In Sweden three out of five illegal file-sharers have ⁵ [_____] back or stopped, with half of these people moving to legal websites supported by ⁶ [_____] .

▶ HELP

Two of the blanks need a plural noun. Listen carefully for plural endings.

Task analysis

4 Work in pairs. What did you find the most difficult about this task? Why?

▶ See **Module 10 Listening 1** for more practice of this task type.

Language development 1

Expressing quantity

▶ EXPERT GRAMMAR page 208

1a Which of these sentences is negative? Which is more positive? Why?
1 For years little action was taken against illegal downloads, with few effects on downloaders.
2 For years, a little action was taken against illegal downloads, with a few effects on downloaders.

b Complete the sentences with the words in the box.

a few   few (x2)   a little   little   many   much
a lot of

1 There was _____ excitement anywhere in the film.
2 The lead actors showed _____ different emotions. It was exhausting to watch!
3 _____ people in the audience enjoyed the film because it was long and slow.
4 _____ people laughed during the film but not many.
5 There was _____ loud music. I wanted quieter music in some scenes.
6 The film was supposed to be a thriller but there wasn't _____ danger in it.
7 There was _____ tension but we wanted more.
8 There were _____ special effects in the film. I wanted more!

c Choose the correct options in *italics* so that the sentences mean the same as those in Exercise 1b. Both options may be possible.
1 There was *enough / too little* excitement.
2 The lead actors *did not show enough / showed too many* emotions.
3 *Too few / Not enough* people in the audience enjoyed the film.
4 *Not enough / Too many* people laughed during the film.
5 There was *not enough / too much* loud music.
6 There *was too little / wasn't enough* danger in the film.
7 There was *enough / too little* tension.
8 There weren't *too many / enough* special effects in the film.

d Work in pairs. Take turns to describe a bad film you have seen. Explain why it was bad using *too much, too little, too few* or *not enough*.

2a Look at the chart and complete the sentences about Australians and leisure time. Replace the percentages in the chart with the phrases in the box.

almost one in five   ~~half~~   just under half
one in every 50   one in five   a quarter

1 _Half_ of the population participate in community activities.
2 _____ read.
3 _____ of men and women do sport or outdoor activities.
4 _____ Australians socialises with friends.
5 _____ people attends sports events.
6 _____ people does arts and crafts.

Participation rate of Australians in selected free-time activities

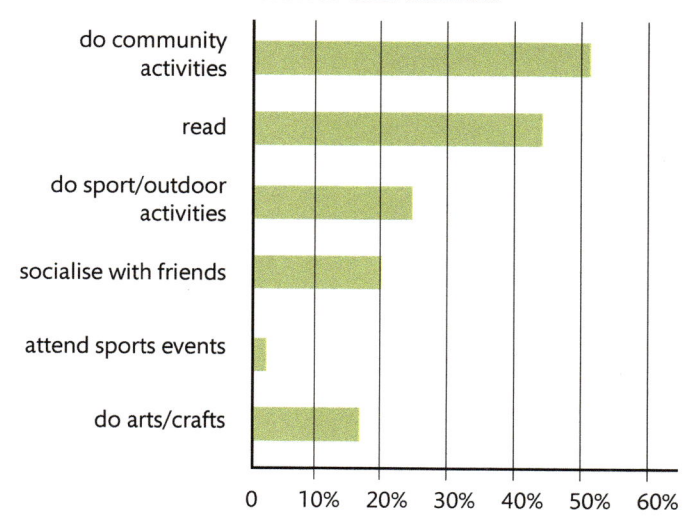

- do community activities: ~50%
- read: ~43%
- do sport/outdoor activities: ~25%
- socialise with friends: ~20%
- attend sports events: ~2%
- do arts/crafts: ~17%

b Write sentences using the prompts.
1 95 percent / the population / listen / music
2 17 percent / people / do / arts and crafts
3 5 percent / women / visit / entertainment venues
4 40 percent / men / read
5 47 percent / women / read
6 1 percent / Australians / attend / courses to learn a hobby
7 56 percent / women / participate in / community activities
8 22 percent / women / and / 17 percent / men / socialise

c Re-write the sentences in Exercise 2b using phrases that are similar to those in the box in Exercise 2a.

3 Work in pairs. Conduct a survey to find out about your classmates and leisure time. Write three questions. Then interview your classmates, calculate the results and present them to the class.

77

5A Module 5
Sensational

Summary writing 1 (Summarize spoken text)

Organising ideas in a summary

In *Summarize spoken text*, after you have listened to the recording and taken notes, you will need to organise your notes into an effective summary.

1a Do you use headphones or in-ear phones when listening to music? What are their advantages and disadvantages?

b 🎧 61 Listen to an interview on the use of in-ear phones and take notes. Then compare notes in pairs.

2a A summary follows the PIE paragraph structure you studied in Module 4. Choose the best topic sentence (1–3) to start a summary of the interview. Use your notes to help you.
1 Doctors suggest that people turn the volume down on their in-ear phones by 80 percent.
2 People turn up the volume on their in-ear phones when there is background noise.
3 If people listen to loud music on in-ear phones, they can damage their hearing.

b Why are the other two sentences in Exercise 2a not appropriate?

3a Supporting points follow a topic sentence. Put these supporting points in a logical order (1–3).
A They do not know their hearing has been damaged until several years later.
B They turn it up too loud in places with a lot of background noise.
C In quiet places most people listen to music at a sensible level.

b Now link the sentences in Exercise 3a. Which sentence should start with *unfortunately*? Which should start with *however*?

4 Choose the best concluding sentence for the summary.
1 So it is important to educate people about how to use in-ear phones safely.
2 It is therefore important for people to get their hearing checked regularly at the doctor's.
3 As a result, it is important for 80 percent of people to learn how to control their volume.

5a 🎧 62 Listen to a lecture about an electronic device called The Mosquito and take notes below.

b Put the sentences in a logical order and link them where appropriate to create a summary of the lecture.
1 Only young people hear the sound so they soon move away.
2 Using this electronic device is against their human rights.
3 We should create better facilities for young people to use.
4 The device could damage their hearing.

▶ See **Summary writing 2** for more practice of this task type.

5B Vision

Listening 2 (Highlight incorrect words)

Before you listen

1 Discuss the questions in pairs.
  1 What mood do you associate with these colours?
     blue   brown   green   red   yellow   white
  2 How many different words do you have for these colours in your language?

Identifying the topic of a text

In *Highlight incorrect words*, you have ten seconds to identify the topic of the text before the recording starts.

2a Look at the strategies for identifying the topic of a text. Time yourself trying each one to find the topic of the text below.
  1 Read the text quickly and look for repeated words or synonyms.
  2 Read the first line.
  3 Read the first and last line.

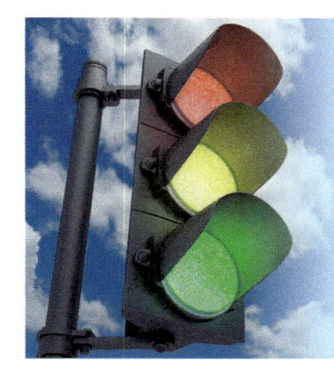

> The way we see colours is not only a matter for our eyes, it's related to language too. A study has shown that Russians are faster and more effective than English speakers at identifying the difference between light and dark blue because they have two words for this colour. English speakers are less able because they only have one. Until the beginning of the last century the Japanese had just one word for *blue* and *green*. The need for a separate word for *green* only arose when foreign materials entered the country. So, interestingly, items like apples, vegetables and traffic lights are still defined as blue in Japan. And yet they're just as green as anywhere else in the world.

  b Which strategy worked best for you? Why?

3 🎧 63 Read and listen to the text in Exercise 2a. Underline the words that are different in the recording.

Test practice
> EXPERT STRATEGIES page 188

4 🎧 64 Complete the task. Follow the text with your pen, underlining the words that are different.

You will hear a recording. Below is a transcription of the recording. Some words in the transcription differ from what the speaker said. Please click on the words that are different.

> Colour theory is the study of colour and its place in art. Humans have been thinking about colours for thousands of years but modern colour theory really arose in the 1800s, when it began to move from science into a pure art. A knowledge of colour theory does require some understanding of basic scientific principles about colour but much of modern colour theory is about the way people perceive, think about and interact with colours – from those used on walls to those selected for a company logo. Colour theory is not only something you see applied to paintings; you can also see it in graphic design, photography, fashion, animation and even video games.

> **HELP**
>
> Listen carefully to the whole of each word as both words might start or end with the same sound but begin or finish differently.

Task analysis

5 🎧 64 Listen again and note down the words that are different in the recording. Think about the following questions for each word.
  1 Does it fit the sentence in the text grammatically?
  2 Does it fit the sentence in the text in meaning?

> See **Module 10 Listening 2** for more practice of this task type.

79

5B Module 5
Sensational

Language development 2

Comparative adjectives

➤ **EXPERT GRAMMAR** page 208

1 Work in pairs and complete the sentences with the correct form of the adjectives in brackets.
1 Russian speakers are _____ (fast) and _____ (effective) at identifying colour than English speakers.
2 English speakers are _____ (able) because they have _____ (few) words for these colours.
3 Japanese apples and vegetables are just _____ (green) anywhere else in the world.
4 Colour theory became _____ (popular) when it became an art.
5 Colour is _____ (important) than it was in the past.
6 Colour was not _____ (common) in other areas of life _____ it is now.

2a Complete the sentences with ... *times* and the comparative form of the adjectives in brackets.
1 The number of people who said they liked art was <u>eight times greater than</u> the number of people who disliked it. (8 x great)
2 The number of people who drew for fun was _____ the number of people who drew professionally. (6 x high)
3 The amount of time spent taking photos was _____ the amount of time spent painting. (10 x great)
4 Visiting art galleries was _____ going to museums. (5 x popular)
5 Buying art postcards was _____ buying larger pictures. (2 x popular)
6 The number of people who enjoyed photography was _____ the number of people who preferred sculpture. (2 x high)

b Work in pairs. Look at the chart and talk about the statistics using comparative adjectives.

Participation in arts and crafts

(Bar chart showing percentages for boys and girls at primary school, secondary school, and young adult levels. Primary school: boys 40%, girls 80%. Secondary school: boys ~18%, girls 60%. Young adult: boys ~5%, girls ~12%.)

Superlative adjectives

➤ **EXPERT GRAMMAR** page 208

3a Complete the sentences with the superlative form of the adjectives in brackets.
1 Who do you think is the _____ (good-looking) person in your country?
2 Where is the _____ (northerly) town in your country? What's it like?
3 When is the _____ (good) time of day to take photographs?
4 Which is the _____ (lovely) place for a picnic?
5 What is the _____ (easy) thing for you to paint: people, places or objects?

b Work in pairs. Choose two questions from Exercise 3a to ask your partner.

Adjectives and adverbs

4a Choose the correct options in *italics* to complete the article.

Four ways science can make things invisible

- You can't [1] *easy / easily* hide something as large as a truck, even in the dark, but a [2] *new / newly* design covers the truck with sheets of hexagonal metal panels which [3] *continual / continually* measure the outside temperature and change rapidly to match. Not even infrared cameras can see it.

- It's not easy to hide something from airport security systems but engineers in Spain and Slovakia have managed it. They took [4] *commercial / commercially* available materials to make a small double-layered cylinder, which becomes [5] *invisible / invisibly* to airport security systems. It can be [6] *easy / easily* produced and used to protect medical equipment such as a pacemaker.

- A [7] *new / newly* developed device in Germany blocks outside noises so you can listen to music at much lower volumes. Sound waves are unable to pass through the high tech disc, which is built into headphones, so the wearer can [8] *simple / simply* walk through a noisy world [9] *quiet / quietly*.

- Very hot surfaces bend light [10] *horizontal / horizontally* and a viewer in, say, a desert, just sees the surface moving like a pool of water. New carbon tubes with an [11] *exceptional / exceptionally* ability to heat up can create the same effect and could [12] *theoretical / theoretically* be used to hide submarines.

b Which of the inventions in Exercise 4a do you think is the most interesting?

80

Module 5 Sensational — 5B

Academic vocabulary 2 [AWL] [ACL]

Academic word list

1a Choose the correct options in *italics* to complete the sentences. Check the meaning of any unknown words in a dictionary.
1. It is difficult to *define / select* the word *art* and what exactly it means.
2. Art can be found everywhere, even in an everyday *item / theory* such as a spoon.
3. Before any object is made, somebody has to *design / interact* it. That's art.
4. A basic *item / principle* of photography is to use natural light.
5. People do not just look at art these days, they also *define / interact* with it.
6. The most popular *principle / theory* is that Da Vinci's *Mona Lisa* was Lisa Gherardini. But perhaps it is better if we do not know.
7. When people choose a favourite piece of art, most of them *perceive / select* a painting.
8. It is right that some people *interact / perceive* computer games as art.

b Work in pairs. Decide which statements in Exercise 1a you agree with. Then compare your ideas with another pair.

Adverbs

2a Match the adverbs in bold in the sentences (1–6) with their meanings (A–F). These adverbs can give us more information about a speaker's attitude.
1. **Basically**, the design of a video game is very important.
2. **Obviously**, a game must be enjoyable or no one will play it.
3. **Interestingly**, today's games will be out of date very soon.
4. Game controls may not seem important but, **actually**, they're essential to its success.
5. **Unusually**, games about the routine of everyday life are very popular.
6. **Personally**, I think games with strong characters are the most enjoyable.

A this is not normal
B this will get your attention
C this is true
D this is my opinion
E this is a simple explanation
F this is easy to understand

b Choose the correct options in *italics* to complete the sentences.
1. Gaming provides many benefits but, *basically / unusually*, it is fun.
2. Video games are still popular but, *actually / obviously*, demand for mobile games is increasing a lot.
3. *Interestingly / Personally*, people become less keen on games as they get older.
4. Many people think gaming is a waste of time but, *actually / basically*, you can learn a lot from it.
5. Gaming used to be a male activity but, *obviously / unusually*, almost as many women play games as men these days.
6. *Interestingly / Personally*, I think playing games with others is more fun.

c Choose one topic from the box and complete the sentences using your own ideas.

| drawing | gaming | photography | reading | television |

1. Basically, I think …
2. Obviously, I …
3. Personally, I prefer …
4. Interestingly, I …
5. Unusually, …
6. Some people think … but, actually, …

The arts

3a Match the verbs and verb phrases (1–7) with the nouns (A–G) to make collocations.
1. write   A novel
2. have an acting B a poem
3. give a live   C gallery
4. enjoy the creative D performance
5. publish a   E work
6. do creative   F role
7. visit an art G process

b Work in pairs. Take turns to ask questions to find out how creative your partner is. Use the collocations in Exercise 3a. Then share the results with the class.

Have you ever … ?

When was the last time you … ?

How often do you … ?

Would you like to … ?

5B Module 5
Sensational

Reading 2 (Reading & writing: Fill in the blanks)

Before you read

1 Work in pairs. Look at the picture for one minute. Then take turns to ask and answer the questions.
 1 Did you find it hard to focus your attention for the full one minute?
 2 Can you describe the picture without looking back at it?
 3 Look back at the picture. What did you forget to mention?

Test practice
➤ EXPERT STRATEGIES page 181

2 Complete the task. Remember to consider the tone of the text.

Below is a text with blanks. Click on each blank, a list of choices will appear. Select the appropriate answer choice for each blank.

Researchers have shown that men and women focus on different things when paying attention. In a new study, they showed that the eyes and attention of men and women move in very different ways. The article, authored by Dr Laurent Itti, [1] _____ the way scientists understand attention and how sensory information is prioritised. [2] _____ studies of vision and attention ignored individual factors such as sex, race and age. Dr Itti's lab studied [3] _____ as they watched videos of people being interviewed. Behind the interview subjects, within the video frame, pedestrians and cars passed by, [4] _____ attention away from the filmed conversation. Researchers discovered that men focused on the speaker's mouth and were most distracted by distinctive movement behind the interview subjects. By contrast, women moved their focus between the interview subject's eyes and body. They also [5] _____ to be more distracted by other people entering the video frame.

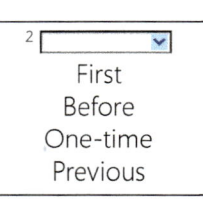

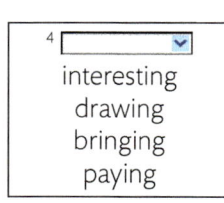

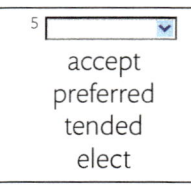

1	2	3	4	5
challenges	First	beings	interesting	accept
annoys	Before	players	drawing	preferred
tests	One-time	participants	bringing	tended
adds	Previous	characters	paying	elect

➤ HELP
• Does Dr Itti agree or disagree with the existing research? What word in blank 1 expresses that?
• Which options cannot come after blank 2? Why?
• Does the option in blank 3 fit in with the context of research?

Task analysis

3 Discuss the questions in pairs.
 1 Which blanks needed a word which matched the context?
 2 What else helped you choose the correct words? Underline the sections in the text that contained clues.

Discussion

4 Discuss this statement in pairs: 'Our first impressions of a person are usually correct'.

82

Module 5
Sensational 5B

Speaking 2 (Describe image)

Comparing data — In *Describe image* you will need to make comparisons between the different data that you have in a graph, chart or map.

1 a Look at the chart in Exercise 5 and write the topic sentence.

  b Now write the overview sentence describing the main data on the chart.

2 a Match the phrases (1–3) with the sections of the chart they describe.

  1 the percentage of people who gave other reasons
  2 the percentage of people who said that the cost prevented them from seeking eye care
  3 the percentage of people who had no eye doctor available

  b Write a phrase for the section of the chart that was not described in Exercise 2a.

3 Complete the description of the chart with the correct form of the adjectives in brackets.

> At 40 percent, cost or the lack of insurance was ^{1} _____ (common) reason why people didn't have their eye problems looked at by a doctor. However, 35 percent of the people said that they didn't think they needed eye care. This was almost ^{2} _____ (high) those who said that the cost prevented them from seeking eye care. In fact, the number of people who gave each of those two reasons was around seven times ^{3} _____ (great) those who had no eye doctor available, with only five percent. This last reason was ^{4} _____ (common). Around 20 percent of the people gave other reasons.

Sample response

4 🎧 65 Listen to two students describing the chart and decide which description is better. Which speaker uses the correct noun phrases? Which speaker uses comparative and superlative forms?

Test practice
> EXPERT STRATEGIES page 172

5 Complete the task in pairs. Take turns to describe the chart. Record your answers.

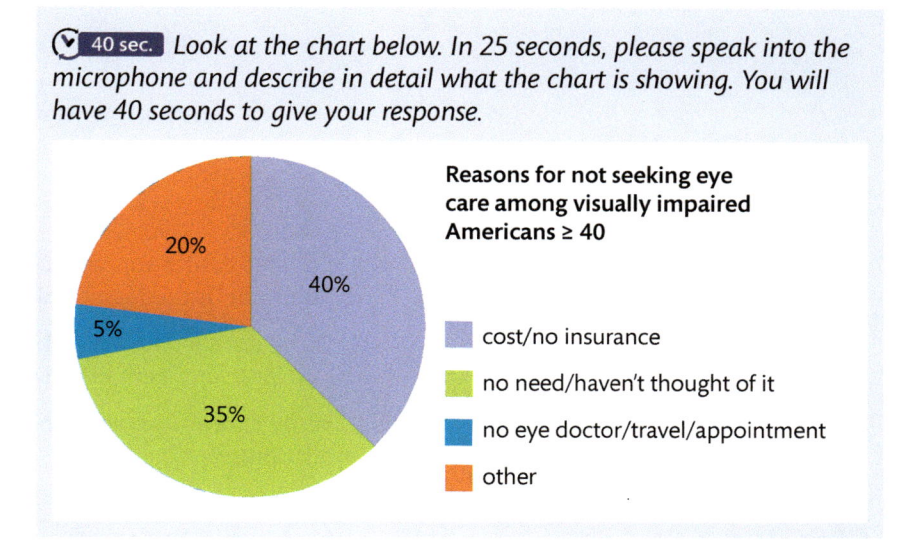

> ⏱ 40 sec. *Look at the chart below. In 25 seconds, please speak into the microphone and describe in detail what the chart is showing. You will have 40 seconds to give your response.*

Reasons for not seeking eye care among visually impaired Americans ≥ 40

- 40% cost/no insurance
- 35% no need/haven't thought of it
- 5% no eye doctor/travel/appointment
- 20% other

Task analysis
> EXPERT SPEAKING page 191

6 Turn to page 191 and complete another timed test practice.

7 Listen to your recording from Exercises 5 and 6. How would you do the task differently if you did it again?

83

5B Module 5
Sensational

Summary writing 2 (Summarize spoken text)

Lead-in

1 Put the sentences about the legal system (A–G) in a logical order (1–7). Check the meaning of the words in bold in a dictionary if you are unsure.

A The police **arrest** a **suspect**. ___
B The police look for **evidence** (e.g. fingerprints, a **weapon**). ___
C The suspect goes to **court**. ___
D The police interview **eyewitnesses** to find out what they saw. ___
E Someone **commits** a crime. _1_
F A **judge** or **jury** decides if the suspect is **guilty**. ___
G The **victim** tells the police what happened to him or her. ___

Understand the task
➤ EXPERT STRATEGIES page 182

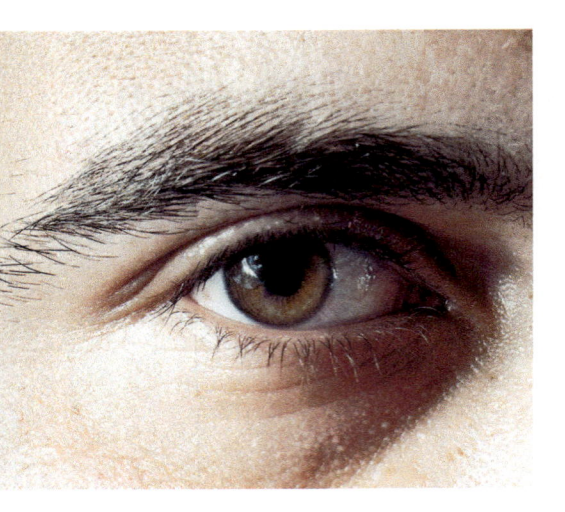

2 Read the instructions and answer the questions.

> ⏱ 10 min. You will hear a short lecture. Write a summary for a fellow student who was not present at the lecture. You should write 50–70 words.
>
> You will have 10 minutes to finish this task. Your response will be judged on the quality of your writing and on how well your response presents the key points presented in the lecture.

1 What are you going to hear?
2 What do you have to write?
3 What is important to remember when writing this task?

3 🎧 66 Listen to the lecture and complete the notes.

- every year 75,000
- but 1/3
- 1974 experiment:
- ppl make mistakes b/c
- argument 4 eyewitnesses:
- argument against eyewitnesses:

Plan your summary

4a Look at your notes from Exercise 3. What is the speaker's main point about the legal system?

b Write a topic sentence that summarises the speaker's main point. Use your answer in Exercise 4a to help you.

5a Write three supporting points that the speaker made to support his opinion.
1 _____
2 _____
3 _____

b You may not be able to include all the supporting points because of the word limit. Choose two points from Exercise 5a to focus on.

84

Module 5
Sensational   5B

c   Work in pairs. What conclusions did the speaker come to about this topic?

Language and content

6a Read the summary and match the punctuation marks (1–4) with their uses (A–F). Two punctuation marks have more than one use.

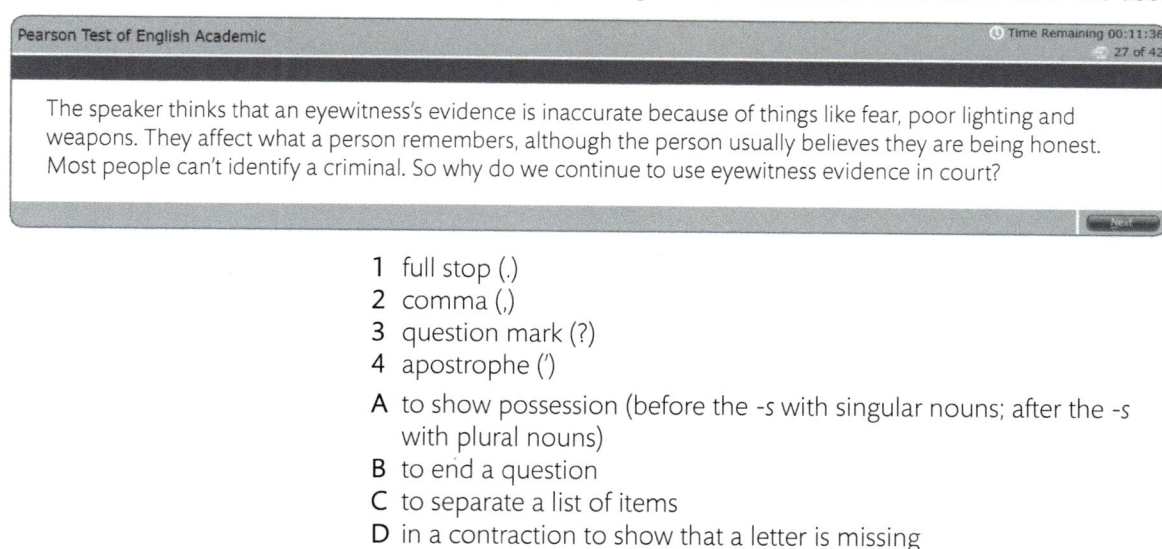

> **Pearson Test of English Academic**   Time Remaining 00:11:36   27 of 42
>
> The speaker thinks that an eyewitness's evidence is inaccurate because of things like fear, poor lighting and weapons. They affect what a person remembers, although the person usually believes they are being honest. Most people can't identify a criminal. So why do we continue to use eyewitness evidence in court?

1 full stop (.)
2 comma (,)
3 question mark (?)
4 apostrophe (')

A to show possession (before the -s with singular nouns; after the -s with plural nouns)
B to end a question
C to separate a list of items
D in a contraction to show that a letter is missing
E to end a sentence
F before a linking word/phrase

b   Punctuate the summary. Start new sentences with a capital letter.

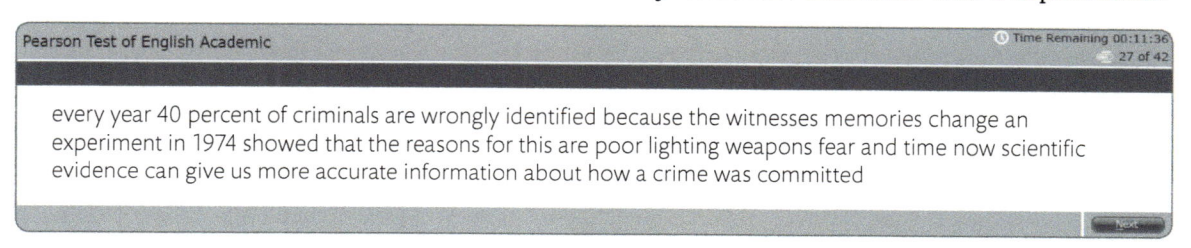

> **Pearson Test of English Academic**   Time Remaining 00:11:36   27 of 42
>
> every year 40 percent of criminals are wrongly identified because the witnesses memories change an experiment in 1974 showed that the reasons for this are poor lighting weapons fear and time now scientific evidence can give us more accurate information about how a crime was committed

c   Look at the summaries in Exercises 6a and 6b. Why are they poor summaries? Use the questions to help you.
1 Is the information accurate?
2 Does the summary introduce the main idea with a topic sentence?
3 Are the ideas organised well?

7   Look at the useful expressions in the table. Which ones could you use in your summary? Choose one from each group.

Describing research	A 1974 study involved over 2,000 people who …
	The results/study suggested that …
	A study which took place in 1974 showed that …
Expressing quantity	More than 75,000 eyewitnesses …
	Over two thousand people …
	… one-third of the time …
	Just/Only 14 percent of viewers …

Write your summary

8   Write your summary. Remember to organise and link your ideas appropriately, and to write 50–70 words.

Check your summary
➤ EXPERT WRITING page 196

9   Check your summary using the checklist on page 196.

5B Module 5
Sensational

Review

1 Complete the comments from a concert review with the words in the box.

a few   few   little   not enough   too many   too much

- There were only ¹ _____ violin players but they played very well.
- The orchestra played very ² _____ music that people knew. They wanted more familiar songs.
- There was ³ _____ talking from some members of the audience during the performance.
- There were ⁴ _____ quiet moments. Everything was too loud.
- There was ⁵ _____ room for everyone to sit down. Some people had to stand.
- There were ⁶ _____ thank-you speeches at the end when people wanted to go home.

2 Put the words in the correct order to make sentences.
1. listen to / music / most / people / once a day
2. group / books / just / of the / read / 50 percent / under
3. teenagers / watching / third / sport / of / enjoy / a
4. an outdoor activity / each week / do / one / people / in five
5. arts and crafts / a quarter / do / of the class
6. children at the school / almost / piano lessons / in ten / have / one

3 Find and correct eight mistakes with comparative and superlative adjectives in the text.

The increase in popularity of e-books means that it is now more common for writers to publish a book themselves and publishers are not as more important as they used to be. However, knowing which is most appropriate choice for you can be difficult. Writers might have a greater chance of being successful if they have the support of a publisher who will spend larger amounts of money on promoting the book. They will also give you an advance, so, financially, it may be the best option. On the other hand, finding a publisher to publish your book is as not easy as publishing your own. For this reason it may be more good for a writer to publish the book themselves and sell it at a price which is less expensive the one you would like to charge. Once readers give positive feedback, other readers will be happy to purchase the book at the more high price. It can also take ten times long to get a book published by a publisher than by yourself, so self-publishing can bring faster results in the less amount of time.

4 Complete the sentences about books with nouns formed from the words in brackets.
1. The world _____ (literate) rate is a little over 80 percent.
2. There has been an _____ (improve) in the number of children who learn to read.
3. For some people, books are the best form of _____ (entertain).
4. Books involve more _____ (creative) than films because the reader uses their imagination.
5. Sometimes _____ (celebrate) from the world of acting or TV write novels.
6. A good thriller writer creates a lot of _____ (tense) for the reader.
7. The _____ (promote) of a new book can be expensive.
8. The _____ (produce) of e-books is increasing each year.

5 Choose the correct options in *italics* to complete the article.

Watching people in an art gallery is an interesting experience. For some, you know the experience is ¹ *emotional / feeling*. They may spend a long time looking at one particular painting in order to ² *perceive / tell* its meaning and admire the artist's creative ³ *process / theory*. For others the creative ⁴ *job / work* they see is ⁵ *cheerful / entertaining* but nothing more. They spend no more than a few seconds looking at a piece of art before moving on to the next one.
Some visitors want to ⁶ *divide / share* their experiences with friends, while others prefer to be alone. There are visitors who want to ⁷ *communicate / interact* with the art and touch it, or read ⁸ *factual / realistic* information about the artist, and there are always some who pay no attention. More serious visitors might want to be more ⁹ *actively / indirectly* involved and spend time drawing the painting in front of them. But no matter how we experience galleries, they continue to be a ¹⁰ *powerful / weak* influence in our culture today.

6 City intelligence

Overview

6A
- **Reading:** Multiple-choice, choose single answer
- **Academic vocabulary:** Cities and towns
- **Speaking:** Repeat sentence; Answer short question
- **Listening:** Highlight correct summary
- **Language development:** Verb patterns
- **Writing:** Write essay

6B
- **Listening:** Highlight correct summary; Write from dictation
- **Language development:** Expressing probability
- **Academic vocabulary:** Social problems
- **Reading:** Multiple-choice, choose single answer
- **Speaking:** Re-tell lecture
- **Writing:** Write essay

Lead-in

1 Discuss the questions in pairs.
1 Do you live in the countryside or in a city?
2 Do you like where you live?
3 What five adjectives would you use to describe your home town/city?
4 Which three cities in the world would you like to visit?

2a Number the items in the box in order of importance for your ideal neighbourhood (1 = least important, 10 = most important).

attractive housing   cinema   college/workplace   fields/woods   nightclubs   parks   public transport
sea/river   shopping centre   sports facilities

b Work in small groups. Compare your ideas and agree on the five most important items.

87

6A Cities for today

Reading 1 (Multiple-choice, choose single answer)

Before you read

1 Work in pairs. How has technology changed the ways cities work in the last century? How will it change them in the future? Think of at least five examples for each.

Identifying a writer's purpose or attitude

In *Multiple-choice, choose single answer*, the question may test your understanding of the writer's purpose or attitude.

2a Match the verbs that express a writer's purpose (1–5) with the explanations (A–E).

1 inform
2 persuade
3 criticise
4 compare
5 contrast

A argue that something is negative and give reasons
B describe what is similar between two or more things
C give facts and/or statistics using neutral language
D describe what is different between two or more things
E argue that something is positive and give reasons

b Words in a text can help you to understand the writer's purpose or attitude. Match the clue words (A–E) with the verbs (1–5) in Exercise 2a.

A similarly, like, both
B however, on the other hand, whereas
C beneficial, must, necessary
D ineffective, poor, concerned
E such as, for example, in addition

3a Read two articles about cities. What is the writer's main purpose in each?

Cities currently house half the world's population, a figure that is predicted to rise in the future. More people will mean an increasing demand on services, so it is important for cities to prepare. In South Korea, Songdo is a newly-created city leading the way. Everything there is monitored by computers, which allows traffic experts to reduce accidents and companies to save energy. 40 percent of the city is green space, with roof gardens that reduce storm water and summer heat; and rain water is recycled, lowering demand for fresh water. If all cities want to be efficient, attractive places to live, they too must invest in this kind of infrastructure.

Songdo in South Korea and California City in the USA are cities created by private individuals with a vision of the perfect city. But while both are situated on privately-owned land, it is hoped the similarities end there. California City sits on 320 km² of desert, divided into plots of land for people to purchase. But demand was overestimated and much of it remains empty. Songdo, on the other hand, is much smaller, at 6 km², and half the expected population has already moved in, despite the fact that it is not yet finished. While California City failed to meet expectations, Songdo will hopefully succeed and become a world-leading city.

Module 6
City intelligence
6A

b Work in pairs. What clue words in the articles gave you the answers to Exercise 3a?

Test practice
> EXPERT STRATEGIES page 177

4 Complete the task. Think about the writer's purpose, using the clue words in Exercise 2b to help you.

Read the text and answer the multiple-choice question by selecting the correct response. Only one response is correct.

Cities around the world are looking at Songdo in South Korea as a template for future urban areas. When completed, it will house 65,000 people and 300,000 commuters. Technology will play a leading role in everyday life there, with everything connected electronically. This 'smart city' may appeal to those people who dream of a futuristic experience or want a more environmentally-friendly living space but do not be mistaken about the potential lack of privacy that accompanies it. Buildings and homes will be monitored at all times and cameras in the streets will see who is doing what and when.

What does the writer want to achieve in this text?

A ○ persuade the reader that living in Songdo is like living in a dream

B ○ criticise the lack of freedom that people in Songdo will have

C ○ inform the reader that Songdo is bad for the environment

D ○ compare life in Songdo with life in other similar cities

> **HELP**
> • Look at options A and C. What does the writer say about *dream* and *environmentally-friendly*? Is it the same as these two options?
> • Look at option B. Does the writer say how people would lose their freedom?
> • Look at option D. What other city or cities does the writer mention?

Task analysis

5a Underline the phrases in the text which can help you to find the correct answer. Compare the phrases you have chosen in pairs.

b Why is each of the other three options incorrect? What would you expect to see in the text if the answers were correct?

Discussion

6 Work in pairs. Student A, persuade Student B that life in a 'smart city' like Songdo is better than in other cities. Student B, persuade Student A that life in a 'smart city' like Songdo is worse than life in other cities.

EXPERT WORD CHECK
appeal to   demand   figure   house (v)   succeed

> See **Reading 2** for more practice of this task type.

6A Module 6
City intelligence

Academic vocabulary 1 [AWL] [ACL]

Cities and towns

1 Choose the correct options in *italics* to complete the collocations in bold. You can find these collocations in the texts in Reading 1.
  1 *Field / Rural* **areas** are better for families than urban areas.
  2 **Green** *ground / spaces* are very important for our health.
  3 *Traffic / Vehicle* **accidents** have increased in recent years.
  4 It's too expensive to buy **privately-owned** *ground / land* to build on.
  5 Families must try harder to **protect** *save* **energy**.
  6 People should pay more for *fresh / clear* **water**.

Academic collocations list

2a Match the beginnings of the sentences (1–6) with the endings (A–F). Then note the collocations in *italics*.
  1 A mayor's job is to *address*
  2 Some *private*
  3 There is an *increasing*
  4 My city does not *meet*
  5 Big businesses play a *leading*
  6 There is more than one *newly-*

  A *the expectations* of visitors.
  B *individuals* invest a lot of time in the community.
  C *demand* for city centre housing these days.
  D *role* in city life.
  E *issues* in a city.
  F *created* area in my town/city.

  b Write the collocations from Exercise 2a in your vocabulary notebook with an example sentence.

Academic word list

3a Complete the text with the words in the box.

  assess   despite   energy   experts   monitors
  potential   similarities

There is a company that ¹_____ the cost of living for foreign residents in world cities. Every year a group of ²_____ look at economic information. They ³_____ the cost of 200 items in each country, including housing and transport, and they produce a list showing ⁴_____ and differences between the cities. Several countries have the ⁵_____ to be number one and each year it changes. ⁶_____ being one of the most famous world cities, New York is surprisingly not usually in the top ten but two African countries which export ⁷_____ such as oil and gas are.

b Work in pairs. Which cities do you think are in the top five? Why?

Prefixes

4a Complete the words in the sentences with the prefixes *mis-*, *re-* or *over-*.
  1 Even rainwater is ____cycled.
  2 Demand was ____estimated and much of it remains empty.
  3 Do not be ____taken about the potential lack of privacy.

b Match the prefixes in Exercise 4a with their meanings (1–3).
  1 too much ___   2 wrong ___   3 again ___

c Complete the words in the article with the prefixes *mis-*, *re-* or *over-*.

An expensive place to live

Every year the cost of living in world cities is ¹____viewed, to give companies an idea of how much it will cost to send employees to work there. This year's report tells us that Luanda continues to be one of the most expensive places for foreigners to live and work. The capital city of Angola is an oil-rich area that's ²____building itself after years of local conflict; a place where new shopping centres and apartment blocks are ³____placing old, damaged buildings every day. It's not uncommon for foreigners to pay $8,000 a month for rent or $50 for a burger but these ⁴____priced goods can be ⁵____leading. While a third of the population are able to afford such products, two thirds of its people live on little money in ⁶____crowded areas with poor facilities. So although much of the city looks richer these days, it ⁷____represents the lives of many people there.

d Choose five words from Exercise 4c and write sentences about your town/city. Then discuss your sentences in pairs.

The council should review our transport system.

Module 6
6A City intelligence

Speaking 1 (Repeat sentence; Answer short question)

Pronunciation: Linking 1

In *Repeat sentence* you are scored on fluency. You will need to link words together to sound fluent.

1 a The letters *a, e, i, o* and *u* are vowels. The other letters of the alphabet are consonants. Look at the linked words in the sentence and answer the questions.

> A new report outlines ways in which cities should address transport issues.

1 Does the first word end with a consonant or a vowel?
2 Does the second word begin with a consonant or a vowel?

b 🎧 67 Listen to the sentence. Is there a pause between each pair of words?

2 a Mark the links between consonant and vowel sounds in the sentences. Then compare answers in pairs.
1 New technology has a role to play in innovation.
2 We could invest in effective public transport.
3 We should attempt to lower the amount of traffic on roads.
4 One solution is a system of electric cars to hire on-demand.
5 Another is an electric bus with an open bottom for cars to drive under.
6 If little action is taken, we could experience energy shortages.

Test practice 1: Repeat sentence
➤ EXPERT STRATEGIES page 171

b 🎧 68 Listen and check your answers. Then listen and repeat the sentences.

3 🎧 69 Complete the task in pairs. You will hear ten sentences. Record your answer if possible.

> ⏱ 15 sec. You will hear a sentence. Please repeat the sentence exactly as you hear it. You will hear the sentence only once.

Task analysis

4 🎧 69 Listen again. Then listen to your recording and answer the questions.
1 How many words did you repeat correctly in each sentence?
2 What did you do when there was an unknown word? What is the best thing to do in this situation?
3 Did you link words or pronounce them separately?

Test practice 2: Answer short question
➤ EXPERT STRATEGIES page 174

5 🎧 70 Complete the task in pairs. You will hear six questions.

> ⏱ 10 sec. You will hear a question. Please give a simple and short answer. Often just one or a few words is enough.

91

6A Module 6
City intelligence

Listening 1 (Highlight correct summary)

Before you listen

1 Discuss the questions in pairs.
   1 What do you know about your capital city's history?
   2 What are the advantages and disadvantages of the location of your capital city?

Classifying and categorising information

The first part of a summary often gives an overview of the structure. This is sometimes tested in summary tasks such as *Highlight correct summary*.

2 Match the beginnings of the sentences (1–4) with the endings (A–D). Then note the categorising phrases in *italics*.
   1 In a city transit system *there are three main component parts*:
   2 For urbanisation to occur, *three factors must be present*:
   3 There are *three main ways in which* cities are preferable to rural areas:
   4 *There are three key stages* in urbanisation:
   A firstly, they offer better work opportunities; secondly, they may be safer than the countryside and, finally, entertainment facilities may be better.
   B a growing economy, dissatisfaction in the countryside and affordable transport.
   C cheap public transport, a network of service roads and link roads with other towns.
   D in the beginning economies are largely farming-based, then as they industrialise, governments invest in roads, etc., making cities more attractive. Finally, populations stabilise when around 70 percent live in towns or cities.

3 🎧 71 Listen to someone categorising reasons for the location of capital cities. What were the reasons behind the location of the capitals?
   1 London, United Kingdom: _____
   2 Wellington, New Zealand: _____
   3 Abuja, Nigeria: _____
   4 Ottawa, Canada: _____
   5 Brasilia, Brazil: _____

Test practice

> EXPERT STRATEGIES page 185

4 🎧 72 Complete the task. Remember to take notes.

You will hear a recording. Click on the paragraph that best relates to the recording.

A ○ There were three reasons why the building of St Petersburg meant Russian Tsar Peter I became famous for being a cruel leader. Many workers died either on the journey or from disease and overwork in the city build itself. The Tsar did not pay his workers or provide food and because of this, many more died.

B ○ Russian Tsar Peter I wanted a new capital city so that he could compete with other European capitals. He built the city on a river so that it would be easier to bring workers and materials into the city to help with the building process.

C ○ There were three challenges with the construction of St Petersburg: the unsuitability of the wet land in the location he chose, the difficulty of transporting builders to the remote location, and the poor conditions they were working in and the lack of raw materials for the construction process.

D ○ St Petersburg was the first city to be built on water and this is why the construction process was so challenging. It was such a big project requiring so many men and materials that building in other parts of Russia stopped while the city was being built.

> HELP

• What are the three reasons/challenges mentioned in options A and C? Is this information correct?
• Underline the linkers in options B and D. Is this the correct relationship between ideas?

Task analysis

5 For this task type, what do you need to practise more: identifying main and supporting ideas, note-taking, reading in detail or something else?

> See **Listening 2** for more practice of this task type.

Module 6
6A City intelligence

Language development 1

Verb patterns

➤ EXPERT GRAMMAR page 209

1a Complete the sentences from Listening 1 with the correct form of the verbs in brackets.
1. Russian Tsar Peter I began _____ (build) a great European city.
2. He decided _____ (construct) his beautiful capital at the mouth of a river.
3. Over 100,000 construction workers died _____ (work) in such difficult conditions.
4. The men were expected _____ (provide) their own tools and food.
5. They were chained together _____ (prevent) them from _____ (run away).
6. Whole forests were cleared _____ (provide) wood for the construction.
7. Stone became so hard _____ (find) that Peter banned anyone else in Russia from _____ (use) it.
8. It was a truly impossible city _____ (build).

b 🎧 73 Listen and check your answers.

c Work in pairs. Find examples of these verb patterns in Exercise 1a.
1. verb + preposition + -ing
2. verb + infinitive
3. verb + infinitive or -ing with no change in meaning
4. adjective + infinitive
5. infinitive of purpose

2a Complete the sentences with the correct form of the verbs in brackets.
1. My home town or city is famous for _____ (attract) tourists.
2. It is difficult _____ (find) things to do at the weekend here.
3. There's plenty of cheap accommodation available _____ (rent).
4. I'm still not comfortable with _____ (find) my way around.
5. There are enough places _____ (walk) around the city.
6. I enjoy _____ (get) out of the city sometimes.
7. I get tired of _____ (live) here sometimes.
8. I'm keen on _____ (visit) big cities when I go on holiday.

b Work in pairs. Are the sentences in Exercise 2a true for you and your town/city?

3a Choose the correct verb forms in *italics* to complete the article.

SLUMS WORTH A FORTUNE

You get to Sagira Londhe's house by ¹*walk / walking* through a half-metre wide alley, ²*to step / stepping* around the mud and old bits of rubbish. It's difficult ³*to find / finding* even the basics of life here, in the Dharavi slum in Mumbai. This is a place where a profit can be made by ⁴*sell / selling* bags of water, even though this illegal business was banned many years before. ⁵*To work / Working* in the pottery and leather businesses around the slums earns people in this neighbourhood approximately $1–2 a day. And yet it may come as a surprise ⁶*to learn / learning* that Sagira has chosen ⁷*to stay / staying*, despite ⁸*to be / being* offered over $100,000 ⁹*to sell / selling* and move. It doesn't look like much but, clearly, there's a real sense of community there that's hard to ¹⁰*leave / leaving*.

Sagira lives on the Dharavi slums, a large area in the middle of Mumbai. Just 300 years ago, the only economic activities in Mumbai were ¹¹*to fish / fishing* and ¹²*to trade / trading*. Few people were prepared ¹³*to live / living* in this area of land that frequently flooded. Today, Dharavi overlooks the Bandra-Kurla Complex, which was built ¹⁴*to become / becoming* the new financial and commercial centre of Mumbai. ¹⁵*To know / Knowing* that the land they occupy has an estimated value of $10 billion does little ¹⁶*to help / to helping* the residents out of poverty, though.

'¹⁷*To live / Living* here is not always easy,' Sagira says, 'but it's better ¹⁸*to be / being* here than homeless. $100,000 may sound like a lot of money but in Mumbai, that money won't go far.'

b Do you think Sagira made the right decision to stay?

6A Module 6
City intelligence

Writing 1 (Write essay)

▶ EXPERT STRATEGIES page 176

To score well in *Write essay*, you need to start your essay with an introductory paragraph.

Introductions
▶ EXPERT WRITING page 199

1 Read the essay prompt and look at the underlined words. Then discuss the questions in pairs.

> Many have argued that the best solution to the problems of <u>overcrowding</u> and <u>transport</u> in modern cities is to <u>encourage people to move back to the countryside</u>. Do you agree with this view?

1 What are the problems of overcrowding in cities?
2 What are the problems of transport in cities?
3 What are the benefits and drawbacks of moving to the countryside?

2 In this test task you have to write a problem-solution essay. Which words in the prompt tell you this? Read about problem-solution essays on page 199. Then answer the questions.

1 Think of one other solution to overcrowding. What are the advantages and disadvantages?
2 Think of one other solution to transport problems. What are the advantages and disadvantages?

3a Read the introduction.

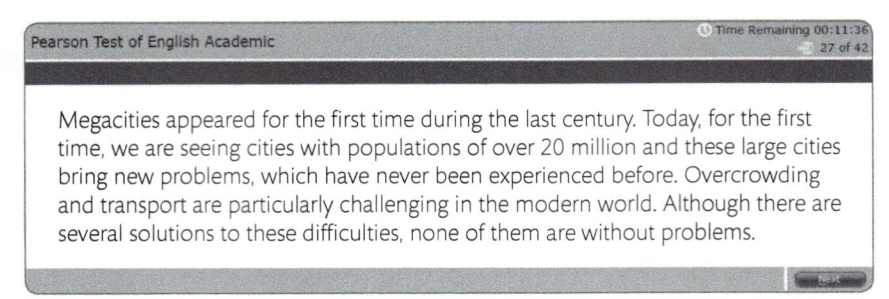

> Pearson Test of English Academic   Time Remaining 00:11:36
> 27 of 42
>
> Megacities appeared for the first time during the last century. Today, for the first time, we are seeing cities with populations of over 20 million and these large cities bring new problems, which have never been experienced before. Overcrowding and transport are particularly challenging in the modern world. Although there are several solutions to these difficulties, none of them are without problems.

b Look at the common features of introductions. Then underline them in the introduction in Exercise 3a.
1 stating the general topic
2 an interesting statistic
3 a reason why this issue is important
4 stating the focus of this essay
5 a thesis statement (a sentence summarising your final conclusion)

c Brainstorm ideas for an introduction for this prompt.

4 Now write your own essay plan. Then plan and write the introduction for your essay.

▶ See **Writing 2** for more practice of this task type.

6B Homes of the future

Listening 2 (Highlight correct summary; Write from dictation)

Before you listen

1 Discuss the questions in pairs.
1 What kind of housing is most popular in your country? Why?
2 What kind of home would you like to live in? Do you think you'll live in a house like this?

Test practice 1: Highlight correct summary
➤ EXPERT STRATEGIES page 185

2 🎧 74 Complete the task. Think about language for classifying and categorising. Remember to take notes.

You will hear a recording. Click on the paragraph that best relates to the recording.

A ○ A new project will look at the problems of housing in London. Because housing is too expensive in the city, people have had to move into garages. Researchers hope their new project will solve this problem by getting people into better homes and also back in work.

B ○ A new project intends to use garages to provide housing for the homeless in London. Although small, there will be areas outside the home to prepare food and clean clothes. The houses will provide both accommodation and training for the people living there.

C ○ A recent project will aim to give homeless people education and training in building houses and garages for key workers in the most expensive neighbourhoods of London. The houses will help people get to work more quickly because of their central location.

D ○ A recent project will aim to put homeless people into their own homes. They will each have their own bedroom, shower room, kitchen and garage and will need to build the homes themselves. Having your own space is generally better than sharing a larger home with others.

Test practice 2: Write from dictation
➤ EXPERT STRATEGIES page 189

3 🎧 75 Complete the task. You will hear three sentences. Then compare answers in pairs.

You will hear a sentence. Type the sentence in the box below exactly as you hear it. Write as much of the sentence as you can. You will hear the sentence only once.

Task analysis

4a 🎧 74 *Highlight correct summary*: Discuss your answers in pairs and underline the phrases which helped you choose the correct summary. Then listen again.

b 🎧 75 *Write from dictation*: Listen again. What examples of consonant–vowel linking can you hear?

6B Module 6
City intelligence

Language development 2

Expressing present probability

▶ EXPERT GRAMMAR page 210

1a Choose the correct options in *italics* to complete the sentences.
1 A home with no central heating *can't / must* get very cold on a snowy day.
2 Having a garden *can't / might* be important for some people but not for everyone.
3 Red walls in a room *may / must* be acceptable but only if you like that colour.
4 Living next to the ocean *can't / must* be wonderful if you enjoy water sports.
5 You *can't / might* have much privacy if you share a room with a brother or sister.
6 A house with many windows *can't / could* be too hot in summer.

b Work in pairs. Say whether you think the statements are true or false. Begin with *It must/might/may/could/can't be true/false because …* .
1 In Siberia people remain in their homes throughout the winter months.
2 In a town in Australia some residents choose to live in caves.
3 Homes in the wettest town in the world, in India, suffer from water shortages.
4 Fishermen who live and sleep on boats often feel sick when they walk on land.
5 Traditional homes in Korea have heated floors.

Expressing future probability

▶ EXPERT GRAMMAR page 210

2a Complete the chart with the words and phrases in the box.

| ~~may~~   may not   might   might not   ~~will definitely~~ |
| will definitely not   will possibly   will possibly not |
| will probably   will probably not |

100% sure	1 <u>will definitely</u>	(+)
	2 _____	(-)
80% sure	3 _____	(+)
	4 _____	(-)
50% sure	5 <u>may</u> _____ _____	(+)
	6 _____ _____ _____	(-)

b Complete the sentences about homes in 2030 to give your opinion. Use the words and phrases in the box in Exercise 2a.
1 Homes _____ be more energy efficient.
2 We _____ control machines with gestures.
3 Robots _____ do the housework.
4 A family's garage _____ recharge their car every evening.
5 Your fridge _____ order food online when you have run out of something.
6 We _____ have access to less fresh water at home.
7 Your kitchen _____ prepare food for your dinner before you get home.
8 Homes _____ be similar to today's homes.

c Compare your answers in Exercise 2b and discuss your opinions in pairs.

3a Look at the more formal ways to express future probability in the table. Re-write your sentences from Exercise 2b using the phrases in the table.

There is a	small possibility	that	homes will be different.
	strong chance		
It is	quite	likely	
	highly	unlikely	

b Work in new pairs. Compare and discuss your answers in Exercise 3a.

4 Find and correct four grammar mistakes and four spelling mistakes in the article.

People imagine all kinds of futuristic buildings when they think about homes of the future but they will not probably look like something from a sci-fi movie. As more poeple move to urban areas, there is highly likely that we will need to build more homes within the space we have. As a result, there is a strong posibility that buildings become taller and individual accomodation smaller. The enviroment definitely will have an impact on these homes too, and will change both the materials used to build the homes and how they run.

Module 6
6B City intelligence

Academic vocabulary 2 AWL ACL

Academic collocations list

1a Choose the correct options in *italics* to complete the text. Then note the collocations in bold.

b Write the collocations from Exercise 1a in your vocabulary notebook with an example sentence.

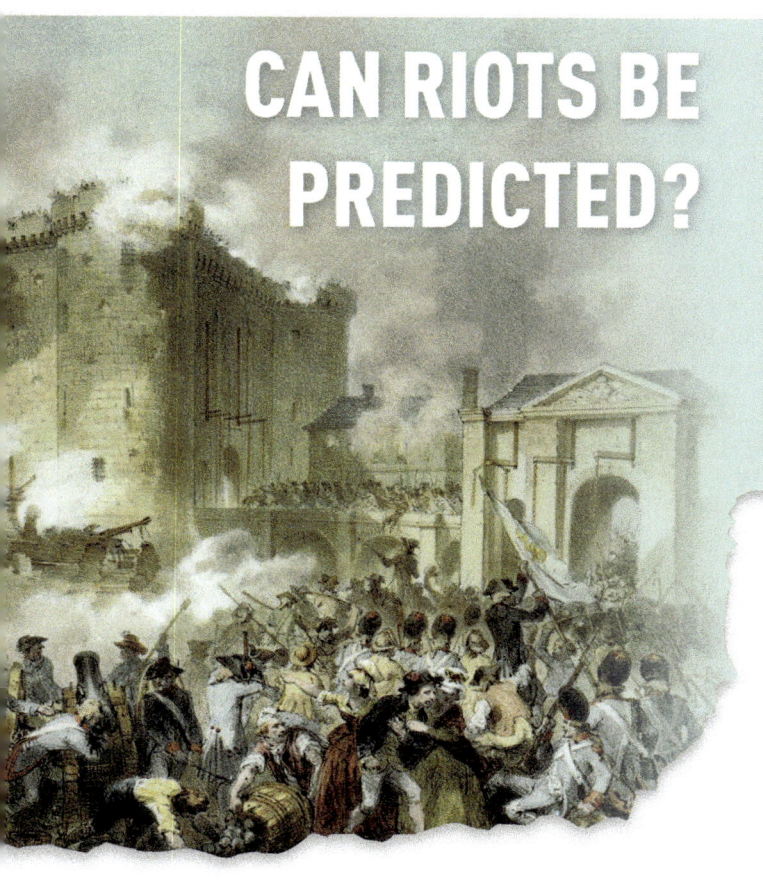

CAN RIOTS BE PREDICTED?

When people stormed the Bastille in France in 1789, they weren't just angry with the King's policies. They were hungry. Can food prices predict when **social** [1] *unrest / unhappiness* will happen? According to new research, the answer is yes. Obviously, there are complex social reasons why people feel unhappy. Access to **educational** [2] *opportunities / circumstances* or **legal** [3] *abilities / rights* are certainly a factor. But studies from around the world have shown food prices are behind dissatisfaction. Food supply is an issue which affects [4] *wider / larger* **society** and more investment is needed in developing the **technical** [5] *facility / skills* to grow food more effectively.

Social problems

3a Match the social problems in the box with the solutions (1–6).

| disability rights | drug abuse | organised crime |
| nuclear power | traffic congestion | unemployment |

1 work with local governments in order to improve public transport
2 develop alternative energy sources able to power industry
3 remove the person at the head of the organisation
4 create strict punishments for people selling illegal substances
5 make all public buildings wheelchair-friendly
6 encourage foreign investment in a country

b What do you think are the advantages and disadvantages of the solutions in Exercise 3a?

4a Complete the sentences with your own ideas. Use the words in the box and language of probability from Language development 2.

| childcare | media influence | ~~obesity rates~~ | plastic |
| retirement | social unrest |

1 If people do not stop eating fast food, *obesity rates will definitely rise.*
2 If the gap between the rich and poor grows, …
3 If women have to work long hours in the future, …
4 If oil runs out, …
5 If the media continues to show violent content, …
6 If more than half the population is over 60, …

b Write the first half of a sentence beginning with *if*. Then find three other students to complete your sentence.

If people start eating more sensibly, …

Academic word list

2a Complete the sentence with a word formed from the word in capitals.

1 The _____ of people in my country are happy. MAJOR
2 Problems with traffic are _____ . REVERSE
3 A _____ wage for workers is the only way to pay fairly. MINIMAL
4 There are serious _____ of not spending on education. CONSEQUENT
5 There was a global economic _____ in 2009. DEPRESS
6 Disabled rights are often _____ by governments. IGNORE
7 Most problems are best solved by _____ government. CENTRE
8 My _____ life is not affected by any social problems. DAY

b Write sentences using the words in capitals in Exercise 2a.

1 *There was a major economic downturn around the world.*

97

6B Module 6
City intelligence

Reading 2 (Multiple-choice, choose single answer)

Before you read

1a Read the text and match the words in bold (1–5) with their meanings (A–E).

> If a terrible natural ¹ **disaster** occurred on Earth and there was a ² **real** possibility that it would not support human life in future, scientists would have to examine the ³ **planet** Mars and assess how they could create an ⁴ **atmosphere** in which people could survive so that it could be ⁵ **transformed** into a human colony.

A   a large, round object in space that moves around the Sun
B   completely changed
C   not imaginary
D   a sudden event which causes great damage or suffering
E   the mixture of gases that surrounds the Earth

b Work in pairs. How likely do you think it is that humans will live on Mars? Why?

Test practice
➤ EXPERT STRATEGIES page 177

2 Complete the task. Remember to think about the writer's purpose.

Read the text and answer the multiple-choice question by selecting the correct response. Only one response is correct.

Mars is an empty, lifeless planet with seemingly little to offer humans. It has a thin atmosphere and no signs of life and yet it holds some promise for the continuation of the human race if disaster hits and destroys Earth. The atmosphere that exists on Mars today is similar to the Earth's atmosphere when it was first formed, making it a real possibility that it will one day be transformed into a planet where plants and animals can live successfully. This could be a natural process billions of years in the future or after just a few centuries of human intelligence, innovation and labour.

The writer compares the atmosphere on Mars and Earth in order to demonstrate how

A ○ different the chemical make-up of each planet is.
B ○ likely it is that both may support human life.
C ○ useful the minerals may be to man in future.
D ○ possible it is that both will be destroyed one day.

Task analysis

3 Match the three incorrect options in Exercise 2 with the reasons why they were incorrect (1–3).
1 The writer does not mention this topic.
2 The writer only talks about this in relation to Earth.
3 The writer says the two planets are similar, not different.

Discussion

4 Work in small groups. Imagine the first humans are moving to Mars. They can breathe with equipment and a small farm has been built. Discuss the questions.
1 What five key skills do the people need to survive?
2 What are the five most important pieces of equipment they need to take?

Module 6
6B
City intelligence

Speaking 2 (Re-tell lecture)

Taking notes on the way ideas are linked

In *Re-tell lecture* you will need to understand the way information is linked in the lecture and take appropriate notes while you listen.

1a Look at the photo in Exercise 4. What is the topic of the lecture?

b 🎧 76 Listen and take notes. What is the main idea?

2a When taking notes, we can use symbols to show how ideas are linked. Match the symbols (1–8) with their meanings (A–H).

1 =	5 +
2 ∴	6 ↛
3 >	7 <
4 →	8 ≠

A leads to/causes/results in ___
B doesn't lead to/cause/result in ___
C also/in addition ___
D more/greater than ___
E less/lower than ___
F equal to/the same as ___
G not equal to/different from ___
H therefore/so ___

b 🎧 76 Use your notes from Exercise 1b to complete the lecture notes. Then listen again and check your answers.

1 employees connect 24/7 w/ tech ∴
2 but new tech ↛
3 non-work activities at home, e.g.
4 working from home can =
5 workers at home >
6 ∴

Sample response

3 🎧 77 Listen to a student re-telling the lecture. Does she link her ideas? Note down the linking words she uses.

Test practice

▶ EXPERT STRATEGIES page 173

4 🎧 76 Complete the task in pairs. Take notes using symbols to help you. Then present the information to your partner.

> ⏱ 40 sec. You will hear a lecture. After listening to the lecture, in 10 seconds, please speak into the microphone and re-tell what you have just heard from the lecture in your own words. You will have 40 seconds to give your response.

▶ HELP

- Start with the speaker's main idea.
- Give the supporting points as you noted them down. Use your linking symbols to help you link the ideas as you speak.

5 🎧 78 Turn to page 194 and complete another timed test practice.

▶ EXPERT SPEAKING page 194

Task analysis

6 Think about the task in Exercise 5. On a scale of 1 to 5, how true are the statements for you? (1 = completely true, 5 = not true).

1 I could understand the main point and supporting points of the lecture.
2 I could understand how the points were linked.
3 I took good notes that I could understand later.
4 I could re-tell the lecture easily because I had good notes.

99

6B Module 6
City intelligence

Writing 2 (Write essay)

Lead-in

1 Discuss the questions in pairs.
   1 Do people generally agree with paying taxes in your country?
   2 If you were a politician, what would you spend public money on?

Understand the task
▶ EXPERT STRATEGIES page 176

2 Read the essay prompt and underline the key words. Then work in pairs. Share ideas on this topic with your partner.

> ⏱ **20 min.** You will have 20 minutes to plan, write and revise an essay about the topic below. Your response will be judged on how well you develop a position, organise your ideas, present supporting details and control the elements of standard written English. You should write 200–300 words.

> Housing is the most basic requirement for a stable society but in many countries there are not enough homes for everyone. Some say government funds should be spent building extra houses and apartments to meet the population's needs. To what extent do you agree with this solution?

▶ HELP
- What essay type is required here? What sentences tell you that?
- What are the benefits and drawbacks with the solution mentioned?
- How else might it be possible to provide more homes?

Plan your essay

To score well in a problem-solution essay for *Write essay*, you should make sure you include an analysis of any solutions you suggest.

3 Read a student's plan for one of the main paragraphs of the essay. What order should the ideas appear in? Number them 1–5. Think about the PIE method you studied in Module 4.

> ___ However, building homes is expensive and it is unfair to expect taxpayers to provide homes for other people who might not always deserve it.
>
> _1_ One solution to this problem is for governments to use taxes to build more homes.
>
> ___ These benefits will reduce the costs of policing and health care for the government in the long term.
>
> ___ The benefits of providing housing for everyone are huge.
>
> ___ For example, having a stable home reduces crime and encourages better health.

4a Look at the first sentence of another paragraph. Complete the paragraph, explaining the advantages and disadvantages of this solution. Remember to use the PIE method.

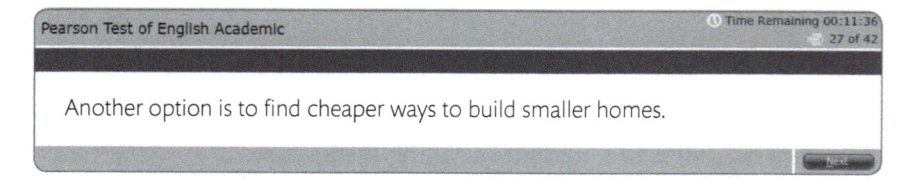

> Another option is to find cheaper ways to build smaller homes.

Module 6
6B City intelligence

b Now write your own essay plan for this prompt. Remember that in a problem-solution essay you should describe the problem and the effects it has in the introduction paragraph. You usually need to recommend one particular solution in the conclusion.

Language and content When you write in academic English, you often need to use the language of probability.

5 a Complete the sentences explaining the advantages and disadvantages of possible solutions. Use the correct form of the words in brackets and add any other words necessary.

1 This *is likely to be* (likely / be) the cheapest solution for the government but it *will definitely not be* (definitely / not be) the best.
2 There _____ (strong / probability) giving homes away free will upset many people.
3 This _____ (unlikely / be) the best solution as it _____ (highly likely / homes / be) even more important in the future.
4 This _____ (cannot / be) the only solution as there _____ (only / small chance / banks / lend) money to poorer people.

b Look at your essay plan. Have you used language of probability to compare options?

6 Read the introduction a student wrote for this prompt. The underlined words and phrases are too informal. Re-write the paragraph using some of the phrases in the table.

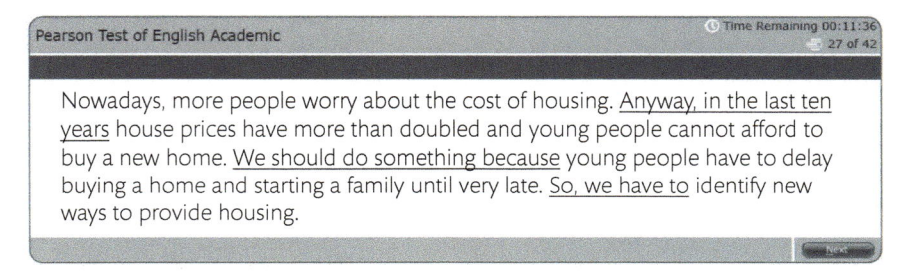

Pearson Test of English Academic   Time Remaining 00:11:36   27 of 42

Nowadays, more people worry about the cost of housing. <u>Anyway, in the last ten years</u> house prices have more than doubled and young people cannot afford to buy a new home. <u>We should do something because</u> young people have to delay buying a home and starting a family until very late. <u>So, we have to</u> identify new ways to provide housing.

Introductions	
Describe the background to the issue	**Over the last decade/century we have seen that** the cosmetics industry has grown. Food for the growing world population **has become an increasingly important issue** in our society. **Many people are concerned that** the money for the beauty industry could be better spent.
Offer a statistic, quotation or fact	**In fact**, the number of people we need to feed in the world is now greater than at any other time in history. **It was suggested** by researchers **that** women now spend over £2,000 a year on their looks.
Say why this topic is important	**This is significant because** that money could make a real difference to people's lives. The effect of spending on beauty products **cannot be underestimated**.
Re-state the question	**It is important to** consider whether this money could make a real difference. **To what extent will/can** people be persuaded to give this money to those who need it?

Write your essay

7 Write your essay. Use your plan from Exercise 4 and the table in Exercise 6 to help you. Remember to write 200–300 words.

Check your essay

8 Check your essay using the checklist on page 196.

> EXPERT WRITING page 196

6B Module 6
City intelligence

Review

1 Complete the sentences with the correct form of the verbs in brackets.

1 Some countries are famous for _____ (locate) their main cities in the least obvious places.
2 The existence of volcano fields below the surface didn't prevent New Zealanders from _____ (construct) the cities of Auckland, Christchurch and Dunedin.
3 It started when Maori used the volcano sites as bases for _____ (train) warriors.
4 Modern residents find it hard _____ (ignore) the fact that Auckland has around 50 volcanic cone heads beneath or around it.
5 In fact, from central Auckland, it's possible _____ (walk) to at least half a dozen of them.
6 None are expected _____ (cause) problems in the near future.
7 However, it's still possible _____ (walk) along footpaths warmed by the heat just below the surface.
8 _____ (spend) the day on Rangitoto Island, which appeared just off the Auckland coast following an eruption 600 years ago, is a popular tourist activity.
9 City officials say that _____ (live) on a volcano field creates few risks.

2 Write responses to the question in the box using the prompts and the words in brackets.

> What would happen if everyone in the world owned a car?

1 congestion / be / a normal part of daily life (a strong chance)
   There is a strong chance that congestion would be a normal part of daily life.
2 people / stop / living in cities (fairly unlikely)
3 traffic jams / last / days, not hours (definitely)
4 pollution / make / it impossible to walk outside (might)
5 manufacturers / develop / smaller, folding cars (a strong possibility)
6 only thinner cars / be / allowed to enter cities (likely)
7 robotic cars / talk / to each other to reduce accidents (a strong chance)
8 self-drive cars / allow / cars to travel closer together safely (highly likely)
9 drivers / be / fined for causing accidents which block roads (a possibility)

3 Complete the article with the words in the box.

> addressed   increasing   leading   meets
> newly-created   potentially   similarities
> suburban

Affordable housing

The [1] _____ demand for housing is a global problem. One South African company has [2] _____ this issue by designing a new construction material which [3] _____ the expectations of the poorer members of society – it's cheap but more importantly, also safe. The [4] _____ homes are made from a removable, reusable, recyclable plastic in the shape of a house, which can be filled with cement when it's in place to make it stronger. It is likely to completely change the nature of [5] _____ areas. It has few [6] _____ with other homes currently available. The whole house takes just one day to build and can be put up by private individuals buying the home, as no skills are required. This dramatically cuts the main cost of homes – labour fees. These homes will [7] _____ improve the quality of life for thousands of families living in poverty and are expected to play a(n) [8] _____ role in cities in the future.

4 Choose the correct options in *italics* to complete the article.

What if we never run out of oil?

The issue of oil was [1] *central / centre* to world politics and economies last century. This century people have worried about how we will learn to live in a world without oil and [2] *glass / plastics*. But what if the oil never runs out?

In recent years, the [3] *scientific / technical* skills behind 'fracking', releasing natural gas from rocks, have made this alternative to petrol impossible to [4] *fail / ignore*. Countries such as the US, Japan, Korea, Canada, China and India are likely to become the new energy producers. In fact, the International Energy Agency predicts that the US will be able to supply all the energy they need – without buying imports – as quickly as 2035.

This will have major [5] *results / consequences* around the world. Global [6] *society / social* unrest may become a problem as the world adapts to a new balance of power. Cheap, plentiful gas is also likely to make climate change worse, affecting the quality of life in the [7] *bigger / wider* society. Although natural gas is considerably cleaner than petrol, it's not completely clean and was always meant to be a 'bridge' fuel, between fossil fuels (coal, petrol and nuclear [8] *fuel / power*) and new, zero carbon forms of energy. Easy access to natural gas reduces the economic arguments for developing those clean energy alternatives.

7 The future of food

Overview

7A
- **Reading:** Reading: Fill in the blanks
- **Academic vocabulary:** Food and food production
- **Speaking:** Read aloud; Answer short question
- **Listening:** Multiple-choice, choose single answer
- **Language development:** The passive
- **Summary writing:** Summarize written text

7B
- **Listening:** Multiple-choice, choose single answer; Write from dictation
- **Language development:** Reduced relative clauses
- **Academic vocabulary:** Business
- **Reading:** Reading: Fill in the blanks
- **Speaking:** Describe image
- **Summary writing:** Summarize written text

Lead-in

1 Discuss the questions in pairs.
  1 Name some of the foods in the pictures.
  2 What are your favourite food items?
  3 Are there any foods you do not like?
  4 The food pyramid above shows how we should be eating. How closely does it match the way you eat?
  5 Do you think it is a good idea to take vitamin and mineral pills?

2 Think of two reasons to agree and disagree with each statement.

'Home-cooked food is better than restaurant meals.'

'Everybody should learn to cook by the time they are 30.'

'In my country food is a really important part of celebrations.'

7A The food we produce

Reading 1 (Reading: Fill in the blanks)

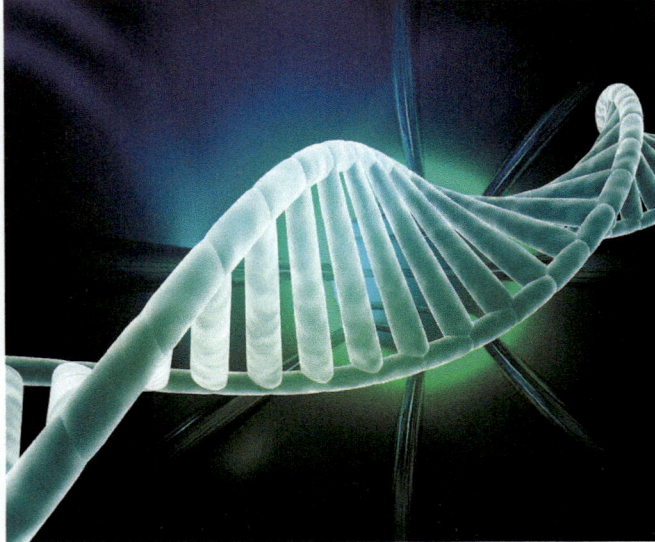

Before you read

1 Discuss the questions in pairs.
1 How important is farming in your country?
2 What plants grow well in your country?
3 What animals are kept on farms in your country?

2 Match the industries in the box with the sentences (1–5). Give reasons for your answers.

farming   pharmaceuticals   both

1 … is/are the business of growing crops or keeping animals.
2 … is/are the business of producing medicines or drugs.
3 … require(s) a large amount of chemicals.
4 … has/have a major effect on people's health.
5 … is/are the subject of a lot of current research.

Identifying words and phrases appropriate to context

Reading: Fill in the blanks tests your understanding of the meaning of words in context.

3a Complete the sentences with one or two words for each blank. Use your own ideas.
1 If it doesn't rain soon, the plants in the fields will _____ .
2 This food is organic – the farmer did not use _____ .
3 My brother loves processed food but I prefer _____ .

b Compare answers in pairs. Were they similar? Why/Why not? Underline the words in the sentences that helped you choose a word to complete each blank.

c Match the sentences in Exercise 3a (1–3) with the clues (A–C) that gave you the answers.
A An opposite was required.
B Further explanation was necessary.
C It was the only logical conclusion.

4a Read the article on page 105 and choose the best title.
1 Gene technology is tested on animals
2 Animals produce drugs in their milk
3 Medicines make animals stronger

Module 7
The future of food
7A

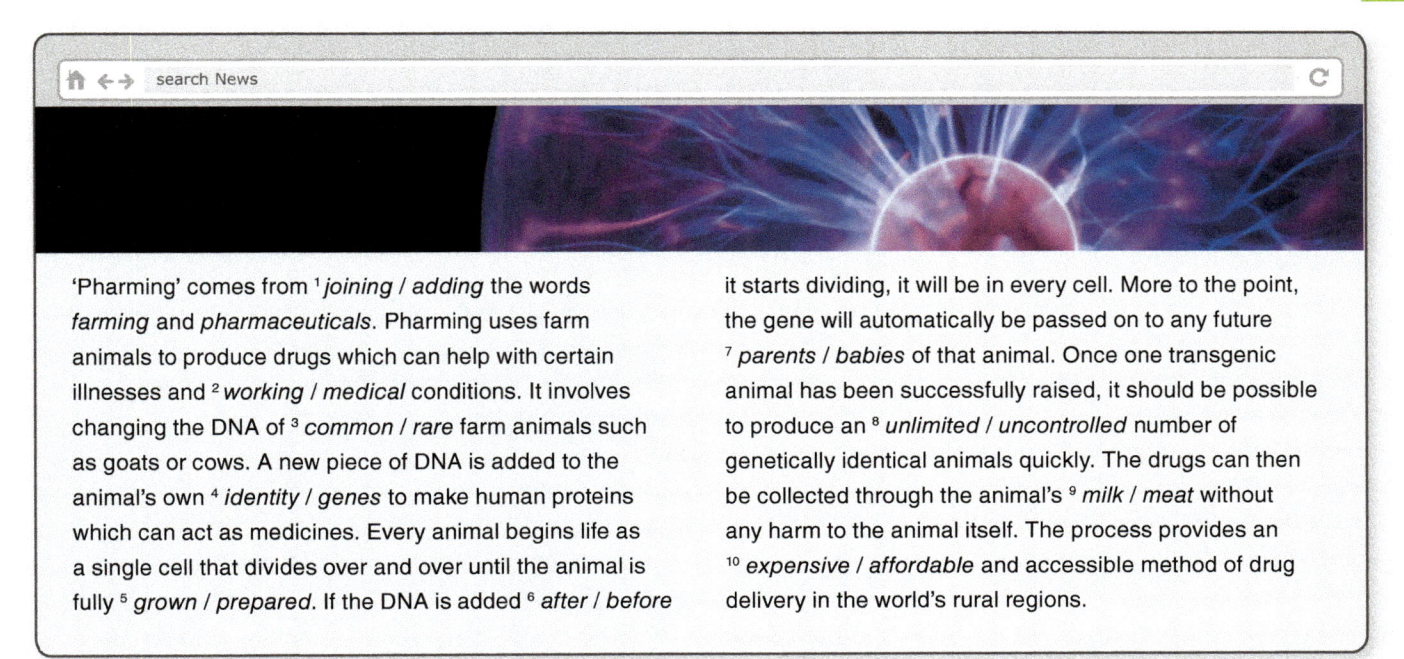

'Pharming' comes from ¹ *joining / adding* the words *farming* and *pharmaceuticals*. Pharming uses farm animals to produce drugs which can help with certain illnesses and ² *working / medical* conditions. It involves changing the DNA of ³ *common / rare* farm animals such as goats or cows. A new piece of DNA is added to the animal's own ⁴ *identity / genes* to make human proteins which can act as medicines. Every animal begins life as a single cell that divides over and over until the animal is fully ⁵ *grown / prepared*. If the DNA is added ⁶ *after / before* it starts dividing, it will be in every cell. More to the point, the gene will automatically be passed on to any future ⁷ *parents / babies* of that animal. Once one transgenic animal has been successfully raised, it should be possible to produce an ⁸ *unlimited / uncontrolled* number of genetically identical animals quickly. The drugs can then be collected through the animal's ⁹ *milk / meat* without any harm to the animal itself. The process provides an ¹⁰ *expensive / affordable* and accessible method of drug delivery in the world's rural regions.

Test practice
> EXPERT STRATEGIES page 180

b   Read the article again and choose the correct options in *italics*. Then underline the phrases that helped you to decide.

5   Complete the task. Remember: there are more words than blanks.

In the text below some words are missing. Drag words from the box below to the appropriate place in the text. To undo an answer choice, drag the word back to the box below the text.

Spider silk is considered the ¹[_____] material ever known, despite its fine width. People have tried starting 'spider farms' to use the silk industrially but the spiders are too ²[_____] to live close together, and like to eat each other. Similarly, attempts to produce the silk in laboratories have ³[_____]. However, when the genes were put into a goat, the animal produced silk proteins in its milk that could be made into a thread with all the ⁴[_____] of spider-made silk.

| aggressive | confused | failed |
| qualities | strongest | thinnest |

> **HELP**
> • Blank 1: What kind of word do you need between *the* and *material*?
> • Blank 2: Do you need a word with a positive or a negative meaning?

Task analysis

6   Discuss the questions in pairs.
    1   Underline the words in the text that helped you rule out certain options. Did you identify them all the first time?
    2   Why is it important to read through the text after you finish?

Discussion

7   Discuss the questions in pairs.
    1   Do you think farms should only be used to produce food?
    2   What might be the dangers of new animals like those discussed in the articles above?

EXPERT WORD CHECK
attempts   cell   certain   thread   width

> See **Reading 2** for more practice of this task type.

105

7A Module 7
The future of food

Academic vocabulary 1 AWL ACL

Academic word list

1a Choose the correct options in *italics* to complete the sentences.

1A What drink is *consumed / consumption* more in your country: tea or coffee?
 B Is it popular to grow plants at home for human *consume / consumption* in your country?
2A What *varied / varieties* of fruit are popular in your country?
 B Is it important to eat a *varied / varieties* diet? Why/Why not?
3A Do you *react / reaction* badly to any particular food?
 B What's normally your *react / reaction* to trying new food?
4A Describe the *process / processed* of making your favourite food.
 B How often do you eat *process / processed* food?

b Discuss the questions in Exercise 1a in pairs.

Academic collocations list

2a Complete the sentences with the words in the box. Then note the collocations in italics.

broad	greater	individual	major	minimum
widely				

1 The _____ *requirement* to stay in good health is around 1,800 calories.
2 Lack of time to cook is a(n) _____ *cause* of weight problems in some countries.
3 Fast food is _____ *available* in many countries.
4 A(n) _____ *range* of vegetables is necessary for good health.
5 Governments should limit salt levels in food, not leave it to _____ *choice*.
6 There is _____ *awareness* of the risks of a poor diet these days.

b Complete the sentences with the collocations in Exercise 2a.

1 There are a(n) _____ of reasons why you should eat well.
2 There is _____ of the calorie content of food today.
3 Vegetables are _____ all year these days.
4 Fast food advertising is a(n) _____ of rising health problems.
5 Diet is a matter of _____ .
6 Eating lots of vegetables is a(n) _____ of healthy eating.

Food

3a Read the article quickly. What is the project under the Arctic Circle? Why is it necessary?

IN CASE OF EMERGENCY, BREAK ICE!

In a mountain deep in the Arctic Circle, 130 metres below the ground, three huge rooms appear. In these rooms are the [1] _seeds_ of the world's most important foods: wheat, [2] _____ and potatoes, as well as vegetables – from [3] _____ to peas. They will be locked away and kept [4] _____ for hundreds, perhaps thousands, of years so that if world disaster ever happens, our children or our children's children will be able to rebuild [5] _____ without losing the 12,000 years' worth of knowledge we've gained so far. There will eventually be all 1.5 million [6] _____ varieties known to man in the room.

Protecting plant varieties matters. In 1948 a man called Jack Harlan was looking for samples of wheat. He found one very unhealthy plant, which was too weak to be worth growing and [7] _____ . He kept a sample anyway. Years later, when a(n) [8] _____ almost killed all the wheat plants in the US, a disaster in terms of world food [9] _____ , Harlan's wheat was the only one that was found to be resistant.

b Read the article again and complete it with the words in the box.

agriculture	crop	disease	frozen	harvesting
lettuce	rice	~~seeds~~	supply	

c Do you think we need this kind of project? Share your ideas with the class.

Word categorisation

4 Complete the table with the headings in the box.

carbohydrates   dairy and calcium   fibre   high-calorie
~~protein~~   vitamins and minerals

1	_protein_	meat, nuts, eggs
2	_____	pasta, potatoes, white bread
3	_____	vegetables, fruit
4	_____	tofu, cheese, milk
5	_____	beans, wholemeal bread, spinach
6	_____	cakes, chips, biscuits

Module 7
The future of food **7A**

Speaking 1 (Read aloud; Answer short question)

Pronunciation: Word stress

In *Read aloud* you will need to stress words accurately.

1 🎧 79 In Modules 3 and 5 you studied word stress. Listen to nine sentences and underline the stressed syllables in the words in the table.

1	science	4	various	7	inform
2	scientific	5	variety	8	information
3	scientifically	6	variations	9	informative

2a Look at the words in *italics* in the sentences. Are they verbs or nouns? How do you know?
  1 A There's been a lot of *progress* in this field.
     B They'll need to *progress* to the next level.
  2 A There's been a *decrease* in the quality of food.
     B The quality of food may *decrease*.
  3 A Professor Jameson *rejects* the idea completely.
     B The food is sorted and the *rejects* are thrown out.
  4 A My country *exports* a lot of food.
     B There were a lot of *exports* last year.

b 🎧 80 Listen to the sentences in Exercise 2a and underline the stressed syllables in the words in *italics*. Do you see any patterns?

c Work in pairs. Practise saying the sentences in Exercise 2a.

Test practice 1: Read aloud
➤ EXPERT STRATEGIES page 170

3 Complete the task. Remember to think about linking words in sense groups, word stress and intonation.

> ⏱ 35 sec. *Look at the text below. In 35 seconds, you must read this text aloud as naturally and clearly as possible. You have 35 seconds to read aloud.*
>
> The great hope of genetically modified foods is that we will be able to increase the number of varieties of plants that can fight off weeds and pests and will grow more quickly and more cheaply. This will allow us to produce more food like rice and use this to feed the hungry.

4 🎧 81 Listen to a model answer. Is it similar to your reading? Did you stress words in the correct places? Try the task again.

Test practice 2: Answer short question
➤ EXPERT STRATEGIES page 174

5 🎧 82 Complete the task in pairs. You will hear six questions.

> ⏱ 10 sec. *You will hear a question. Please give a simple and short answer. Often just one or a few words is enough.*

genetically modified food or plants have had their genetic structure changed so that they are not affected by particular diseases or harmful insects

107

7A Module 7
The future of food

Listening 1 (Multiple-choice, choose single answer)

Before you listen

1 Discuss the questions in pairs. Check the meaning of the words in bold in a dictionary if you are unsure.
   1 Do you have a big **agricultural industry** in your country? What **crops** do farmers grow in their **fields**?
   2 Is your country **dependent on** others for food, i.e. do you **consume** more than you grow? What food do you **import**?

Identifying the organisation of a text

In *Multiple-choice, choose single answer* you will need to identify the organisation of a text in order to follow the speaker's ideas.

2a 🎧 83 Listen to an agriculture expert talking about farming in Japan. What is the main topic?

b 🎧 83 Listen again. Which pattern does the speaker use to organise his ideas? Which words from his talk tell you this?
   1 comparison + contrast
   2 problem + solution
   3 cause + effect
   4 description of a situation + example + conclusion
   5 event 1 + event 2 + event 3

c Match the words and phrases (A–E) with the text organisation patterns (1–5) in Exercise 2b.
   A issue, problem, plan, solve
   B first, then, next, finally
   C because, caused by, result, consequence
   D such as, for instance, therefore
   E similar, like, in comparison, difference

3a 🎧 84 Listen to three more people talking about farming in Japan. Which pattern from Exercise 2b does each speaker use to organise his/her ideas?

b 🎧 84 Listen again. Which words helped you choose a pattern for each speaker?

Test practice
> EXPERT STRATEGIES page 186

4 🎧 85 Complete the task. Remember to take notes and use the organisation of the text to help you answer the question.

> *Listen to the recording and answer the multiple-choice question by selecting the correct response. Only one response is correct.*
>
> What conclusion does the speaker draw about possible new farming techniques?
>
> A ○ Farmers will need to start using more advanced tools.
> B ○ Farmers will grow a much larger number of crops.
> C ○ Farmers will produce crops at a competitive price.
> D ○ Farmers will have a different relationship with nature.

> **HELP**
>
> When does a speaker usually present their conclusion?

Task analysis

5 Work in pairs. How useful are these strategies for this task? Did you use them?
   1 Read the instructions carefully.
   2 Use the organisation of the lecture to help you answer the question.
   3 Eliminate options which include information not in the lecture or opposite to what the speaker said.

> See **Listening 2** for more practice of this task type.

Module 7
The future of food 7A

Language development 1

The passive

> EXPERT GRAMMAR page 210

1a Underline the active verb forms and circle the passive verb forms in the sentences.
1. Less than 12 percent of the land will be farmed in the future.
2. The government has created a plan to try to solve the problem.
3. Just 40 percent of food in Japan is produced by Japanese farmers.
4. The farm will be run by these boys once the farmer reaches retirement age.
5. Many farms consist of small plots of land between apartment blocks.

b Look at the passive verb forms in Exercise 1a and identify who carried out the actions. Is this always mentioned? Why/Why not?

c Re-write the sentences in the passive.
1. Fresh food which supermarkets sell is not always fresh.
2. You can store most fruit for a few weeks in the right temperature.
3. Producers chill them as quickly as possible.
4. Producers pick some fruit before it is ripe.
5. Producers sometimes spray fruit with a chemical to stop them going bad.

2a Look at the diagram. What does it show?

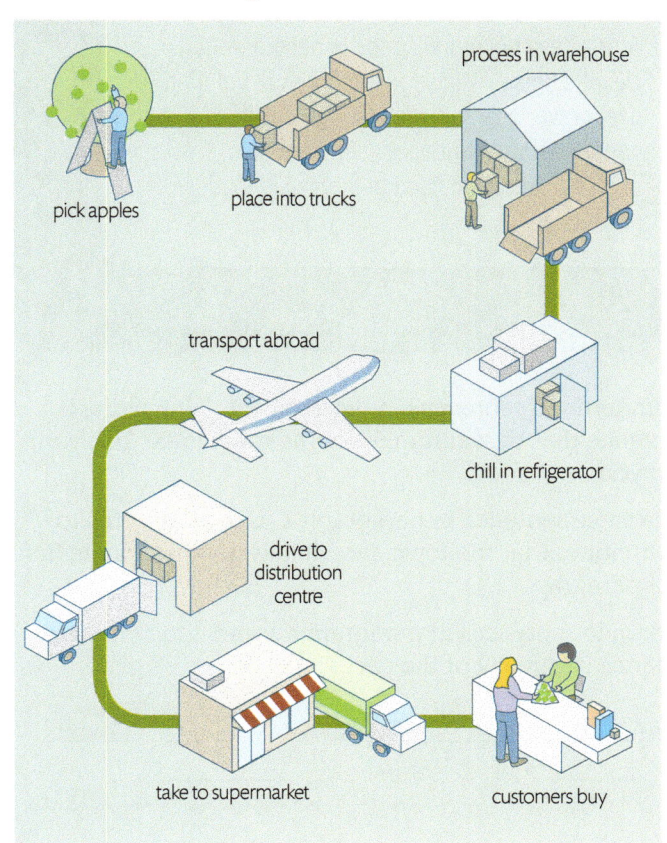

(diagram showing: pick apples → place into trucks → process in warehouse → chill in refrigerator → transport abroad → drive to distribution centre → take to supermarket → customers buy)

b Write passive sentences to describe each step of the process in the diagram in Exercise 2a.

c Work in pairs. Take turns to describe the diagram to your partner without looking at your sentences. Check that your partner uses the passive correctly.

3a Complete the first part of an article with the correct passive form of the verbs in brackets.

Will meat on your plate disappear?

Scientists are warning that water and food shortages could force the world into vegetarianism in a report which [1] _____ (release) yesterday. 20 percent of a human's protein [2] _____ (take) from animal-based products but this may drop to just five percent in the future. This is because the population [3] _____ (expect) to rise by two billion before 2050, which will increase demand for food and water. Scientists say that a larger population cannot [4] _____ (feed) if common eating habits in western nations continue. Five to ten times more water [5] _____ (consume) by a meat diet than a vegetarian diet, so they believe that in the future water for animals [6] _____ (limit) and less meat [7] _____ (produce).

b Complete the second part of the article with the correct active or passive form of the verbs in brackets.

Increasingly, our water levels [1] _____ (affect) by our changeable climate. Droughts and poor monsoon rains all [2] _____ (contribute) to this problem. Adopting a vegetarian diet is one solution, as one third of the world's farmland [3] _____ (use) to grow crops that feed animals. But there are other solutions, too. For example, waste levels could [4] _____ (reduce) and international trade could [5] _____ (increase). These may help to solve water shortages at a time when water [6] _____ (also / need) to satisfy global energy demand. This demand [7] _____ (rise) by 60 percent over the next 30 years as more electricity [8] _____ (generate) for the 1.3 billion people currently without it.

c Do many people eat a vegetarian diet in your country? Share your ideas with the class.

109

7A Module 7
The future of food

Summary writing 1 (Summarize written text)

Bringing information together in one sentence

In *Summarize written text* it is important to understand the key information in the text and bring it together to create a one-sentence summary.

1 Read the article and make notes of the key information. Use the key words in the text, as you did on page 14 of Module 1.

A revolution of a different kind

Agriculture today would not be the same without the Green Revolution that significantly increased the amount of crops produced per acre of land. The Revolution describes the changes in agricultural practices which started in Mexico in the 1940s. Scientist Norman Borlaug developed new varieties of wheat that were disease-resistant and produced high quantities. Along with new mechanised agricultural technologies, innovations in the way land is watered and the use of chemical fertilizers, Mexico was able to produce more wheat than was needed by its own citizens, leading to it becoming an exporter of wheat by the 1960s. Prior to this, the country had imported almost half of its wheat supply.

The technologies soon spread worldwide. India, which was close to a mass famine in the early 1960s, was able to become one of the world's leading rice producers with help from Borlaug, who developed a new variety of rice. There have been criticisms of the Green Revolution, however. The first is that the increased amount of food production has led to overpopulation worldwide. The second is that places like Africa have not significantly benefited from it. Despite these criticisms, the Green Revolution has forever changed the way agriculture is conducted worldwide, benefiting people of many nations in need of increased food production.

2 Look at the underlined sentences in paragraph 1. Which one is the topic sentence that best summarises the main idea? Use your notes to help you.

3 Underline the topic sentence in paragraph 2. Use your notes to help you. Remember that the topic sentence is not always the first sentence in a paragraph.

4 Combine the topic sentences in paragraphs 1 and 2 to complete the one-sentence summary of the text.

Agriculture today _____ because it _____ and _____ , despite some _____ .

> See **Writing 2** for more practice of this task type.

7B The food we eat

Listening 2 (Multiple-choice, choose single answer; Write from dictation)

Before you listen

1a Work in pairs. Complete the sentences using your own ideas.
1 Our five senses are …
2 Cells on our tongue can identify tastes such as …
3 A human's sense of smell is less sensitive than a(n) …

b Discuss the questions in pairs.
1 What is your favourite smell? Your favourite taste?
2 Why do you think our bodies have a sense of smell and a sense of taste?

Test practice 1: Multiple-choice, choose single answer
➤ EXPERT STRATEGIES page 186

2 🎧 86 Complete the task. Remember to take notes.

> Listen to the recording and answer the multiple-choice question by selecting the correct response. Only one response is correct.
>
> According to the speaker, a dog's sense of smell is better than a human's because
>
> A ○ its cells are more sensitive.
> B ○ it has a better memory.
> C ○ it has more cells.
> D ○ it trains itself effectively.

Test practice 2: Write from dictation
➤ EXPERT STRATEGIES page 189

3 🎧 87 Complete the task. You will hear three sentences. Then compare answers in pairs.

> You will hear a sentence. Type the sentence in the box below exactly as you hear it. Write as much of the sentence as you can. You will hear the sentence only once.

Task analysis

4a Match three incorrect options in Exercise 2 with the reasons why they were incorrect.
1 The speaker did not mention this.
2 The speaker talks about humans in relation to this topic but he does not talk about dogs.
3 The speaker says the opposite.

b 🎧 87 Listen to the sentences from Exercise 3 again. If you made mistakes, what caused them? You did not hear the words? Unknown vocabulary? Spelling? Lack of concentration?

111

7B Module 7
The future of food

Language development 2

Reduced relative clauses

> EXPERT GRAMMAR page 211

1a Look at the graph. What changes have there been in food consumption?

Purchases of food products among 1,000 people in a UK city in 2001 and 2011

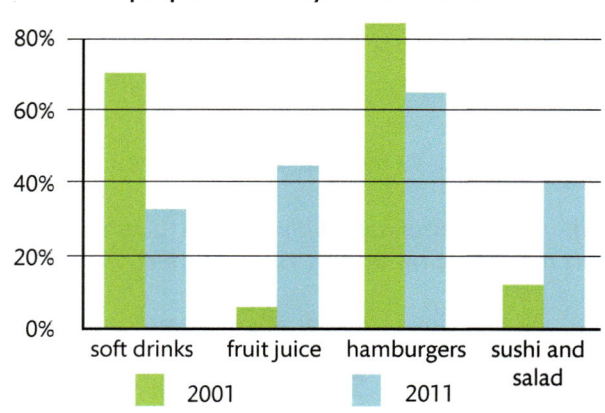

(Bar graph showing percentages for soft drinks, fruit juice, hamburgers, sushi and salad in 2001 and 2011)

- soft drinks: 2001 ~70%, 2011 ~33%
- fruit juice: 2001 ~5%, 2011 ~45%
- hamburgers: 2001 ~85%, 2011 ~65%
- sushi and salad: 2001 ~12%, 2011 ~40%

b Complete the sentences with the words in the box. You can use the words more than once.

amount	level	number

1 The _____ of people *who participated* in the survey was quite low.
2 The _____ of fast food consumption *which was recorded* in this survey fell.
3 The _____ of hamburgers *which were eaten* dropped by 10 percent.
4 The _____ of fruit juice *which was drunk* increased considerably.
5 The _____ of individuals *who made* healthier choices rose.
6 The _____ of sushi *which was bought* went up more than any other category.

2a Look at the full and reduced relative clauses in the sentences and answer the questions.

> 1 A People *who are trained* to recognise smells are not necessarily any more sensitive.
> B People *trained* to recognise smells are not necessarily any more sensitive.
> 2 A Perfume experts *who work* with smells are better at retrieving them from memory.
> B Perfume experts *working* with smells are better at retrieving them from memory.

1 Are the verbs in the full relative clauses in Exercises 1b and 2a active or passive?
2 When do we replace *who* + verb with a past participle?
3 When do we replace *who* + verb with an *-ing* form?

b Complete the reduced relative clauses in the sentences with the correct form of the verbs in brackets.

1 Do you enjoy eating food _____ (pre-cook) in a factory?
2 Do you think foods _____ (use) a lot of colourings are safe?
3 Do people in your country eat foods _____ (grow) in their own garden?
4 Do you think there will be more people _____ (work) in farming in future?
5 Are recipes _____ (involve) a lot of cooking time popular in your country?

3a Rewrite the sentences in Exercise 1b changing the full relative clauses in *italics* to reduced relative clauses.

1 *The number of people participating in the survey was quite low.*

b Work in pairs. Take turns to describe the graph in Exercise 1a to your partner. Use reduced relative clauses where possible.

4a Read the article. Then change the full relative clauses in *italics* to reduced relative clauses.

Looking at junk food makes you feel hungry, study confirms

Researchers have proven something [1] *which was already widely known*: the sight of delicious food makes you hungry. This scientific evidence, though, raises questions about images of food [2] *which are shown in the media*. It is likely that they contribute to the weight increases [3] *which have been seen in Western populations*. A research group from Max Planck Institute created a test [4] *which involved a series of pictures* [5] *which contained either images of delicious food or non-edible objects*, which they showed to healthy males. The scientists tested levels of a chemical [6] *which controls how hungry we feel*, ghrelin. Previously, scientists believed that this chemical was produced by factors [7] *which could only be found inside the body, not in the environment*. The scientists recommend that anyone [8] *who is concerned about their weight* should avoid looking at photographs [9] *which show high-calorie food*.

1 ... *something already widely known* ...

b Do you think the use of photos of food in adverts should be more controlled? Share your ideas with the class.

Academic vocabulary 2 AWL ACL

Prepositions

1a Complete the sentences with the prepositions in the box. Does each preposition follow a verb or an adjective?

at   between   by   from   to (x2)

1 What are you influenced _____ when choosing food at the supermarket?
2 Can you tell the difference _____ the taste of famous brands and supermarket own brands? How are they different?
3 Are you sensitive _____ the amount of calories food contains?
4 Has your diet today changed compared _____ ten years ago? How?
5 Are you better _____ cooking now than you were a few years ago?
6 If someone reached into the back of your fridge, what could they retrieve _____ there?

b Discuss the questions in Exercise 1a in pairs.

Business

2a Choose the correct options in *italics* to complete the sentences.

1 Walmart is an example of a large supermarket *brand / chain*.
2 Walmart has *branches / industries* in many different areas of the US and abroad.
3 The food *industry / market* involves businesses such as supermarkets, restaurants, farms, etc.
4 Some supermarkets *form / manufacture* their own branded products.
5 It can be difficult to *do / run* a large business such as a supermarket.
6 The head of a supermarket must make sure that the company makes a *profit / wage* and not a *loss / miss*.

b Where do people tend to do their food shopping in your country? Why?

3 Complete the sentences with a noun formed from the words in capitals.

1 Big supermarket chains have a significant _influence_ on what people buy. **INFLUENTIAL**
2 Supermarkets often have a price _____ system to show that their products are cheaper. **COMPARE**
3 The amount of money spent in a supermarket can indicate if a country's _____ is healthy or not. **ECONOMIC**
4 Supermarkets often pay other food _____ to make branded products for them. **MANUFACTURE**
5 The arrival of a new supermarket can be positive and lower _____ in a town. **EMPLOY**
6 The _____ system in a large organisation must be strong to succeed. **MANAGE**
7 Many small shop owners enjoy their _____ and do not want to be part of a large organisation. **DEPENDENT**
8 _____ that own many stores can often afford to keep their prices low. **RETAIL**

4a Complete the words in the article to form collocations. Then note the collocations in *italics*.

In [1] e_____ *times* food shopping involved going to a number of [2] *sp*_____ *shops* to buy vegetables, meat, bread, etc. But in the last century the supermarket was born and shoppers can now buy all the food they need in one place, as well as clothes, household goods and electrical equipment. Many are even offering [3] *f*_____ *services*.

Today a few large supermarket chains dominate the [4] *r*_____ *sector*. By becoming large, they receive many [5] *e*_____ *benefits* which often appear to be passed onto the customer. For example, they [6] *m*_____ *contracts* with farmers to sell their produce at low prices and they purchase [7] *l*_____ *quantities* at one time. This allows them to keep prices low and attract *new* [8] *c*_____. They also provide other social benefits such as *employment* [9] *o*_____ for thousands of people.

The negative side of this is that small [10] *in*_____ *retailers* have found it difficult to keep up with the *increased* [11] *c*_____ and there are far fewer *family* [12] *f*_____ today than there were in the past.

b 🎧 88 Listen and check your answers. Then write the collocations in your vocabulary notebook with an example sentence.

113

7B Module 7
The future of food

Reading 2 (Reading: Fill in the blanks)

Before you read

1 Discuss the questions in pairs.
1 Would you like to have dinner in the place in the photo?
2 Which is your favourite and least favourite type of restaurant?

2 Chose the correct options in *italics* to complete the sentences.
1 Most *diners / dinners* prefer to eat outside.
2 High *calory / calorie* food is OK, occasionally.
3 It's not healthy to eat *desert / dessert* every day.
4 People want to eat in a restaurant with a good *atmospher / atmosphere*.

Test practice
> EXPERT STRATEGIES page 180

3 Complete the task. Remember to think about the context around the blanks.

In the text below some words are missing. Drag words from the box below to the appropriate place in the text. To undo an answer choice, drag the word back to the box below the text.

Lighting and music can affect people's consumption of food as well as ¹[_____] of meals. In ²[_____], a restaurant's atmosphere can cause people to ³[_____]. This is because individuals tend to stay longer and order dessert, even if they hadn't ⁴[_____] to do so on arrival. However, bright lights and loud noise at fast food restaurants can make individuals feel stressed rather than ⁵[_____]. In fact, atmosphere can increase food intake by as much as 175 calories.

| contrast | enjoyment | entertainment | feed |
| particular | overeat | planned | relaxed |

Task analysis

4 Compare answers in pairs. Then discuss the questions.
1 What do you think you need to practise most: learning new vocabulary or learning to use words in context?
2 Did you re-read the text after you finished? Did it make sense?

Discussion

5 How do people make a room look special when friends come round for dinner? Do you do any of these things? Why/Why not?

Module 7
7B The future of food

Speaking 2 (Describe image)

Developing a complex idea within a spoken discourse

To score well on *Describe image*, you will need to show that you can develop a complex idea and reach conclusions or discuss the implications of what you can see.

1 Look at the diagram in Exercise 3, illustrating the benefits of machine-drilled wells over hand-drilled wells and discuss the questions in pairs.
   1 What is the purpose of a well?
   2 The main issue illustrated in the diagram is that
      A people who make wells by hand cannot go very deep.
      B wells made by hand might not provide safe drinking water.
      C wells with a pump at the top are more efficient.

Sample response

2a 🎧 89 Listen to two students describing the diagram in Exercise 3. Which student has correctly developed the main idea in the diagram? Why?

b Complete the second student's description with the words in the box.

| firstly | for these reasons | however | secondly | so |
| this | two |

> The diagram shows the differences between a hand-dug well and a machine-drilled well. The machine-drilled well has [1]_____ key advantages. [2]_____, it's much deeper. The man-made well can only reach the water just below the soil, [3]_____ chemicals and agricultural waste can enter the water supply. [4]_____ can be avoided by drilling through the rock to the purer water below. [5]_____, contaminants can also enter the water supply through the open top. A well with a mechanical hand pump, [6]_____, is sealed and keeps contamination out. [7]_____, water from the machine-drilled well is safer.

c 🎧 90 Listen and check your answers.

Test practice

➤ EXPERT STRATEGIES page 172

3 Complete the task on the right in pairs. Take turns to describe the diagram. Record your answers if possible.

🎬 40 sec. Look at the chart below. In 25 seconds, please speak into the microphone and describe in detail what the chart is showing. You will have 40 seconds to give your response.

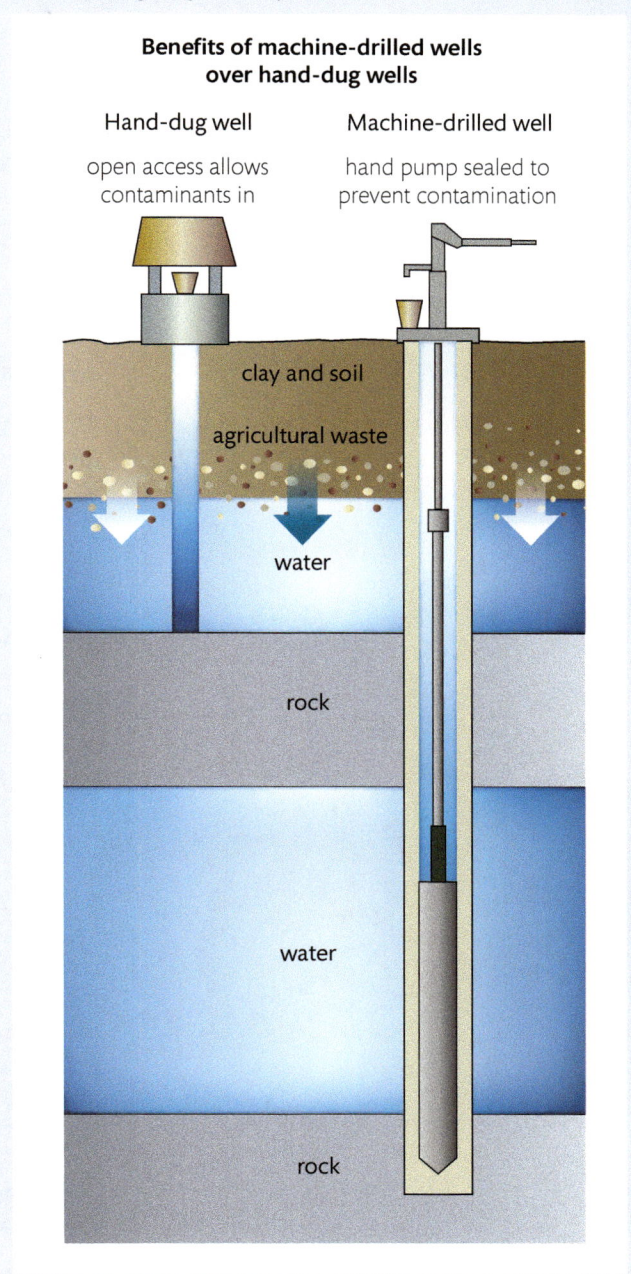

Benefits of machine-drilled wells over hand-dug wells

Hand-dug well — open access allows contaminants in

Machine-drilled well — hand pump sealed to prevent contamination

clay and soil
agricultural waste
water
rock
water
rock

4 Turn to page 192 and complete another timed test practice.

➤ EXPERT SPEAKING page 192

Task analysis

5 🎧 91 Listen to a model answer for the task in Exercise 4. Compare it with your description. What differences were there? Try the task again.

7B Module 7
The future of food

Summary writing 2 (Summarize written text)

Lead-in

1a Complete the questions with the words in the box. Check the meaning of any unknown words in a dictionary.

alternative   blamed for   controversial   ingredients   subsidies
sweetener   tariffs

1 Do people in your country tend to put sugar or _____ in their tea/coffee?
2 Are there any types of food that are _____ in your country (e.g. bad for you)?
3 Which types of food are usually _____ weight gain?
4 Do farmers in your country receive _____ from the government to grow certain crops?
5 Is honey a good _____ to sugar? Why/Why not?
6 What _____ can you find in fizzy drinks?
7 What do you know about international trade taxes such as _____ ?

b Discuss the questions in Exercise 1a in pairs.

Understand the task
➤ EXPERT STRATEGIES page 175

2a Read the instructions for *Summarize written text* and answer the questions.

1 How many sentences should your summary have?
2 In the test, where do you type your summary?
3 How much time do you have to complete the task?
4 How is your summary scored?

b Read the text quickly. What is the topic?

> **10 min.** *Read the passage below and summarize it using one sentence. Type your response in the box at the bottom of the screen. You have 10 minutes to finish this task. Your response will be judged on the quality of your writing and on how well your response presents the key points in the passage.*
>
> In the 1970s international tariffs caused sugar prices to rise, which created a problem for some manufacturers. As a result, they began to look for alternative products that were more cost effective. Until this time, high fructose corn syrup (HFCS) had not been used a lot. It was a good alternative to sugar and was cheaper because of the government subsidies that American farmers received for growing corn. The use of HFCS steadily rose and is now regularly used as an ingredient in processed food such as tinned vegetables and ketchup. In the 1980s two of the largest fizzy drinks manufacturers stopped using sugar completely and replaced it with HFCS, which made the sweetener more acceptable.
>
> Today HFCS is a controversial product, regularly blamed for the rising weight gain occurring in the USA. There are also concerns that it has the potential to cause other health problems such as diabetes, heart and liver disease because it is processed and is not a natural form of sugar. As a result, some health groups have argued that it should be banned. Despite these worries, there is little scientific evidence to suggest that HFCS is any more harmful than other types of sweeteners, including sugar.

Module 7	7B
The future of food	

Plan your summary sentence

3 a Read the text more carefully. Find the key words and use them to help you write notes on the key information.

b Compare your notes in pairs. Have you noted down similar key words?

c Underline the topic sentence in each paragraph. Does the writer come to a conclusion at the end of the text? Discuss your answers in pairs.

d Write two or three sentences to describe the main idea of the text. Use your notes and the topic sentences to help you. Then compare and discuss your answers in pairs. Explain your decisions to your partner.

Language and content

4 a Find and correct three spelling mistakes in each of the summary sentences of texts related to food.
1 Some people believe it is the goverment's responsability to fight weight gain issues, wich have increased in recent years, <u>so that</u> people lead healthier lives and rely less on state health care systems.
2 A psychologist claims that it is neccesary for people to control there consumption of fatty food from a young age <u>so as not to</u> become dependant on it.
3 Labels are placed on food items <u>in order to</u> seperate healthy products from those that are not so good for you and allow consumors to acheive better diets.
4 The writer believes that our eating habits will definately change in the future <u>to</u> ensure we do not consistantly eat more than our enviroment can provide.

b Look at the underlined phrases in Exercise 4a and answer the questions.
1 What do they all express?
2 Which phrases are followed by an infinitive? Which is followed by a clause?

c Complete the sentences using your own ideas.
1 In some countries fast food advertising to children is banned in order to …
2 Some sweet manufacturers use natural flavouring so as not to …
3 Food packaging should be recyclable to …
4 Fizzy drinks sometimes have high amounts of sugar in them so that …

5 When writing a one-sentence summary, three pieces of information is probably the most you will be able to include. Join the pieces of information to make one sentence.
1 Food advertising to children is banned in some countries. It makes them want to eat junk food. It is considered to be negative.
    Food advertising to children is banned in some countries because it makes them want to eat junk food, so it is considered to be negative.
2 Many sweet manufacturers use natural flavouring. Parents will buy them. The parents are worried about their children's health.
3 Food packaging uses a lot of resources. It produces a lot of waste. We should try to reduce this.
4 Some people drink a lot of fizzy drinks. They can contain a lot of caffeine. Too much caffeine can cause anxiety.

Write your summary sentence

6 Write your summary sentence. Use your notes from Exercise 3a and the language in Exercise 4a to help you.

Check your summary sentence

7 Check your summary sentence using the checklist on page 196.

> EXPERT WRITING page 196

117

7B Module 7
The future of food

Review

1 Complete the article with the correct active or passive form of the verbs in brackets.

> The five basic tastes are sour, sweet, salty, bitter and umami. All of the sensations that we experience can ¹_____ (describe) as a combination of these five basic tastes. Our tongue ²_____ (cover) in taste cells called 'buds' but each bud is sensitive to just one of these five basic tastes, so when we ³_____ (eat) a particular type of food, certain cells ⁴_____ (activate). Two types of food that activate similar buds ⁵_____ (taste) almost the same. But it's not just our taste buds that ⁶_____ (influence) our sense of taste. It ⁷_____ (depend) heavily on smell. Many qualities of food that we think we taste are actually a function of smell. That's why when you have a cold and your nose ⁸_____ (block), it is often impossible to taste food properly.

2 Complete the sentences about carrots with the words in the box.

consumption   crops   diseases   frozen   harvest
imports   ingredient   minerals   order   processed
retailers   varieties   vitamin

1. One thousand years ago there were several _____ of carrot, including black and purple.
2. In the 1200s, the Dutch cross-bred carrots in _____ to create an orange one.
3. The _____ of carrots is recommended for health reasons.
4. Carrots are full of _____ A and _____ .
5. _____ vegetables, like carrots, can be just as healthy as fresh vegetables.
6. Carrots can be a(n) _____ of both savoury and sweet dishes.
7. If you grow carrots in the same place each year, _____ will start to kill the plants.
8. In Asia carrot _____ are grown during the winter.
9. Germany _____ some of their carrots from the Netherlands.
10. When carrots are _____ , people carefully check the quality of them.
11. Supermarket _____ have specific requirements for the carrots they buy.
12. Around 40 percent of the UK carrot _____ is rejected because it does not meet supermarket requirements.

3 Read the article. Then change the relative clauses in *italics* to reduced relative clauses.

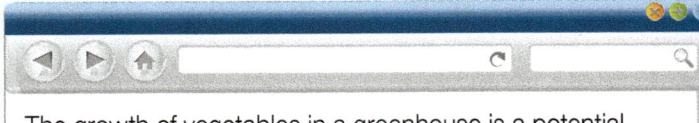

> The growth of vegetables in a greenhouse is a potential business opportunity. However, people ¹*who are interested in this opportunity* must be aware of all the factors ²*which are involved*. Firstly, you must learn about customers ³*who buy vegetables in your area* to help you decide which kinds of vegetables to grow. Market research ⁴*which is conducted in this industry* is very important and should not be forgotten. The next thing is to find a site ⁵*which offers good quality water*, access to energy, potential customers and employees. Individuals ⁶*who build a greenhouse on such a site* may need to get permission from local government.
>
> Another factor to consider is energy. Growers ⁷*who investigate different energy solutions* want to avoid any increase in natural gas prices. Therefore, new farmers may want to look at cheaper forms of power such as energy ⁸*which is created by the sun or wind*. Finally, farmers must decide how to sell their products. Having one supermarket which sells all of your products is easier but results in less income. Customers who want to sell their vegetables at the side of the road will need a licence.

1. *interested*   5. _____
2. _____   6. _____
3. _____   7. _____
4. _____   8. _____

4 Choose the correct options in *italics* to complete the text.

> Max is an experienced ¹*free / independent* retailer. He owns a ²*special / specialist* shop that sells fruit and vegetables grown by local farmers. His business started as a family ³*agent / firm* 20 years ago, managed by his father and uncle. Max now ⁴*makes / runs* the business with his cousin Sarah and her husband Al. These days the business ⁵*does / makes* a good profit because of the ⁶*broad / long* range of products that it sells. However, this was not always the case. It was only when people began to develop a ⁷*greater / larger* awareness of the chemicals used in the ⁸*agricultural / farmer* industry that the demand for ⁹*natural / organic* food increased. Today customers visiting the shop comment on the quality of these products that are not ¹⁰*largely / widely* available elsewhere in the area.

8 Being human

Overview

8A
- **Reading:** Reading & writing: Fill in the blanks
- **Academic vocabulary:** Science and technology
- **Speaking:** Repeat sentence; Answer short question
- **Listening:** Select missing word
- **Language development:** Expressing obligation and permission
- **Writing:** Write essay

8B
- **Listening:** Select missing word; Write from dictation
- **Language development:** Academic language
- **Academic vocabulary:** Health
- **Reading:** Reading & writing: Fill in the blanks
- **Speaking:** Re-tell lecture
- **Writing:** Write essay

Lead-in

1. Discuss the questions in pairs.
   1. How does technology improve your daily life? Think of five ways.
   2. In what ways does technology make you feel frustrated?
   3. What is your favourite gadget? Why?

2. How does technology help these people? Think of at least three ways for each.
   1. bankers   2. doctors   3. engineers   4. police officers   5. sailors

3. Work in small groups. Think of a piece of technology that you would like to be invented in future. Present your ideas to the class explaining what the invention is and how it will benefit you and others. Which group has the best idea?

8A Man and machine

Reading 1 (Reading & writing: Fill in the blanks)

Before you read

1 Work in pairs. Discuss how technology can be used to improve quality of life in these situations. Check the meaning of the words in bold in a dictionary if you are unsure.
   1 You are **raising** a **deaf** child.
   2 Your legs are **paralysed**.
   3 You are old and do not have **flexibility** in your hands.
   4 You need an **operation** to **cure** an illness.

Identifying grammatical links

In *Reading & writing: Fill in the blanks* and other reading tasks it is important to understand how grammar helps to link ideas.

2 Read the article quickly. What is the main point?

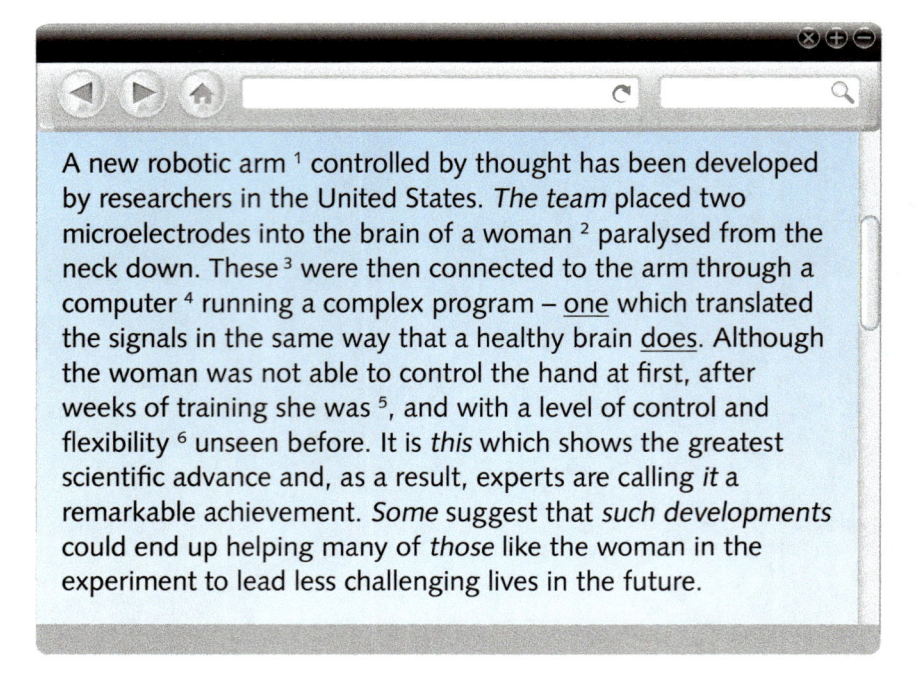

A new robotic arm [1] controlled by thought has been developed by researchers in the United States. *The team* placed two microelectrodes into the brain of a woman [2] paralysed from the neck down. These [3] were then connected to the arm through a computer [4] running a complex program – <u>one</u> which translated the signals in the same way that a healthy brain <u>does</u>. Although the woman was not able to control the hand at first, after weeks of training she was [5], and with a level of control and flexibility [6] unseen before. It is *this* which shows the greatest scientific advance and, as a result, experts are calling *it* a remarkable achievement. *Some* suggest that *such developments* could end up helping many of *those* like the woman in the experiment to lead less challenging lives in the future.

3a In texts, words are sometimes left out on purpose. Look at 1–6 in the article in Exercise 2 and decide where in the text the words in the box belong.

   able to control the hand   microelectrodes   which had been   which is   which was   who is

b Match the words in the box in Exercise 3a with the reasons they were left out (A–B).
   A to avoid repetition of a word(s)   B to reduce a relative clause

4 In texts, nouns are sometimes replaced by *one(s)* and verbs are sometimes replaced by *do/does/did (so)* to avoid repetition. Look at the two underlined words in the article in Exercise 2. Which words do they replace?

5 In texts, words like pronouns, articles, etc. are sometimes used to refer to things mentioned somewhere else and avoid repetition. Look at the words in *italics* in the article. What do they refer to?
   The team = The researchers

Module 8
Being human — 8A

Test practice
> EXPERT STRATEGIES page 181

6 Complete the task. Think about how grammar is used to link ideas in the text.

Below is a text with blanks. Click on each blank, a list of choices will appear. Select the appropriate answer choice for each blank.

For many hearing parents who have a deaf child, the decision to give their son or daughter the ability to hear is an easy one. But for deaf parents in the same [1] _____, it may not be the case. Some people in the deaf community do not support *cochlear implants*, the electronic [2] _____ that can restore some form of hearing, because they believe that deafness is not a disability. They say it is simply a cultural difference which should [3] _____ as normal and not something that needs to be cured. Another reason for their decision is that an operation by a surgeon is needed to insert the implants behind the ear. This presents a risk that parents may not [4] _____ to take. In addition, those that receive the implant do not suddenly hear normally. It can help them to hear some sounds and to communicate more effectively but it is not the same as normal hearing and can be unpleasant for some. As a result, a number of deaf parents choose not to use [5] _____ technology and instead raise their children to communicate using sign language.

1	2	3	4	5
event	device	accept	fancy	such
background	stuff	accepted	wish	one
situation	facility	is accepted	desire	it
conditions	too	be accepted	require	these

> **HELP**
>
> Blank 3: Is this an active or passive sentence? Think about who does the action.

Task analysis

7 Match the three incorrect options in each question in Exercise 6 with the reasons why they were incorrect.
1 The meaning is incorrect.
2 The word does not fit grammatically.
3 The word is too informal for the tone of the text.
4 The word does not collocate with words around it.

Discussion

8 a Work in small groups. In Exercise 6 you read arguments *against* a deaf person having an implant to help them hear. What are the arguments *for*? Think of at least three.

b Now argue the reasons *for* and *against*. Try to come to a consensus as a group.

> **EXPERT WORD CHECK**
> insert   normal   remarkable   restore   scientific advance

> See **Reading 2** for more practice of this task type.

8A Module 8: Being human

Academic vocabulary 1 AWL ACL

Science

1a Imagine a group of scientists are working on a research project. Put the actions in the correct order (1–6). Check the meaning of the words in bold in a dictionary if you are unsure.

- ___ They **carry out** research and **gather data** to help them understand the problem.
- ___ Finally, if they are lucky, their discovery **makes history**.
- ___ They **examine the data** they collect.
- _1_ They **identify a problem**.
- ___ They **publish their research** results.
- ___ They **find evidence** in the data that explains the cause.

b Complete the article with the words in the box.

| collect | conduct | discovered | international |
| natural | research | significant | |

To answer a scientific question, most researchers go to a laboratory and do some ¹_____ into the issue. They ²_____ an experiment, ³_____ data, analyse it and then publish their work in a(n) ⁴_____ journal. But a(n) ⁵_____ increase in *citizen scientists* is changing all that. Citizen scientists are no experts and have no professional understanding of ⁶_____ science (e.g. biology, chemistry or physics) but they work together and do research online. In a recent project, a group of citizen scientists ⁷_____ a protein structure in just three weeks – something that real scientists had failed to do.

c Find four pairs of synonyms in Exercises 1a and 1b.

problem – issue

d Discuss the questions in pairs.
1 What are the benefits of citizen scientists doing research online?
2 Are there any potential problems?

Phrasal verbs

2a Match the beginnings of the sentences (1–8) with the endings (A–H). Then note the phrasal verbs in *italics*.
1 I can never *work*
2 Whenever I touch a piece of equipment, it *breaks*
3 I am good at *coming*
4 I sometimes *note*
5 I think men are better at *dealing*
6 I would like to *carry*
7 I always *go*
8 Because of my bad memory, I often have to *look*

A *out* some research into the way our brains work.
B *down*!
C *up* words in a dictionary.
D *out* difficult maths problems.
E *up* with new ideas.
F *over* notes from lessons later that day.
G *with* science topics than women.
H *down* English words I see on the internet.

b Replace the phrasal verbs in Exercise 2a with a different verb that has a similar meaning. Use a dictionary to help you.

I can never ~~work out~~ solve difficult maths problems.

c Write the phrasal verbs in Exercise 2a in your vocabulary notebook. Then work in pairs and tell your partner if the sentences are true for you or not.

Technology

3a Choose the correct options in *italics* to complete the sentences. Then note the collocations in bold.
1 You have a **computer** *sickness / virus* which is deleting your files.
2 You want to *insert / install* a new **program** but you don't know how.
3 You want to *load up / upload* a **video** on a website but your connection is too slow.
4 You can't **enter your** *password / protection* because you've forgotten it.
5 You **click on a** *connection / link* and it takes you to a different website.
6 You try to *download / fetch* an **app** but it takes too long.
7 You've **lost a** *document / paper* and hours of work because you didn't save it properly.
8 You've got a *technical / technological* **problem** and no one you can ask for help.

b Work in pairs. Which of the computer problems in Exercise 3a have you experienced?

c Write the collocations from Exercise 3a in your vocabulary notebook with an example sentence.

Module 8
Being human

8A

Speaking 1 (Repeat sentence; Answer short question)

Pronunciation: Sentence stress

In *Repeat sentence* you may hear speakers place more stress on one word in a sentence in order to communicate a particular message.

1 a 🎧 92 A social robot is a robot which communicates with humans. Listen to two speakers giving the same opinion. Which word does the second speaker stress more? Why does she do this?

> I don't think social robots are good for society.

b 🎧 93 Listen to four more speakers giving the same opinion. For each speaker, write a number (1–4) under the word that is stressed in the speech bubble above.

c Now think about how sentence stress changes meaning. Match the follow-up sentences (A–D) with the speakers (1–4) in Exercise 1b.
  A But it's possible.
  B Other types of robots are OK though.
  C Although they might be good for individual people.
  D But other people might disagree with me.

d 🎧 94 Listen and check your answers.

e 🎧 94 Listen again and repeat the sentences.

2 a Underline the word in the first sentence that should be stressed. Use the stressed (underlined) word in the second sentence to help you.
  1 Social robots are being created to help people. They won't <u>hurt</u> us.
  2 Talking to a robot is not the same as talking to a human. It's very <u>different</u>, actually.
  3 Loneliness won't disappear. However, it could be <u>reduced</u>.
  4 Some people might enjoy talking to a robot. But it's not for <u>everyone</u>.
  5 Social robots might help some people. But I'm <u>not</u> completely <u>sure</u>.
  6 This is a terrible idea. Although some people think it's a <u>good</u> one.

b 🎧 95 Listen and check your answers. Then work in pairs and practise saying the sentences.

Test practice 1: Repeat sentence
➤ EXPERT STRATEGIES page 171

3 🎧 96 Complete the task in pairs. You will hear ten sentences. Record your answers if possible.

> ⏱ 15 sec. *You will hear a sentence. Please repeat the sentence exactly as you hear it. You will hear the sentence only once.*

Task analysis

4 🎧 97 Listen to a student repeating the sentences. How many sentences does he repeat correctly?

Test practice 2: Answer short question
➤ EXPERT STRATEGIES page 174

5 🎧 98 Complete the task in pairs. You will hear six questions.

> ⏱ 10 sec. *You will hear a question. Please give a simple and short answer. Often just one or a few words is enough.*

123

8A Module 8
Being human

Listening 1 (Select missing word)

Before you listen

1 Work in pairs. Compare the two people in each photo. What do you think their relationship is?

2 Work in pairs. Take turns to do the actions in the box.

| blink   breathe deeply   shrug your shoulders   twitch |

Predicting how a speaker will continue

In *Select missing word* you will hear a recording where the final word has been replaced by a beep. You should listen carefully for clues that will help you predict how the speaker will continue.

3a Look at the extract from a lecture on robots. What word or phrase do you think finishes the sentence?

> 'The use of industrial robots removes the need for humans to perform certain dangerous and harmful jobs. However, robots themselves can also create ...'

b 🎧 99 Listen to extracts from the lecture and answer the questions. In each extract, the final word or group of words has been replaced by a beep.

1 A What is the benefit of using industrial robots?
  B Think: what could be a negative result of this?
2 A What has happened abroad?
  B Think: what could be introduced to prevent this?
3 A When do the fewest accidents happen?
  B Think: what would be the opposite of this?
4 A What causes an operator to enter a robot's working space?
  B Think: what is the opposite of this?
5 A What is recommended to prevent accidents?
  B Think: where is an obvious place to put these?

c 🎧 99 Listen again and choose a word or phrase from the box to complete each extract.

| accelerates   dangerous conditions   safety rules |
| easy-to-reach locations   unexpected movement |

1 _____   3 _____   5 _____
2 _____   4 _____

Test practice

▶ EXPERT STRATEGIES page 187

4 🎧 100 Complete the task. Remember to take notes as you listen.

> You will hear a recording about a new kind of robot. At the end of the recording the last word or group of words has been replaced by a beep. Select the correct option to complete the recording.
>
> A ○ acting differently
> B ○ walking around
> C ○ appearing elsewhere
> D ○ discussing politics

▶ HELP

- Why did Professor Ishiguro make the robot? Which option does that rule out?
- What limitation does the robot have?

Task analysis

5 How important do you think it is to listen closely up to the end? How helpful are linkers in this task type?

▶ See **Listening 2** for more practice of this task type.

Module 8 — Being human — 8A

Language development 1

Expressing obligation and permission

▶ EXPERT GRAMMAR page 211

1 Complete the sentences about robots with the verbs in the box.

| must | mustn't | have to | don't have to | had to |
| didn't have to | will have to | ~~should~~ |

1 As an industrial robot operator, I know I __should__ respect the risks involved in my job.
2 Companies _____ introduce safety measures for employees by law.
3 Robot operators _____ go near the robot when it is switched on.
4 Companies _____ use robots in their factories but they improve the production process a lot.
5 Robot creator Hiroshi Ishiguro _____ attend lectures but sometimes his robot does it instead.
6 Ishiguro _____ look carefully at his own face so he could make a robot that looked like him.
7 Ishiguro _____ build a robot that looked like him but he chose to do it.
8 Ishiguro _____ create legs for his robot in the future if he wants it to walk.

2a Read the article about robots and the law. What is Kate Darling's main point?

> Kate Darling, a research specialist at the MIT Media Lab, believes that we will have to give legal rights to social robots in the future, similar to those we give animals. Although robots cannot feel pain, she says that the laws will stop humans from feeling uncomfortable if a robot is hit. As robots become more like humans, she thinks it will become more difficult for people, especially young children, to tell the difference between the robots and animals.

b Complete the sentences using your own ideas to make rules for protecting social robots.
1 You must not …
2 You have to …
3 You must …
4 You do not have to … but you should …
5 You have to …
6 You must not …

c Work in pairs. Compare your rules and correct any grammar mistakes.

3a Choose the correct options in *italics* to complete the first part of an opinion essay.

> Most children today are given too much freedom, especially when it comes to technology. They [1] *can / cannot* sit and play computer games or chat on social networking sites for as long as they like. A generation ago young people [2] *cannot / could not* stay inside all day. They were sent outside where they [3] *were / were not* allowed to play until it got dark. Today adolescents who [4] *can / are not* allowed to sit and stare at a screen all day are likely to grow up to be healthier adults.

b Complete the sentences about using technology as a child so they are true for you. Use *had to, didn't have to, could, couldn't* and the verbs in the box.

| chat | do | download | put away | share | take |
| turn off | watch |

1 I _____ my homework on a computer.
2 I _____ the TV after watching it for two hours.
3 I _____ a mobile phone to school.
4 I _____ to my friends via computer.
5 I _____ a computer with my family.
6 I _____ TV in my bedroom.
7 I _____ music onto a phone/an MP3 player.
8 I _____ all of my gadgets at dinnertime.

Other ways to express obligation and permission

4a Match the more formal ways of expressing obligation and permission (1–4) with the modal verbs (A–D).
1 It was necessary (for me) to do it.
2 It was not necessary (for me) to do it.
3 I was prohibited from doing it.
4 I was allowed to do it.

A I could do it.
B I didn't have to do it.
C I had to do it.
D I couldn't do it.

b Re-write your sentences from Exercise 3b using the expressions (1–4) in Exercise 4a.

c Do young children today have a stricter or more relaxed childhood than their parents did? Write a paragraph giving your opinion and supporting points. Remember to use the PIE method.

8A Module 8
Being human

Writing 1 (Write essay)

Writing conclusions
> EXPERT STRATEGIES page 176

To score well in *Write essay*, you need to end your essay with a conclusion paragraph.

1 Read the essay prompt and look at the underlined words. Then discuss the questions in pairs.

> <u>Modern science</u> has changed <u>the way human beings relate to each other</u> forever. <u>Society</u> was better when technology was simpler. Discuss whether you agree or disagree with this statement with reference to one culture which you are familiar with.

   1 What are the main inventions of the last 100 years? What has their impact been?
   2 How have these inventions changed human relations?
   3 What historical period in society should you compare modern society to? What do you know about that time?

2 In this test task you have to write a case study essay. Which words in the prompt tell you this? Read about case study essays on page 200. Then answer the questions.
   1 You can only describe one culture. Which culture will you choose? Why?
   2 What examples *specifically* and *only* from your chosen culture could you use as evidence of the views you expressed in Exercise 1?

> EXPERT WRITING page 200

3a Read three conclusion paragraphs.

1
> So, because of improved communication and the fact that modern medicine keeps families together longer, I believe that modern technology has improved social relationships in Taiwan. If we introduce laws to control the worst aspects of technology, we will continue to enjoy the benefits in future.

2
> In conclusion, the evidence suggests that people are more likely to live alone and experience loneliness in Latvia today more than at any other time in history. Unless we take action to strengthen communities, these problems may become worse in future.

3
> To sum up, the changes in Bahrain have taken place very rapidly. It is too early to say whether this will have a negative effect on family and social relationships. More research is needed to better understand these changes.

b Look at the common features of conclusion paragraphs. Then underline them in the paragraphs in Exercise 3a.
   1 summarising what was said
   2 reaching a conclusion
   3 making a positive prediction
   4 giving a warning for the future
   5 recommending an area for further research

c Brainstorm ideas for a conclusion paragraph for this prompt.

4 Now write your own essay plan and conclusion for this prompt. How will you summarise your ideas? What conclusion will you reach? How will you end your essay?

> See **Writing 2** for more practice of this task type.

8B Body and soul

Listening 2 (Select missing word; Write from dictation)

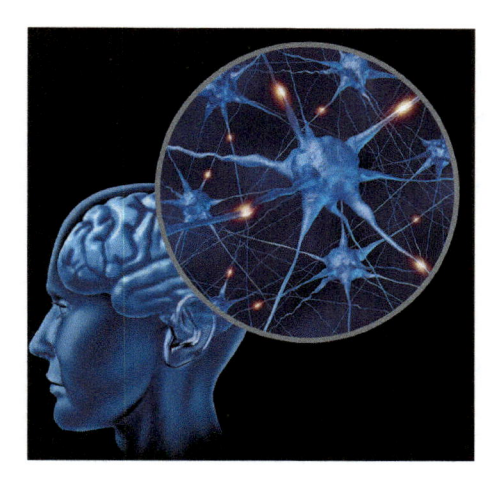

Before you listen

1 Look at the photo and discuss the questions in pairs.
  1 What does the photo show?
  2 What do you know about how the brain works?

2 Complete each pair of sentences with one of the words in the box. You will need to use some words more than once.

functions   gut   nerves

1 A I had to sit down to calm my _____ .
  B My dad has a condition that affects the _____ in his back.
2 A I had a _____ feeling that something was going to happen.
  B It can take 72 hours for food to pass through the _____ .
3 A The nervous system controls bodily _____ .
  B This room is often hired for wedding _____ .

Test practice 1: Select missing word
➤ EXPERT STRATEGIES page 187

3 🎧 101 Complete the task. Remember to use clues to predict how the speaker will continue.

You will hear a recording about the stomach. At the end of the recording the last word or group of words has been replaced by a beep. Select the correct option to complete the recording.

A ○ a complex spinal cord
B ○ an inactive mind
C ○ a second brain
D ○ a sensitive stomach

Test practice 2: Write from dictation
➤ EXPERT STRATEGIES page 189

4 🎧 102 Complete the task. You will hear three sentences. Then compare answers in pairs.

You will hear a sentence. Type the sentence in the box below exactly as you hear it. Write as much of the sentence as you can. You will hear the sentence only once.

Task analysis

5a Discuss the questions in pairs.
  1 Exercise 3 tested your understanding of the whole recording. Did you take notes on the content to help you?
  2 Which options in Exercise 3 were you able to rule out because they were definitely wrong? Did you know the correct answer or did you have to guess?

b 🎧 102 Listen to the sentences for *Write from dictation* again. How many words did you write correctly? How many were incorrect? Why?

127

8B Module 8
Being human

Language development 2

Academic language

▶ EXPERT GRAMMAR page 211

1 Look at the features of academic language (A–E). Then match them with the words and phrases in italics (1–5) in the text.

A using speculative language (e.g. *may*, *could*) rather than concrete language (*is*, *will*, etc.)
B using passive voice
C using formal word choice
D using *this/these* instead of *it/they*
E using complex noun phrases

> There have been ¹ *many clues to the nature of the brain materials in the gut*. A frightening or worrying experience, such as a job interview, ² *may result in* pain in the stomach region. ³ *This* is ⁴ *further* confirmed by reports of 'butterflies in the stomach' before a high stress situation. These ⁵ *have always been explained* by theories of the main brain.

2a Complete the article with the words in the box. You will need to use some words more than once.

> claimed   is/are likely   suggests

> Recent research ¹ _____ that legal drugs, like caffeine, which make you perform better in mental tasks, ² _____ to become more popular in future. An informal opinion poll run by *Nature* states that one in five people ³ _____ they had used drugs to improve focus and memory. One scientist goes much further and ⁴ _____ that people have an ethical responsibility to take them and perform to the best of their mental ability. It ⁵ _____ that new laws will be needed to control the use of these drugs as they ⁶ _____ to lead to personal advantages such as higher grades, better jobs and more money. This all ⁷ _____ that social inequality may increase in the future, as newer, more effective drugs are introduced for those who can afford them.

b Discuss the questions in pairs.
1 Do you agree that people have a responsibility to perform to the best of their abilities?
2 Do you think these drugs are a good idea?

3 Complete the second sentence with a noun + preposition collocation that is similar in meaning to the words in *italics* in the first sentence.

1 Detailed genetic descriptions of people will be common because the costs *will go down*.
Detailed genetic descriptions of people will be common because of a(n) _decrease in_ costs.

2 *We will probably* download DNA from a computer to a human.
The _____ downloading DNA from a computer to a human will be greater.

3 People *will use* this information in the future and this may cause problems.
The future _____ this information may cause problems.

4 The market for personal genetic information *will grow*.
There will be a(n) _____ the market for personal genetic information.

5 Individuals might *fail* to get a job because they have the gene for an illness.
The _____ individuals to get a job might result from having the gene for an illness.

6 We are likely *to introduce* new laws to stop people experiencing unfair treatment.
The _____ new laws is likely to prevent unfair treatment.

4 Find and correct four mistakes in the use of the passive and four spelling mistakes in the text.

> Pharmaceuticals is used to treat or prevent illness, whereas cosmetics are use to make people look better. *Cosmeceuticals*, drugs wich make someone more attractive, haven't appeared in shops yet but this is mostly because the law requires that drugs are more thorouhly testing than cosmetics. The distinction between cosmetics and pharmaceuticals is already unclear at times. In the US, for example, sunscreen and some shampoos are considerd to be drugs. However, as long as people put pressure on companies to produce these products, it is likely that the curent regulation will be relax over the next ten years and we will see cosmeceuticals much more often.

Academic vocabulary 2 AWL ACL

Academic collocations list

1a Choose the correct options in *italics* to complete the text. Then note the collocations in bold.

Physical well-being has been [1] *strongly / highly* **linked** to mental well-being. Stress, while fine for a [2] *little / short* **period**, can have a very negative effect on health in the long term. The pressure on workers to do more in less time is [3] *well / strongly* **documented**. This kind of pressure, however, can have [4] *serious / thoughtful* **consequences**. Maintaining a [5] *single / positive* **view** of life is perhaps the solution. In one study, individuals [6] *made / set* **themselves a target** of listing five things they were happy about three times a day. They showed [7] *partly / relatively* **few** signs of stress. They also [8] *showed / set* **a tendency** to suffer from fewer infections.

b Complete the questions with the correct form of the collocations in Exercise 1a.
1 Do you think it is OK to ignore unhealthy habits for a(n) _____ of time?
2 What health problems have been _____ in your country?
3 Do you think there are _____ people who feel sad in the world or quite a lot?
4 Which do you think has more _____ : poor diet or lack of exercise?
5 Have you _____ yourself any healthy-living _____ for this year?
6 Do you think our health is _____ to the life choices we make?
7 Do you think some health problems _____ to run in families?
8 Do you have a(n) _____ of your future?

c Discuss the questions in Exercise 1b in pairs.

'I'm making sure I get my five daily portions.'

Academic word list

2a Match the beginnings of the sentences (1–8) with the endings (A–H).
1 Many *factors* can lead
2 Poor *lifestyle* choices
3 There are several *schemes* to encourage
4 Governments cannot stop us coming into
5 There is financial help available to people
6 Many older people face
7 People experience more
8 *Mental* health problems are not

A *potential* health problems.
B to a poor diet.
C who are *registered* as disabled.
D *contact* with infections like bird flu.
E *injuries* at home than work.
F openly discussed in my country.
G have a negative effect on health.
H good health which have worked.

b Choose three of the words in *italics* in Exercise 2a and write your own sentences.

Health

3a Complete the article with the words in the box.

alternative   healing   healthy   ill   medicine
physical   sickness   systems

THE RISE OF THE BIOMEDICAL MODEL OF HEALTH

Health and *illness* are words that are culturally and socially defined. Cultures differ in what they consider to be [1] _____ and normal. All cultures have known concepts of being physically well or [2] _____ but most of what we now recognise as [3] _____ is a consequence of developments in western science over the past three centuries. In pre-modern cultures the family was the main institution coping with [4] _____ . There have always been individuals who specialised in [5] _____ which use a mixture of [6] _____ and magical remedies and many of these traditional [7] _____ of treatment survive today in non-western cultures throughout the world. A large number of them fall into the category of [8] _____ medicines.

b What alternative medicine is popular in your country? Share your ideas with the class.

129

8B Module 8
Being human

Reading 2 (Reading & writing: Fill in the blanks)

Before you read

1a Read the sentences and check the meaning of the words in bold in a dictionary.
1 There is a **shortage** of blood donors.
2 **Organ transplants** are a normal part of the culture.
3 Donors do not **register** on a **list**. Instead, the **state automatically** adds the names of all adults to the list.

b Work in pairs. Which of the sentences in Exercise 1a describe the situation in your country?

Test practice

➤ EXPERT STRATEGIES page 181

2 Complete the task.

Below is a text with blanks. Click on each blank, a list of choices will appear. Select the appropriate answer choice for each blank.

Currently, if an English person wants to donate their organs after their death, they register their name on a list. However, some argue that a person's name should automatically appear on the list ¹ [ ] they ask for it to be taken off. The ² [ ] is that there are 8,000 people in the UK who need a transplant but there is a shortage of donors. This means that fewer than 3,000 transplants ³ [ ] out annually. Due to medical advances, the number of people whose lives could be saved by a transplant is rising more quickly than the number of donors who are ⁴ [ ]. Automatic donation is a system used in Spain and Austria but people who disagree with it say that our bodies would belong to the state ⁵ [ ] of to ourselves and such donation would be very upsetting for families.

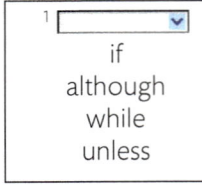

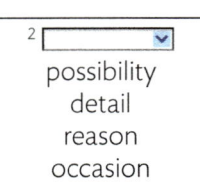

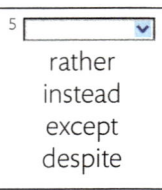

1	2	3	4	5
if	possibility	carry	prepared	rather
although	detail	carried	delighted	instead
while	reason	are carried	ready	except
unless	occasion	had been carried	available	despite

Task analysis

3 Discuss the questions in pairs.
1 Did you read the text quickly first? If so, how did this help you?
2 How much time did you spend trying to guess the missing word before looking at the options?
3 How helpful was it to look at the words before and after each blank?
4 Why are the incorrect options wrong?

Discussion

4 Work in groups of four. Read the statement. Two of you argue *for* the statement and two argue *against* it. Prepare your arguments and then have a debate.

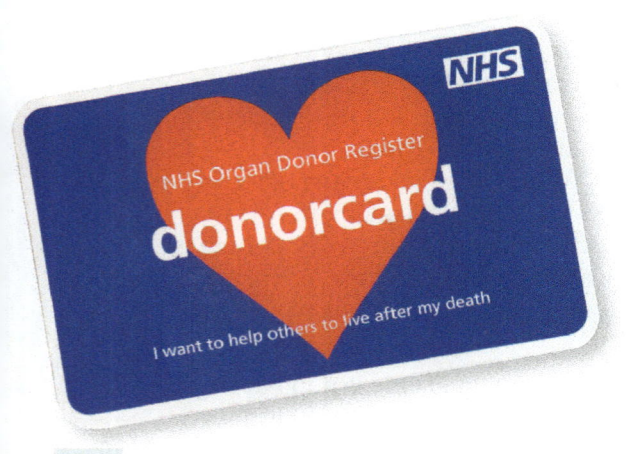

> An automatic organ donation system is fair for everyone.

Speaking 2 (Re-tell lecture)

Taking notes on a speaker's conclusion

In *Re-tell lecture* you will need to take notes on the speaker's main point, supporting points and the conclusions that he or she draws.

1 a You will hear a lecture. Look at the photo in Exercise 4. What is the topic of the lecture?

b 🎧 103 Listen to the lecture and take notes.

c Compare your notes in pairs. Did you write down the same main idea, reasons and examples?

2 a In which part of a talk do you expect to hear the speaker draw a conclusion?

    1 the beginning   2 the middle   3 the end

b Which of the words and phrases in the box are likely to introduce a speaker's conclusion?

> afterwards   as a result   because   however   so
> the effect of this is that   then   to conclude

c 🎧 103 Listen to the lecture again and complete the notes on the speaker's conclusion.

> *conclusion: body changes represent* _____

Sample response

3 🎧 104 Listen to a student re-telling the lecture. Does he use the same structure as the speaker? What information from the lecture does he choose not to include? Why?

Test practice
> EXPERT STRATEGIES page 173

4 🎧 103 Complete the task in pairs. Take notes, then present the information to your partner.

> ⏱ 40 sec. You will hear a lecture. After listening to the lecture, in 10 seconds, please speak into the microphone and re-tell what you have just heard from the lecture in your own words. You will have 40 seconds to give your response.

> EXPERT SPEAKING page 194

5 🎧 105 Turn to page 194 and complete another timed test practice.

Task analysis

6 Discuss the questions in pairs.
1 How did you decide what information to include in your summary?
2 What information did you choose not to include? Why?

8B Module 8
Being human

Writing 2 (Write essay)

Lead-in

1 Discuss the questions in pairs.
   1 Do you think beauty products work?
   2 Why do you think the cosmetics industry is worth so much money?

Understand the task
➤ EXPERT STRATEGIES page 176

2a Read the essay prompt and underline the key words. What kind of essay do you need to write?

> ⏱ **20 min.** You will have 20 minutes to plan, write and revise an essay about the topic below. Your response will be judged on how well you develop a position, organise your ideas, present supporting details and control the elements of standard written English. You should write 200–300 words.

> The cosmetics industry has grown from nothing into a multi-million-dollar industry. All of this money has been wasted and could be spent on providing better health care. To what extent do you agree with this view? Write with reference to one culture that you know well.

➤ **HELP**

Who depends on the cosmetics industry for employment/business?

b Work in pairs. Share ideas on this topic. Brainstorm as many as possible in two minutes.

Plan your essay

To score well in a case study essay for *Write essay*, you should analyse and answer the question but you will need to make sure that all your examples come from only ONE culture or region.

3a Read the comments from a blog on the subject. Which bloggers argue in support of the cosmetics industry? Can you think of an argument against each point?

search News

1 **Blogster:** A million dollars is a lot to one person but it won't change the health of a whole country.

2 **ShopGirl:** In my country the beauty business gives thousands of people jobs – loads of them are women.

3 **Duncan29:** Spending on hospitals is a better idea – nothing else matters without good health.

4 **MintSweet:** Popular magazines are much cheaper in my country because they're paid for by adverts for make-up.

b Are any of the comments in Exercise 3a true of your country? Can you include these ideas in your essay?

c Write an essay plan. Write an outline of the topic sentences and evidence you would like to use in your essay. What can you put in the introduction and conclusion?

Module 8
Being human — 8B

Language and content

When you write your essay, you should try to use all the features of academic English.

4a Complete the sentences with the words in the box so that they have a similar meaning to the comments in Exercise 3a but are written in a more academic style.

| a large amount | are employed | essential | helps | mostly | much |
| on health | seems | the media | | | |

1 A million dollars _____ like _____ of money to an individual but nationally, it will not make _____ difference.
2 In my country thousands of people _____ by the cosmetics industry and they are _____ women.
3 Spending the money _____ is a better idea. Good health is _____ in life.
4 Advertising by the cosmetics industry _____ pay for a lot of _____ we enjoy.

b Which of these features of academic English do the sentences in Exercise 4a use?

1 using a more specific, technical or formal word
2 softening strong views
3 using passive voice and complex noun phrases

5 Read the conclusion a student wrote for this prompt. The underlined words are too informal. Re-write the paragraph using some of the expressions in the table.

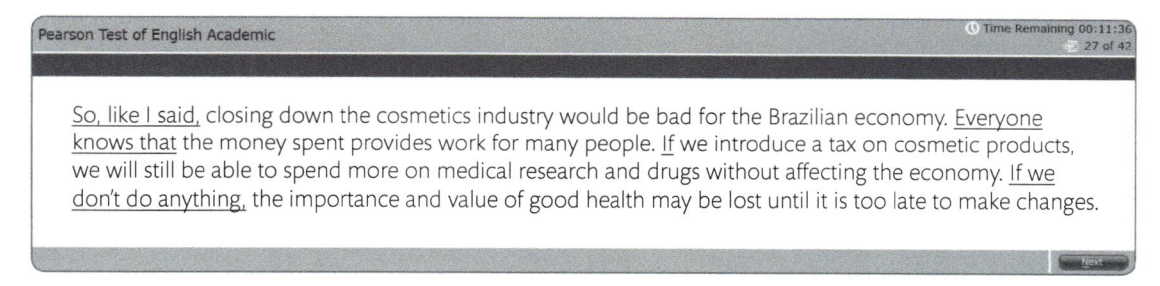

Pearson Test of English Academic — Time Remaining 00:11:36 — 27 of 42

So, like I said, closing down the cosmetics industry would be bad for the Brazilian economy. Everyone knows that the money spent provides work for many people. If we introduce a tax on cosmetic products, we will still be able to spend more on medical research and drugs without affecting the economy. If we don't do anything, the importance and value of good health may be lost until it is too late to make changes.

Conclusions	
Summarise what was said before	**So the evidence suggests that** my country benefits from the cosmetics industry. **To sum up**, spending on make-up is a waste of money that could be better used.
Offer a conclusion (Why is this important?)	**What this means is that** more people could enjoy a healthier, happier life. **Clearly**, the money could be spent on medical research and make a real difference.
Make a positive prediction	**Provided that** we act now, many lives will be saved. **The change is likely** to benefit the poorest members of society.
Offer a warning	**Unless we take this action now**, future generations will suffer. **The government / Individuals / Scientists must take immediate action.** Otherwise there may be real problems in the future.

Write your essay

6 Write your essay. Use your plan from Exercise 3 and the table in Exercise 5 to help you. Remember to write 200–300 words.

Check your essay
➤ EXPERT WRITING page 196

7 Check your essay using the checklist on page 196.

8B Module 8 being human

Review

1 Work in pairs. Complete the article with the words in the box.

cannot   could   couldn't   didn't have to
don't have to   had to   have to   mustn't

SMELL

An effective sense of smell is important in many areas of life. It acts as a warning system. People know that they [1]_____ hang around once they detect the smell of smoke. You [2]_____ put in any effort with smells, as our nose is 10,000 times more sensitive than your tongue and you [3]_____ identify many tastes without it. In an experiment, participants [4]_____ eat chocolate while holding their noses. There were able to identify the sweetness but [5]_____ identify the chocolate flavour. This is because the flavours of foods such as chocolate or coffee [6]_____ be sensed through smell rather than through taste. Smell is also directly connected to the emotional part of the brain and to memories, too. Participants in one test [7]_____ easily associate smells with people and events decades after the actual experience. They [8]_____ be exposed to the smell for very long either. Just 0.5 seconds was enough to make the connections.

2 Read the article and look at the phrases in *italics*. Choose the more academic phrase in each pair to complete the article.

Do emotions come from the heart, or from the gut?

As far back as 1996 people had identified [1] *the importance of the gut / how important the gut was* in chemical production. A *New York Times* article [2] *told everyone / pointed out* that about 95 percent of the brain chemical serotonin is produced in the gut. Now, serotonin is important to you and me because [3] *it / this chemical* controls how calm we feel. [4] *People know it best because it is / It is best known as* the chemical that gives you a good night's sleep. Other chemicals like dopamine and histamine, to name just a few, are also made in the gut. [5] *These / They* are all chemicals which [6] *send / communicate* positive emotions to the brain. So, although we [7] *are / might only be* aware of the negative things in the gut like pain or feeling full and uncomfortable, it's clear that the gut has [8] *a role to play / a lot to do* in creating emotions.

3 Match the beginnings of the sentences (1–8) with the endings (A–H).
1 Early Hollywood films came
2 One of the main problems
3 But this was challenged by scientists carrying
4 One astronaut made
5 He survived the cold despite
6 After examining the nature of
7 Scientists also worked
8 In fact, the only significant

A the significant drop in temperatures.
B problem would be the lack of oxygen.
C history when his space suit broke open outside the spaceship.
D out research into space exploration.
E vacuums, researchers realised they maintain temperatures very well.
F out that his blood system was able to deal with the air pressure.
G that they identified was surviving the pressure.
H up with the idea that bodies would not survive in space.

4 Complete the article with the words in the box.

alternative   factors   lifestyle   potential   relatively
short period   strongly linked   well-documented

SO YOU THINK YOU KNOW WHAT YOU ARE

All human life starts as a single-cell; this has been [1]_____ . However, did you know that a single cell, with the [2]_____ for life, was formed before your mother was born? So if your mother was 30 when she had you, on your 18th birthday you could arguably consider yourself 48 years old!

But what about the chemicals which make up your body? Well, they're borrowed for a fairly [3]_____ . Hydrogen, the most common chemical, was formed 13.7 billion years ago. Carbon and oxygen were made in the middle of stars 12 billion years ago. You are, in fact, stardust!

But, of course, not all of the human body is human. In fact, there are [4]_____ few human cells, compared to bacteria – ten times fewer, in fact. Many [5]_____ influence health and bacteria are definitely one of them. One experiment [6]_____ bacteria to well-being when a scientist attempted to raise animals in a bacteria-free environment. Many died and those that did survive needed a(n) [7]_____ diet to keep them alive. It seems bacteria are a necessary part of the [8]_____ we enjoy.

9 Winning counts!

Overview

9A
- **Reading:** Re-order paragraphs
- **Academic vocabulary:** Sports
- **Speaking:** Read aloud; Answer short question
- **Listening:** Multiple-choice, choose multiple answers
- **Language development:** Articles
- **Summary writing:** Summarize spoken text

9B
- **Listening:** Multiple-choice, choose multiple answers; Write from dictation
- **Language development:** Grammatical linkers
- **Academic vocabulary:** Money and industry
- **Reading:** Re-order paragraphs
- **Speaking:** Describe image
- **Summary writing:** Summarize spoken text

Lead-in

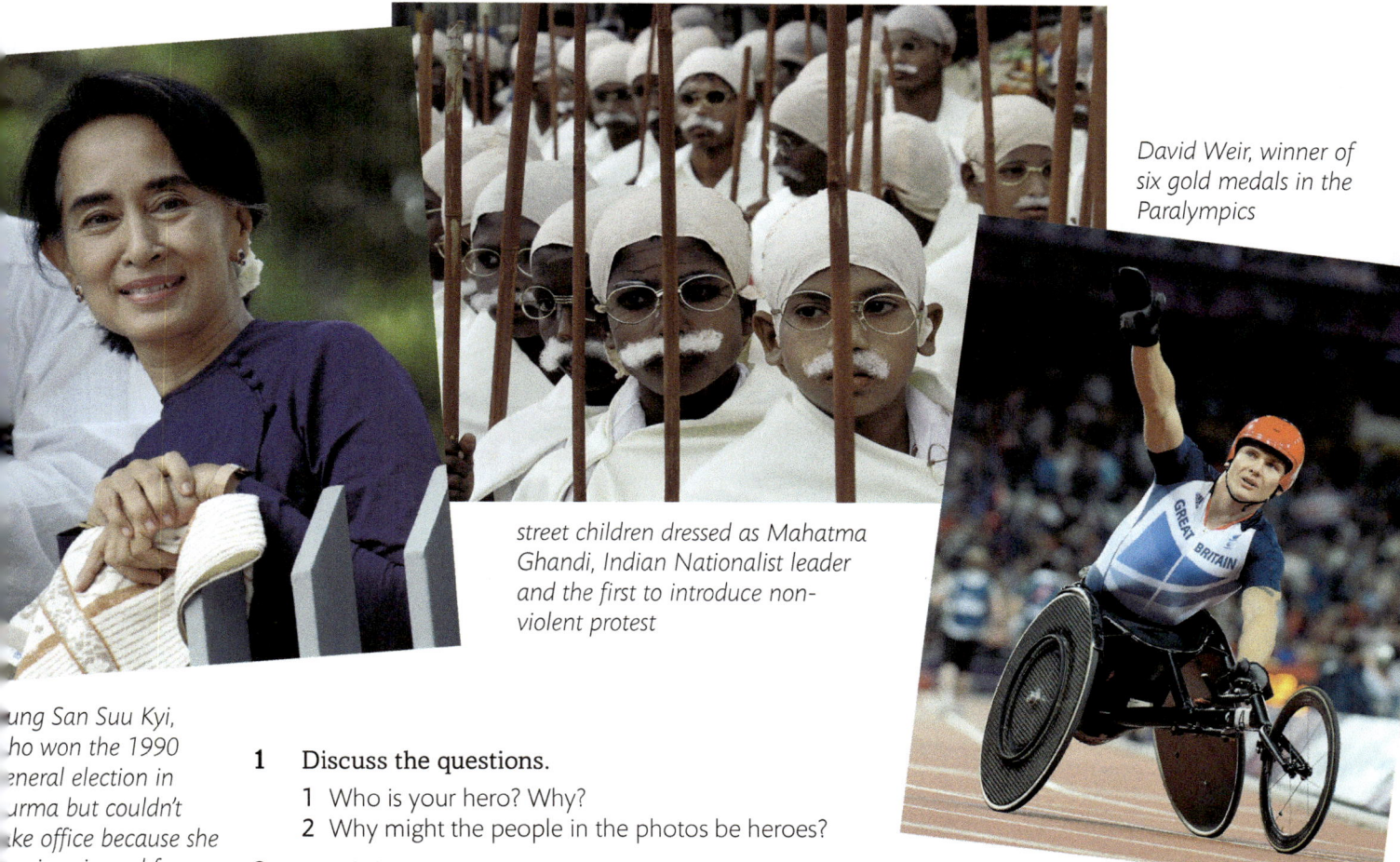

David Weir, winner of six gold medals in the Paralympics

street children dressed as Mahatma Ghandi, Indian Nationalist leader and the first to introduce non-violent protest

Aung San Suu Kyi, who won the 1990 general election in Burma but couldn't take office because she was imprisoned from 1989 to 2010

1 Discuss the questions.
  1 Who is your hero? Why?
  2 Why might the people in the photos be heroes?

2 Read the quotes. Do you agree or disagree with each one?

'Success has a simple formula: do your best and people may like it.' Sam Ewing, baseball player

'I've missed more than 9,000 shots in my career. I've lost almost 300 games. 26 times I've been trusted to take the game-winning shot and missed. I've failed over and over and over again in my life. And that is why I succeed.' Michael Jordan, basketball player

'A hero is no braver than an ordinary man but he is brave five minutes longer.' Ralph Waldo Emerson, poet

3 Complete the sentence using your own ideas.
  A hero is …

135

9A A sporting chance

Reading 1 (Re-order paragraphs)

Before you read

1 Discuss the questions in pairs.
  1 Which sports are taught in schools in your country?
  2 Which sports does your country generally do well in?

Following a logical or chronological sequence of events

In *Re-order paragraphs* you will need to be able to identify both logical links and chronological (time) links.

2a Which sentence in each pair logically comes first? Why?

1
  A If you are an athlete in Australia, then about $40 million will buy you a gold.
  B How much support, financial or medical, would you need to be a sporting winner?

2
  A Complaints that drug use is unfair miss the point: competitive sport is not fair.
  B It is no accident that a country which can afford $17 million for a swim research centre wins the gold.

3
  A It is now an industry with a massive system that trains, tests and manipulates athletes almost to death.
  B Elite sport long ago moved away from the amateur athlete, training in their spare time.

4
  A There is a simple reason why African athletes perform well in running events but not swimming.
  B It is because running requires very little in the way of equipment.

5
  A Of course, in the case of someone 1.6 seconds off a world record, they might just help but that kind of athlete wouldn't even be there without a lot of financial support.
  B Drugs affect sporting performance but the difference is small unless you are already a top athlete.

b Match the pairs of sentences in Exercise 2a (1–5) with the types of logical sequence (A–E).
  A idea → reason
  B argument → opposite argument
  C idea → example
  D question → answer
  E past → present

136

Module 9 — Winning counts! 9A

Test practice
> EXPERT STRATEGIES page 179

3 Complete the task. Remember to look for logical relationships between the sentences.

The text boxes in the left panel have been placed in a random order. Restore the original order by dragging the text boxes from the left panel to the right panel.

Source | Target

A | He began by taking DNA samples but found that they all had a very different genetic make-up.

B | So he then looked at the East African way of life and found that as children, 68 percent of all top Ethiopian or Kenyan runners ran, rather than walked, to school and back home, from the age of five onwards.

C | Dr Pitsiladis has spent years trying to identify why Ethiopian runners from the mountain region are so successful.

D | He tested those children and found that their bodies processed oxygen more efficiently than many adult elite athletes in Britain.

E | From this he concluded that there was nothing that could be identified genetically as East African.

> **HELP**
> - In which sentence does Dr Pitsiladis' name appear? Where is this most likely to come in the paragraph?
> - Find and underline the words *he concluded*. What idea does this refer back to?

Task analysis

4 Discuss the questions in pairs.
1 Did you put the sentences in pairs before looking for the overall structure? Was this more helpful?
2 How did linkers and other grammatical links in the sentences help you in this task?

Discussion

5 Discuss the questions in pairs.
1 Do you think some countries naturally produce people who are better at certain sports?
2 Do you think money spent on sports is a waste?

EXPERT WORD CHECK
amateur   elite   genetic make-up   manipulate   sample

> See **Reading 2** for more practice of this task type.

9A Module 9
Winning counts!

Academic vocabulary 1 AWL ACL

Academic collocations list

1a Match the beginnings of the sentences (1–6) with the endings (A–F). Then note the collocations in *italics*.

1. Do you think people have an *individual*
2. Does the state play a *key*
3. Is it in the *national*
4. Are passive lifestyles a *major*
5. What kind of facilities do you think *increase*
6. Are there any *newly*

A *interest* to encourage people to keep fit?
B *the likelihood* of people choosing to do more sport?
C *concern* among people in your country?
D *responsibility* to lead a healthy lifestyle?
E *created* sports clubs in your country?
F *role* in providing sports clubs and facilities?

b Change the questions in Exercise 1a to statements which are true for you.

I think people only have an individual responsibility to lead a healthy lifestyle if they have children or someone they need to look after.

Academic word list

2 Complete the sentences with the words in the box.

dramatic   eventually   exceed   ignore   relaxed   so-called

1. People have a more _____ attitude to fitness these days.
2. Exercise is good for you but you shouldn't _____ your limits.
3. _____ 'weight loss medicines' rarely work.
4. There's a(n) _____ increase in the amount of sport done in the warmer months.
5. Schools will _____ stop offering sport.
6. Young people _____ the benefits of walking.

Verb + preposition

3 Complete the sentences with the prepositions in the box.

about   by   for   in   to (x3)   with

1. Do you worry _____ your levels of fitness?
2. What do you blame _____ the lack of exercise in modern society?
3. Do you think physical inactivity adds _____ other problems, like sleeping?
4. Who are sports campaigns usually led _____ , politicians or sports celebrities?
5. Why should the amount of sport we do matter _____ politicians?
6. Is it acceptable for children to succeed _____ sport but not academic subjects?
7. Do you think children are provided _____ enough space to practise sports in schools?
8. Do you think spending time on sport could lead _____ improvements in education?

Sports

4a Choose the correct options in *italics* to complete the article.

DO SPORTS MAKE YOUR CHILDREN SMARTER?

A large amount of economic literature suggests that sporting activities among [1] *adolescents / adolescence* has a positive effect on educational achievement and [2] *work / professional* success later in life. Our study focused on German children who attend sports [3] *clubs / businesses*, the main institution for encouraging sport for leisure or for [4] *competitions / fights* in this country. The results showed that sports could do as much for a child's success as large-scale academic educational programmes. But why? Certainly, sports participation reduces the time spent on [5] *still / passive* activities such as watching television. It also exposes children to [6] *co-operation / share* with other children in a team. Victory in competitions may raise young people's [7] *self-esteem / value*, while [8] *fail / defeat* may teach them to deal with challenges. The study highlights how important locally available sports [9] *places / facilities* are. Good [10] *equipment / tools* is also necessary, as are adults with [11] *teaching / coaching* skills. This is particularly important in cities where there may be limited public space for [12] *recreational / hobby* activities.

b Why do you think participating in sport has such a strong influence on a child's future success?

Module 9
9A Winning counts!

Speaking 1 (Read aloud; Answer short question)

Pronunciation: Linking

In *Read aloud* you are scored on fluency. You will need to link words together to sound fluent.

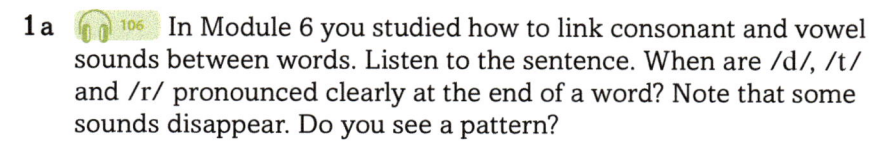

1 a 🎧 106 In Module 6 you studied how to link consonant and vowel sounds between words. Listen to the sentence. When are /d/, /t/ and /r/ pronounced clearly at the end of a word? Note that some sounds disappear. Do you see a pattern?

> The New Zealand men's national rugby team, known as The All Blacks, are accepted by many in the world of professional sport as the world's most successful team ever.

b Read the sentences. When are the /d/, /t/ and /r/ sounds in bold clearly pronounced?

1 In ove**r** a hundre**d** years only five separa**te** nations have been able to bea**t** them and they've accumulate**d** a historic win ra**te** of 75 percent.
2 Only the United States' basketball team has a simila**r** pas**t** record but with a population of 350 million, compare**d** to New Zealan**d**'s four million, they'**re** mo**re** likely to produce a winning team.
3 Befo**re** every match they perform the Haka, a Maori wa**r** dance that is closely associa**te**d with New Zealan**d**'s cultural history an**d** is designe**d** to terrify opponents.

c 🎧 107 Listen and check your answers.

Test practice 1: Read aloud
➤ EXPERT STRATEGIES page 170

2 Complete the task. Think about linking sounds between words before you speak.

> ⏱ 40 sec. Look at the text below. In 40 seconds, you must read this text aloud as naturally and clearly as possible. You have 40 seconds to read aloud.

➤ **HELP**
- Try saying *modern era* as one word. Stress the first syllables: *mo*dern *e*ra.
- Try making the *d* and *t* disappear while you say: *an(d), while it's accepte(d) tha(t) no team ...*

> In the highly scientific modern era success in professional rugby careers can come down to tiny details and, while it's accepted that no team should have an obvious advantage physically, the precise movement of this war dance is designed to give a clear and unfair psychological advantage.

Task analysis

3 🎧 108 Listen to a native speaker reading the text and answer the questions.
1 Did you use similar pronunciation?
2 Were you able to link words together in a similar way?

Test practice 2: Answer short question
➤ EXPERT STRATEGIES page 174

4 🎧 109 Complete the task in pairs. You will hear five questions.

> ⏱ 10 sec. You will hear a question. Please give a simple and short answer. Often just one or a few words is enough.

139

9A Module 9
Winning counts!

Listening 1 (Multiple-choice, choose multiple answers)

Before you listen

1 You will hear a lecture about how ancient humans were able to survive in a world with dangerous animals. Look at the words in the box. What do you think the speaker is going to say?

chase   collapse   distance   energy   marathon   speed   sweat   track (v)

Identifying specific details

In *Multiple-choice, choose multiple answers* you may be tested on your ability to identify details, facts or opinions in a recording.

2a 🎧 110 Listen to the lecture and take notes.

b Discuss the questions in pairs.
1 What is the main topic of the lecture?
2 What did you learn about the topic?

3a 🎧 111 Listen to the first half of the lecture and answer the questions.
1 What running skill do cheetahs lack?
2 When do horses and dogs run long distances?
3 What do millions of people do each year?
4 Which parts of our bodies help us to run far?

b 🎧 112 Now listen to the second half of the lecture and complete the sentences.
1 We sweat in order to _____ .
2 Human breathing is different because _____ .
3 Ancient humans caught animals by _____ .

Test practice
➤ EXPERT STRATEGIES page 183

4 🎧 110 Complete the task. Use your notes from Exercise 2a and your answers to Exercises 3a and 3b to help you.

Listen to the recording and answer the question by selecting all the correct responses. You will need to select more than one response.

According to the speaker, what gave ancient humans an advantage over faster animals?

A ☐ They could run further.
B ☐ They were more intelligent.
C ☐ They kept lower body temperatures.
D ☐ They did not give up easily.
E ☐ They had longer arms and legs.
F ☐ They thought running was satisfying.
G ☐ They had weapons to help them.

➤ HELP

The recording may use different words to the options. What are different ways to say *intelligent, kept lower body temperatures, did not give up easily, satisfying* and *weapons*?

Task analysis

5 Which of the incorrect response options:
1 were not mentioned in the recording?
2 were the opposite of what was mentioned in the recording?

Module 9 — 9A
Winning counts!

Language development 1

Articles

▶ EXPERT GRAMMAR page 212

1a Choose the correct options in *italics* to complete the sentences about running.
1 Ancient people had to run long distances to get *a / an* advantage over fast animals.
2 *A / The* million people around the world choose to run marathons.
3 Our ability to sweat might not seem like *an / the* advantage but it allows us to lose heat.
4 Our feet store energy, which makes it easier for us to take *a / the* second step.
5 Ancient humans caught animals by tracking them. They chased *an / the* animals again and again.

b Look at the underlined nouns in Exercise 1a. Why is there no article before each of them?

2a Complete the quiz with *a*, *an*, *the* or – (no article).

1 Which athlete holds _____ world record for _____ fastest 100 m?
2 Did _____ Austrian man fly faster than light or sound when he did _____ highest skydive?
3 Approximately how many calories do _____ female runners use when doing _____ marathon somewhere?
4 When athletes compete in _____ professional competition, how fast does _____ javelin they throw travel?
5 Is it _____ UK or _____ France that has produced the world's fastest downhill cyclist on snow (222 kph)?
6 How many kilometres does _____ footballer run on average in _____ match?

b Work in pairs. Do the quiz in Exercise 2a.

3a Complete the text with *a*, *an*, *the* or – (no article).

Scientists at ¹_____ university in London have discovered that ²_____ person's perception of time slows down when they prepare to do ³_____ physical action. And it slows down even more for ⁴_____ professional athletes like tennis players and F1 drivers. ⁵_____ scientists suggest that preparing to hit ⁶_____ ball, for example, affects ⁷_____ way our brain processes ⁸_____ information. This is because our brain takes in a lot more visual information than normal and so we feel as if time is longer and slower than it actually is. ⁹_____ university team carried out simple experiments to calculate ¹⁰_____ reaction time of ¹¹_____ group of volunteers. ¹²_____ next step will involve using ¹³_____ scanner to see what is happening in ¹⁴_____ visual part of each volunteer's brain.

b Are there any occasions when time seems slower for you? Or when time speeds up? Why do you think this happens? Share your ideas with the class.

4a In each pair, which sentence is about something general and which is about something specific? Work in pairs and try to work out the rule.
1 A A group of runners has arrived.
  B The group of runners has arrived.
2 A The boy is faster than the girl.
  B Boys are faster than girls.
3 A People can go to a stadium to watch a match.
  B People can go to the stadium to watch the match.
4 A The runner should wear the hat.
  B Runners should wear a hat.
5 A I think athletes are overpaid.
  B I think the athletes are overpaid.
6 A He wrote an article about a tennis player for a local sports paper.
  B He wrote the article about the tennis player for the local sports paper.

b Write six generalisations about speed and distance by putting the nouns into the correct singular or plural form.
1 man / drive faster than / woman
   Men drive faster than women.
2 car / move around my city more quickly than / motorbike
3 astronaut now / travel further into space than / astronaut 40 years ago
4 older person / walk for longer distances than / younger person
5 marathon runner / mentally stronger than / speed runner
6 travelling by car / slower than / travelling by train

c Choose a topic from the box and write three generalisations about it. Then work in pairs. Read your sentences to your partner and find out if he/she agrees with you.

family   free time   money   sport   travel   work

> Children from big families are generally more sociable than children from smaller families.

> I agree.

141

9A Module 9
Winning counts!

Summary writing 1 (Summarize spoken text)

> **EXPERT STRATEGIES** page 182

Giving an opposing opinion

In *Summarize spoken text* you may hear a speaker giving an opposing opinion as well as their own. You will need to identify and summarise this.

1 Look at the spectators in the photo. What is happening to them physically and mentally?

2a 🎧 113 Listen to six people talking about watching sport and underline each speaker's stronger opinion.
  1 boring to watch / produce exciting moments
  2 crowded / great sense of community
  3 more fun to watch / playing it offers more benefits
  4 good atmosphere / see more on TV
  5 winning / wanting your team to win
  6 expensive / worth it for special day out

  b Does the speaker usually start with his/her opinion or the opposing opinion? Why?

  c 🎧 113 Listen again. Which word or phrase from the box does each speaker use to introduce the opposing opinion? Number the words and phrases 1–6.

  admit that   agreed   although   some people argue that
  while it's true that   while

3a Write sentences that represent your opinion. Use the prompts and the phrases in brackets. You can change the order of the ideas.
  1 watching sport is fun / watching sport is uninteresting (some people argue that / but in my view)
  2 being a spectator can be thrilling / being a spectator can be stressful (while / also)
  3 watching sport is inspiring / watching sport is frustrating (while it's true that for some people / in my opinion)
  4 booing another team is part of the game / booing another team is rude (I admit / but)
  5 watching sport with friends is more sociable / watching sport alone is more enjoyable (although)
  6 playing sport is important / watching sport is exciting (agreed / but)

  b Compare your sentences in pairs. Do you and your partner have the same views?

4a 🎧 114 Listen to someone talking about watching sport and take notes.

  b Write a sentence giving the speaker's opinion and the opposing opinion about each of the items in the box. Use your notes from Exercise 4a to help you.

  watching football is a spectator sport   watching a match is harmless
  length of the physical effects   excitement in a person's life

> See **Summary writing** 2 for more practice of this task type.

142

9B Do your best!

Listening 2 (Multiple-choice, choose multiple answers; Write from dictation)

Before you listen

1a Work in pairs. What do you think the words in bold mean?
1 I'd like to be an **entrepreneur** with a successful company.
2 I have the **qualities** needed to be a good manager.
3 I'm **knowledgeable** about my favourite subject area.
4 I've got good **people skills**.
5 I'm **imaginative** and think of ideas quickly.

b Which of the sentences do you both agree with?

Test practice 1: Multiple-choice, choose multiple answers
▶ EXPERT STRATEGIES page 183

2 🎧 115 Complete the task. Remember to take notes as you listen.

Listen to the recording and answer the question by selecting all the correct responses. You will need to select more than one response.

According to the speaker, what are the key things that entrepreneurs need in order to run a successful business?

A ☐ They need to have a high level of motivation.
B ☐ They need to communicate well with colleagues.
C ☐ They need to have a high level of intelligence.
D ☐ They need to know a lot about their subject area.
E ☐ They need to provide good customer service.

Test practice 2: Write from dictation
▶ EXPERT STRATEGIES page 189

3 🎧 116 Complete the task. You will hear three sentences. Then compare answers in pairs.

You will hear a sentence. Type the sentence in the box below exactly as you hear it. Write as much of the sentence as you can. You will hear the sentence only once.

Task analysis

4a Compare your notes from Exercise 2 in pairs. Which of these points did you note down? How helpful were your notes when answering the question?
1 the main point   2 supporting details   3 concluding sentence

b 🎧 116 Listen to the sentences for *Write from dictation* again. What examples of consonant–vowel linking can you hear?

143

9B Module 9
Winning counts!

Language development 2

Grammatical linkers

> EXPERT GRAMMAR page 212

1a Complete the sentences with *this, these, that, those* or *so*.
1. These days work is seen as a sign of status. _____ means that people care more about their position in society than in the past.
2. Both financial status and marital status mattered in older societies but _____ are not so important now.
3. It's necessary to work very hard to succeed but even if you do _____ , there are no guarantees you will achieve your goal.
4. Status isn't always about money: the income of footballers is higher than _____ of many businessmen but not their status.
5. There has been a rise in the number of people increasing their social status. _____ is largely because of education.
6. There is a large gap between _____ who are at the top of the social scale and _____ who are at the bottom.

b Work in pairs. What word or phrase in each sentence do the words in the blanks in Exercise 1a replace?

2a Match the beginnings of the sentences (1–6) with the endings (A–F).
1. Many people in the US have recently reported feeling happier.
2. It's important not to mix up Dante Gabriel Rossetti and Dante.
3. Few projects have tried to explain the connection.
4. Over 30 percent of people said they had lied to their partner in the last month.
5. The survey confirmed **what they originally suspected**.
6. Success depends on two main factors: hard work and luck.

A **The former** can be planned for, whereas **the latter** is hard to predict.
B **A similar situation** has been recorded in other countries.
C A minimum amount of money can buy happiness.
D **The number** would be much **higher** if you included members of the wider family.
E **One** was an 18th-century artist, **the other** a 13th century poet.
F **This one**, however, intends to **do just that**.

b Look at the words and phrases in bold in Exercise 2a. What do they refer to?

3a Complete the article with the words in the box.

former   latter   similar situations   such   then   these   this   what

Psychologist shows why we 'choke' under pressure

Many people may remember when golfer Greg Norman choked in the 1996 US Masters. He had played brilliantly for the first three days, taking a huge lead, [1] _____ on his final day he stopped playing like a pro and lost everything. [2] _____ have been observed in others: a brilliant student fails a test; a smart business person blows a key presentation. Each of [3] _____ people has suffered the same problem: they have just choked under pressure. Choking in [4] _____ cases happens when the brain stops working as predicted. Thinking too much about [5] _____ you are doing because you are worried about failing can lead to 'paralysis by analysis'. [6] _____ only affects experts who normally rely on doing things automatically. Even a simple trick such as singing helps stop portions of the brain from shutting down. In her laboratory, psychologist Sandra Beilock gives people lessons in meditation. The [7] _____ can offer a quick fix for bad nerves but the [8] _____ has proven to be successful among students in actually improving performance.

b Write a one-sentence summary of the article in Exercise 3a in no more than 75 words. Try to use some of the linking words in this section.

4 Complete the sentences with the words in the box. Use two words for each sentence.

benefits   ~~feelings~~   mistake   problems   skill   such (x2)   these   this (x2)

1. Work can often make people anxious, irritable or depressed. However, *such feelings* are also a sign of stress.
2. Stress sufferers might also have difficulties sleeping. _____ often leave you less able to work the next day.
3. Regular exercise increases energy, improves focus and relaxes the body and mind. _____ can be felt up to 24 hours later.
4. Most people underestimate how long jobs take, and _____ can lead to problems.
5. Anyone can limit the amount of stress they suffer, though, by learning emotional intelligence. _____ can be easily taught.

Module 9
Winning counts!
9B

Academic vocabulary 2 AWL ACL

Academic collocations list

1a Choose the correct word in *italics* to complete the sentences. Then note the collocations in bold.
1. An entrepreneur tries to *build / grow* a **company** and *do / make* large **profits**.
2. They have a *big / high* **level of** intelligence and are very knowledgeable about their **subject** *area / topic*.
3. They are *highly / strongly* **motivated** and work hard to *achieve / meet* their **goals**.
4. They are very good at *developing / thinking* creative **ideas**.
5. They want to *achieve / make* **success** quickly.
6. They do not want to *lose / miss* **opportunities**.
7. They are not always very good at **communicating** *completely / effectively*.

b Write the collocations in Exercise 1a in your vocabulary notebook with an example sentence. Try to personalise the sentences.

build a company (v + n) – My mother built a company when she was in her thirties.

Money

2a Which of the verbs in the box collocate with *money*? Write them in the spidergram.

afford borrow change charge count do earn
hire lend owe pay save spend waste

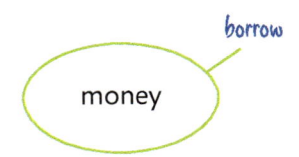

borrow → money

b Complete the sentences with words from Exercise 2a.
1. It is never good to _____ money to friends because they may not return it.
2. When you _____ someone money, it is best to pay it back as soon as possible.
3. It feels good to _____ money on other people.
4. It is important to _____ money as you might need it in the future.
5. You should never buy things you can't _____ .
6. All students over 16 should _____ some spending money by doing a part-time job.
7. It is common for people to _____ money by buying clothes that they never wear.
8. It is common for couples to _____ money from their parents when they start a family.

3a Complete the article with the words in the box.

borrow budget charges debt earn income lend
loans pay back profit start worth

In poor communities around the world people are trying their best to [1] _____ a small business so they can [2] _____ money and improve their lives. Most big banks prefer not to [3] _____ these people the small amounts of money they need because of the low [4] _____ they will make, so people go to microfinancing companies for help instead. These companies [5] _____ money from the big banks and give small [6] _____ to people on low incomes. In 2006 Bangladeshi banker Mohammad Yunus won the Nobel Peace Prize for his work in this area and in many countries, such as India, this idea was considered to be a solution to their poverty problem. However, it has ended up creating problems of its own. On top of the money the person borrows, the bank also [7] _____ interest, sometimes as high as 30 percent. This makes the [8] _____ much larger than it was at first. If something affects the person's monthly [9] _____ or if they cannot [10] _____ their spending well, they may not be able to [11] _____ the monthly loan repayments. Although microloans have been very positive for thousands of people, some may feel that the stress the loan brings is not [12] _____ the benefits it provides.

b What things do you need to make a successful company, other than money? Share your ideas with the class.

4 Complete the sentences with the words in the box. Use some words more than once.

considerable significantly slight slightly

1. The amount of money borrowed increased _____ from $100 to $110.
2. There was a _____ rise in loans from 1,025 to 10,400 per year.
3. The number of loans that weren't repaid grew _____ from 436 to 2670.
4. There was a _____ decrease in interest from 2 percent to 1.9 percent.
5. The number of loan applications is expected to increase _____ this year, by 1.5 percent.
6. There is likely to be a _____ rise in loans given. It could be as high as 60 percent.

145

9B Module 9
Winning counts!

Reading 2 (Re-order paragraphs)

Before you read

1 Discuss the questions in pairs.
   1 Which of the items in the list do you think is the riskiest? Why?
   - air travel
   - car accident
   - fire
   - overeating
   - natural disaster
   2 The photo shows Thomas Midgley, a scientist, who has been described as 'the one human responsible for more deaths than any other in human history'. What do you think he did?

Test practice
> EXPERT STRATEGIES page 179

2 Complete the task. Remember to look for logical relationships between the sentences.

The text boxes in the left panel have been placed in a random order. Restore the original order by dragging the text boxes from the left panel to the right panel.

	Source	Target
A	At that time additives could reduce the noise but none effectively got rid of it, until Midgley realised that adding lead to petrol solved the problem completely.	☐
B	These two chemicals gradually ate away at the atmosphere and poisoned millions of people's health for 50 years until their true impact was finally identified.	☐
C	Thomas Midgley started his career working on a major problem of the day, called 'engine knock', where fuel burnt in an uncontrolled explosion.	☐
D	He then turned to refrigerators and was asked to work on safer alternatives to the toxic cooling chemicals used at that time, coming up with CFC gas as a solution.	☐

Task analysis

3 Work in pairs. Compare and discuss how you approached the task. What were the links between each sentence?

Discussion

4 Discuss the questions in small groups.
   1 Do you think that Thomas Midgley deserves the title of the world's most dangerous man?
   2 Do you think that scientists today could make similar mistakes as those that Thomas Midgley made?

Module 9
Winning counts! — 9B

Speaking 2 (Describe image)

Dealing with more than one image

In *Describe image* the information may be expressed in more than one chart. You should try to find connections between the two charts.

1 a Work in pairs. Look at the charts in Exercise 3 and answer the questions.
   1. Around the world, what is the gap between female and male participation in secondary education?
   2. Is the situation similar in Latin America and the Caribbean?

b Complete the overview sentence summarising the data in the charts.

> Although around the world girls are less likely _____ , in some regions, such as _____ , this trend is reversed.

Sample response

2 a 🎧 117 Listen to two students describing the charts. Which student seems to have a better understanding of the charts? How can you tell?

b 🎧 118 Listen to the first student again and complete the description.

> The two charts show the differences in participation rates between boys and girls in secondary school in 2009. [1]_____ there's a gap between the boys and girls, although it's not a large gap – 82 percent for males compared to 79 percent for females. But in [2]_____ this trend is reversed, with 100 percent female attendance compared to 96 percent for boys. So, although [3]_____ girls are less likely to attend secondary school than boys, this is not true of the Latin American and Caribbean region.

Test practice
▶ EXPERT STRATEGIES page 172

3 Complete the task in pairs. Take turns to describe the charts. Remember to compare the information between the two charts. Record your answers if possible.

⏱ 40 sec. Look at the chart below. In 25 seconds, please speak into the microphone and describe in detail what the chart is showing. You will have 40 seconds to give your response.

Differences between participation rates in secondary school in 2009

Latin America and the Caribbean participation rates: girls 100, boys 96

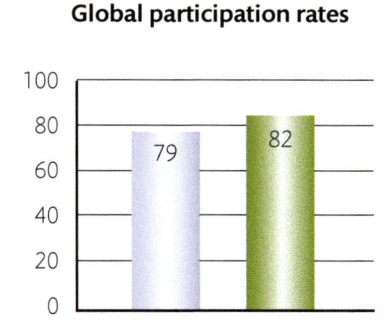

Global participation rates: girls 79, boys 82

Task analysis
▶ EXPERT SPEAKING page 192

4 Turn to page 192 and complete another timed test practice.

5 Compare and discuss which task (Exercise 3 or 4) you found harder to complete in the time limit. Did you manage to compare both the pass rates and the fail rates of boys and girls in Exercise 4?

147

9B Module 9
Winning counts!

Summary writing 2 (Summarize spoken text)

Lead-in

1a Choose the correct options in *italics* to complete the questions. Check the meaning of any unknown words in a dictionary.
1. If you had a lot of money, would you choose to give some of it *away / out*?
2. What good *aims / causes* would you choose to support?
3. What kind of charity would you like to *begin / found*?
4. Would you make a *donation / donor* to a charity in another country?
5. Would opening a *private / public* library in your name be worthwhile?
6. Would you spend it all now or save it so you have a *contribution / pension* when you retire?

b Discuss the questions in Exercise 1a in pairs. Do you know of any famous philanthropists? Who do/did they give their money to?

Understand the task
▶ EXPERT STRATEGIES page 182

2 Read the instructions and answer the questions.

> **10 min.** You will hear a short interview. Write a summary for a fellow student who was not present at the interview. You should write 50–70 words.
>
> You will have 10 minutes to finish this task. Your response will be judged on the quality of your writing and on how well your response presents the key points presented in the interview.

1. What are you going to hear and write?
2. How many words should you write?
3. How much time do you have to do this?

3a 🎧 119 Listen to the interview and take notes below.

b Compare your notes and discuss the questions in pairs.
1. What do you think about Andrew Carnegie's actions?
2. Would you do the same? Why/Why not?

Plan your summary

4a Write a topic sentence to summarise the main point of the interview.

b Write five sentences on supporting points made in the interview.

Module 9
Winning counts!
9B

c It is unlikely that you will to be able to include all the information from Exercise 4b in your summary without exceeding the limit of 70 words. Look at your sentences and number them in order of importance (1 = most important, 5 = least important).

d Did the speaker draw any conclusions? If so, write a concluding sentence.

e Work in pairs. Discuss your answers in Exercises 4b–d and explain your decisions.

Language and content

5a Read the sentences. Which of the underlined phrases describe the cause of an action? Which describe the effect of an action?
1 A childhood experience led to the opening of 2,000 public libraries.
2 Because of his poor beginnings, he gave 90 percent of his money away.
3 Owing to Carnegie's donation, teachers were able to get a pension.
4 A kind act from a rich man resulted in his interest in books.
5 Due to his beliefs, Carnegie gave away much of his money.

b Write sentences using the prompts below and the underlined phrases in Exercise 5a. Use each phrase once.
1 Carnegie's donation / millions of people have access to public libraries today
   Due to Carnegie's donation, millions of people have access to public libraries today.
2 Carnegie's influence / other wealthy people gave away money
3 Carnegie's generosity / the availability of pensions for teachers
4 the Carnegie Institution / more science research was done
5 Carnegie's beliefs / the decision to give away most of his money

6 Look at the useful expressions in the table. Then finish the incomplete sentences in each section. Use your notes from Exercise 3a to help you.

Writing about someone's life	He was a Scottish-American industrialist. He began work aged 12. In 1902 he _____ . Throughout his life _____ . When he was young, _____ . By 1911 _____ . Still today he _____ .
What people say/ think about someone	He is considered to be (one of the greatest philanthropists) of all time. He is said to be _____ . He is thought to be _____ .

Write your summary

7 Write your summary. Remember to organise and link your ideas appropriately. Remember to write 50–70 words.

Check your summary
➤ EXPERT WRITING page 196

8 Check your summary using the checklist on page 196.

9B Module 9
Winning counts!

Review

1 Complete the article with the words in the box.

achieve   added   attitude   co-operation
gave away   recreational   spent   wasted

Doing things to help other people can make you feel as if you have more free time and not less, according to recent research. An experiment carried out at Harvard Business School involved three groups of people who ¹_____ time in different ways. One group helped other people, one group ²_____ time by counting how many times the letter e occurred in a text and the third group participated in their own choice of ³_____ activities. In each experiment, the people who ⁴_____ their time to a good cause felt that they had more time than the people who did not. Before the experiment, the study authors believed that this was because a high level of ⁵_____ between people provides them with a more relaxed ⁶_____. But the research showed that it actually made people feel more useful and ⁷_____ to their self-esteem, as they felt that they could ⁸_____ goals.

2a Match words 1–8 with words A–H to make collocations.

1 communicate   A a company
2 a dramatic   B concern
3 exceed   C effectively
4 highly   D facilities
5 a major   E increase
6 sports   F motivated
7 start   G skills
8 people   H your limits

b Complete the sentences with the collocations in Exercise 2a.
1 If you want to _____, you need to have money and a good idea.
2 There has been _____ in the number of people who want to run their own business.
3 Making a profit is _____ for all new business owners.
4 To be successful in life, you need to be _____ to work hard.
5 Business managers must _____ with their staff.
6 Without _____, you are not able to get on well with your team.
7 If you believe you can do more than is possible, you will _____.
8 Some companies provide _____ for staff to use at lunchtime.

3 Complete the article with *a*, *an*, *the* or – (no article).

search News

It's not always possible to have more ¹_____ time but you can do things that make you feel as if you do. You might choose to do ²_____ activity you enjoy when you take ³_____ break, like reading ⁴_____ book, but this actually makes time seem faster. It's better to pick ⁵_____ activity like helping others, which makes you feel as if you can do more with ⁶_____ time you have. Thinking about ⁷_____ present time can also help make time feel longer. And in ⁸_____ experiment where people concentrated on their breathing for five minutes, people who took long, slow breaths felt time was slower than those who took short breaths. So, taking ⁹_____ long deep breath every now and then is ¹⁰_____ good idea.

4 Complete the article with the words in the box.

former   it   latter   so   such   these   this

Failure is a negative word for most business people, but ¹_____ can actually encourage creativity, either for an individual or an organisation. There seem to be two ways that people view failure, which I describe as type 1 and type 2. The ²_____, type 1, is being afraid of it. Most individuals, managers and businesses are like ³_____. They think that failure is embarrassing and painful and as a result, there is very little creativity in a company, producing low results. But the ⁴_____, type 2, is being afraid of missing opportunities. Places like Silicon Valley in California are full of ⁵_____ people. What is embarrassing to them is sitting around and watching other people think of a great idea when they could do ⁶_____. What type 2 people know is that failure is not bad; it can actually be exciting. In ⁷_____ a situation, you can actually get ideas for the next big thing. When we are children, we are all type 2, full of energy and creativity. But somewhere between childhood and adulthood, we change to type 1 because failure is just not allowed.

10 Let's talk!

Overview

10A
- **Reading:** Multiple-choice, choose multiple answers
- **Academic vocabulary:** Research
- **Speaking:** Repeat sentence; Answer short question
- **Listening:** Fill in the blanks
- **Language development:** Present perfect and past simple
- **Writing:** Write essay

10B
- **Listening:** Highlight incorrect words
- **Language development:** Reported speech
- **Academic vocabulary:** Shops and advertising
- **Reading:** Multiple-choice, choose multiple answers
- **Speaking:** Re-tell lecture
- **Writing:** Write essay

Lead-in

1. Look at the photos and discuss the questions.
    1. How does each photo represent the topic of *communication*? How is the communication different in each?
    2. How has the way we communicate changed in the last 50 years? Think of at least three ways.
    3. How do you prefer to communicate with people? Why?

2. In what different ways do these groups of people communicate? Who do they communicate with?
   - employees
   - journalists
   - politicians
   - students

3. Work in small groups. Think of five ways you communicate your ideas or feelings using facial expressions or gestures. Do you all do similar things?

151

10A Now you're talking!

Reading 1 (Multiple-choice, choose multiple answers)

Before you read

1 Check the meaning of the words in bold in a dictionary. Then answer the questions about your country/culture in pairs.
   1 Do young people **respect** the older generation?
   2 Is it common for students to **question** their teachers?
   3 Is **power** shared between everyone or just a small group of people?
   4 Do all groups of people have **equality** in the workplace?
   5 Does your government **measure** how happy people are?
   6 Do you think the people in your country would be high or low on a happiness **index**?

Inferring information in a text

In *Multiple-choice, choose multiple answers* you may need to infer information from the text in order to answer the question.

2 Read the text in Exercise 5 and answer the questions. Does the writer directly state this information?
   1 What does the Power Distance Index measure?
   2 What are the features of countries with a high index?
   3 What are the features of countries with a low index?
   4 In which subject areas has the index been used for research?

3 A reader often has to infer information from a text because the writer does not state it directly. What information in the text tells us that:
   1 Hofstede has an interest in cultural differences? (paragraph 1)
   2 employees respect management in a high index culture? (paragraph 2)
   3 the writer has a particular interest in Germany? (paragraph 3)
   4 developing countries are likely to have a high index? (paragraph 3)
   5 the Power Distance Index is respected by other academics? (paragraph 4)

4a In each pair of sentences, which information can we infer from the text? Which information can we not infer?
   1 paragraph 1
      A Not all people believe that power should be shared equally.
      B Hofstede believes that cultures with a low index are better.
   2 paragraph 2
      A People in authority in low index countries are weak.
      B People in authority in high index countries make the decisions.
   3 paragraph 3
      A People in Austria believe in equality for everyone.
      B European countries all have a low Power Distance Index.
   4 paragraph 4
      A The index can help business people understand each other better.
      B It is important to use the index when doing research.

b Work in pairs. Discuss your reasons for your answers in Exercise 4a.

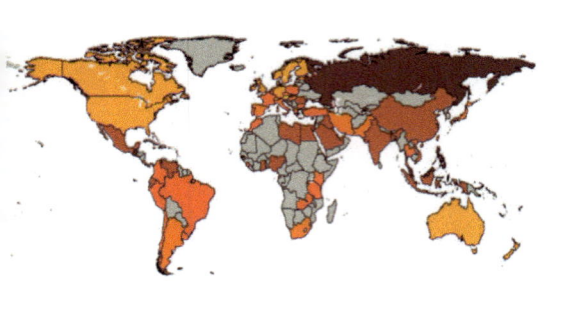

Module 10
Let's talk! — 10A

Test practice
> EXPERT STRATEGIES page 178

5 Complete the task. Think about what the writer states directly and what you can infer from the text.

Read the text and answer the question by selecting all the correct responses. More than one response is correct.

Professor Geert Hofstede has developed a theory about culture and its likely impact on individual people. One feature of this theory is the Power Distance Index. This index measures how much people accept the unequal share of power in society. In a culture with a high Power Distance Index people accept that power is shared unequally, whereas members of a culture with a low Power Distance Index expect it to be shared evenly.

Countries with a high index generally have centralised authority, with many levels which people respect. People tend not to question the decisions that people in authority make. However, in countries with a low index there are fewer levels of authority and people respect individualism more than authority. Furthermore, decisions made by people in authority are regularly questioned.

Germany has an index of 35. Compared to many Arab, Latin, African and Asian countries, where the power distance is high (70–80), and Austria, where it is very low (11), Germany is somewhere in the middle. Germany does not have a large gap between the wealthy and the poor and there is a widespread belief in equality for each citizen. Germans have the opportunity to rise in society. On the other hand, the power distance in the United States scores a 40 on the cultural scale. The US has a more unequal distribution of wealth compared to German society.

The Power Distance Index has been used in research in the fields of sociology, psychology, international management and cross-cultural communication because it can significantly affect both verbal and written forms of communication across cultures.

What can be inferred about companies in a country with a high Power Distance Index?

A ☐ They have a structure with many managers and rules.

B ☐ They expect all team members to give their opinions.

C ☐ They do not mind employees who doubt their managers.

D ☐ They have many low level staff who are told what to do.

E ☐ They believe that all staff have the same rights.

> **HELP**
>
> Focus on the two paragraphs that say what a high index is.

Task analysis

6 Discuss the questions in pairs.
1. Which parts of the text gave you the answers?
2. Why are the incorrect options wrong?

Discussion

7 Work in pairs. Do you think your country has a high or low Power Distance Index? Why?

EXPERT WORD CHECK
centralised   feature   gap   individualism   score (v)

> See **Reading 2** for more practice of this task type.

10A Module 10
Let's talk!

Academic vocabulary 1 AWL ACL

Academic nouns

1a Complete the article with the words in the box.

authority   communication   cultures   decisions
impact   research   theory

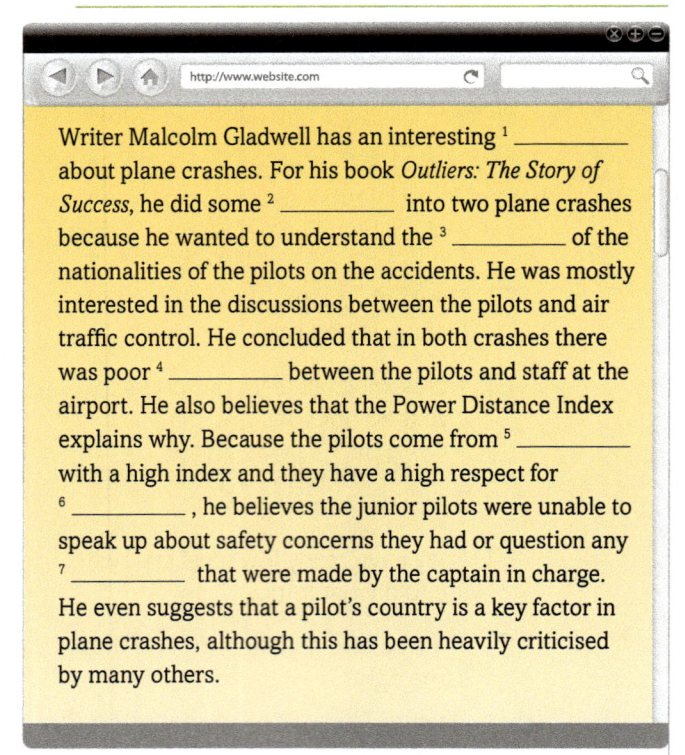

Writer Malcolm Gladwell has an interesting [1] _____ about plane crashes. For his book *Outliers: The Story of Success*, he did some [2] _____ into two plane crashes because he wanted to understand the [3] _____ of the nationalities of the pilots on the accidents. He was mostly interested in the discussions between the pilots and air traffic control. He concluded that in both crashes there was poor [4] _____ between the pilots and staff at the airport. He also believes that the Power Distance Index explains why. Because the pilots come from [5] _____ with a high index and they have a high respect for [6] _____, he believes the junior pilots were unable to speak up about safety concerns they had or question any [7] _____ that were made by the captain in charge. He even suggests that a pilot's country is a key factor in plane crashes, although this has been heavily criticised by many others.

b Why do you think people have criticised Malcolm Gladwell's ideas? Share your ideas with the class.

Academic collocations list

2a Match the beginnings of the sentences (1–6) with the endings (A–F). Then note the collocations in *italics*.

1 Age has a *likely*
2 Levels of authority *significantly*
3 Forms of *verbal*
4 Young people *have*
5 Decision-making powers are *shared*
6 There is a *widespread*

A *the opportunity* to develop their communication skills at school.
B *communication* are more important than written communication.
C *belief* that women talk more than men.
D *affect* the way people speak to each other.
E *equally among* people in a family.
F *impact* on the way people speak to each other.

b Think about the way people communicate in your culture. Write five sentences using collocations from Exercise 2a.

Research

3a Choose the correct options in *italics* to complete the article.

The [1] *data / research* that Professor Albert Mehrabian conducted in the [2] *field / goal* of communication in the 1960s still influences our understanding today. His [3] *analysis / theory* showed that only seven percent of a message is communicated by the words we use. The other 93 percent comes from non-verbal communication. To [4] *evaluate / source* the importance of voice tone and facial expression, he carried out two [5] *experiments / research*. The [6] *distribution / process* involved people listening to a word repeated three times to express either like, dislike or a neutral position. Sometimes they also saw photos of facial expressions. The results provided [7] *concepts / evidence* that 38 percent of communication comes from our tone of voice and 55 percent comes from our facial expression. The [8] *concept / method* of 7-38-55 is widely used by people who carry out communication [9] *results / studies* today, although it is often misunderstood. It is not [10] *joined / linked* to all communication; it is only [11] *involved in / related to* feelings and attitudes. More recently, research [12] *evidence / findings* have [13] *seen / shown* that tone of voice is actually more important than facial expressions but [14] *conclusions / evaluation* tend to vary.

b What do you pay attention to the most: words, tone of voice or facial expressions? Share your ideas with the class.

4a Match the verbs in bold in the sentences (1–6) with their meanings (A–F).

1 Mehrabian **argued** that body language is more important than words.
2 He **claimed** that words give just seven percent of a message.
3 He **estimated** that 38 percent of communication comes from tone.
4 He **concluded** that non-verbal communication is more important than verbal communication.
5 The writer of the article **pointed out** that people often misunderstand Mehrabian's research.
6 Recent research **proves** that the topic is a very difficult one.

A provide evidence for something
B give your opinion
C guess the value
D decide something is true after looking at evidence
E say something people did not know
F say that something is true even though it has not been proved

b Write three sentences about Malcolm Gladwell in Exercise 1a using verbs from Exercise 4a.

Module 10
Let's talk! — 10A

Speaking 1 (Repeat sentence; Answer short question)

Pronunciation: Stress timing and weak forms

English is a stress-timed language, so some words are stressed and some are unstressed. In *Repeat sentence* it is important that you say the sentence with the correct stress.

1a Work in pairs. Take it in turns to say each group of words at a normal speed. Approximately how long does it take you to say each group of words?
  1 colleague, sent, email
  2 having, email, exchange
  3 shocked, said, sounded, impatient
  4 talked, phone, minutes, solve, problem

b 🎧 120 Read four sentences in which the words from Exercise 1a are the stressed words. Then listen to someone saying the stressed words and then the full sentences. Does she take more time to say the words or the full sentences, or the same amount of time for both?
  1 *A* colleague sent me *an* email.
  2 *We were* having *an* email exchange.
  3 *I was* shocked when she said *that I* sounded impatient.
  4 *We* talked *on the* phone *for a* few minutes *to* solve *the* problem.

c 🎧 120 Look at the words in italics in Exercise 1b. These words have a weak form (they are unstressed). Listen to how each weak form is pronounced. Then repeat the sentences.

2 🎧 121 Underline the stressed words and circle the weak forms in the sentences. Then listen, check your answers and repeat the sentences.
  1 Email's quick and convenient.
  2 But there's no context for the words we read.
  3 When we talk, we use tone and expressions to understand.
  4 Email increases the chances of miscommunication.

Test practice 1: Repeat sentence
➤ EXPERT STRATEGIES page 171

3 🎧 122 Complete the task in pairs. You will hear ten sentences. Record your answers if possible.

> ⓥ 15 sec. You will hear a sentence. Please repeat the sentence exactly as you hear it. You will hear the sentence only once.

Task analysis

4 🎧 123 Listen to five students repeating some of the sentences in Exercise 2. How many use appropriate sentence stress and weak forms?

Test practice 2: Answer short question
➤ EXPERT STRATEGIES page 174

5 🎧 124 Complete the task in pairs. You will hear six questions.

> ⓥ 10 sec. You will hear a question. Please give a simple and short answer. Often just one or a few words is enough.

155

10A Module 10
Let's talk!

Listening 1 (Fill in the blanks)

Before you listen

1 Discuss the questions in pairs.
  1 Look at the cartoon. Have you ever had problems communicating in a different language?
  2 Who do you find it easiest to communicate with? Why?

Checking your work

In *Fill in the blanks*, it is important to read through the text after you have finished to make sure that it makes sense.

2a 🎧 125 Listen and complete the text.

We miscommunicate more commonly than we communicate [1] _____ . Often, the words we have are at least [2] _____ inadequate to express how we feel. The first words we think of are often poor [3] _____ of what we really mean. We might at times even want to take our words back for a second [4] _____ . But once those words have left our mouths, our partners are already [5] _____ to whatever we have just said. Most conversations happen too fast to allow us to [6] _____ what we really meant to say.

Miscommunication

b Work in pairs. Choose the correct spelling for the words you heard in Exercise 2a. Does the word make sense in the rest of the sentence?

  1 acurately / accurately
  2 somewhat / somewant
  3 reflections / refleccions
  4 attemt / attempt
  5 replying / reply
  6 figured / figure

Test practice
▶ EXPERT STRATEGIES page 184

3 🎧 126 Complete the task. Remember to note down the words as you listen.

You will hear a recording. Type the missing words in each blank.

People rarely translate another person's [1]_____ way of saying things with any degree of [2]_____ . This is because when we learn the meaning of words, we pick up their broad meanings but we've added subtle [3]_____ of difference which we get from our personal experiences. If you grew up in an aggressive household, the phrase 'I'm angry with you' had different [4]_____ than for a person from a family where people talked through problems. We're left having to work out meaning from our own experience. So despite the fact that, say, Bob and Gina are both speaking English, Bob is really speaking 'Bob-English' and Gina is turning that into 'Gina-English' and the [5]_____ is never going to be perfect.

Task analysis

4 Discuss the questions in pairs.
  1 Which part of speech was each blank?
  2 Which of the blanks was the most difficult? Why?

Language development 1

Present perfect and past simple
➤ EXPERT GRAMMAR page 213

1 Choose the correct options in *italics* to complete the sentences.
1 But once those words *have left / left* our mouths, our partners are already replying to whatever we *just said / have just said*.
2 Most conversations happen too fast to allow us to figure out what we really *meant / have meant* to say.
3 We *added / have added* subtle shades of difference.
4 If you grew up in an aggressive household, the phrase 'I'm angry with you' *had / has had* different associations than for a person from a family where people *talked / have talked* through problems.

2a Complete the sentences with the present perfect or past simple form of the verbs in brackets.
1 Who _____ (be) the first person you _____ (make) friends with at school? _____ (you / stay) in touch?
2 Where _____ (you / meet) your closest friend? How long _____ (you / know) each other?
3 _____ (you / ever / meet) a famous person? If so, _____ (that person / make) a good first impression?
4 _____ (you / ever / speak) to someone from another country? _____ (you / get on) well?
5 When _____ (you / start) this book? _____ (you / finish) it yet?

b Discuss the questions in Exercise 2a in small groups.

3a Read the article and choose the best title.

1 Fidgeting may release stress ... for men!

2 KEEP STILL IF YOU WANT TO SUCCEED IN INTERVIEWS!

So, you ¹ _____ (perfect) your CV and you ² _____ (choose) the perfect tie before you go to that interview tomorrow. But ³ _____ (you / think) about how much you should fidget?
In a study out last year scientists at Roehampton University ⁴ _____ (find) that men who repeatedly ⁵ _____ (touch) their face, ⁶ _____ (bite) and ⁷ _____ (lick) their lips, ⁸ _____ (yawn) and ⁹ _____ (scratch) during an interview were calmer and ¹⁰ _____ (not make) as many mistakes. They ¹¹ _____ (hypothesise) that fidgeting ¹² _____ (have) a relaxing effect. The test ¹³ _____ (since / be) repeated with female interviewees but they ¹⁴ _____ (find) that the opposite was true among women.

b Work in pairs. Complete the article in Exercise 3a with the present perfect or past simple form of the verbs in brackets.

4a Work in pairs. Read the questions graduates asked future employers at job interviews. Complete them with the present perfect or past simple form of the verbs in brackets.
1 _____ (you / look) at my references yet?
2 How _____ (the company / recognise) good work in the past?
3 Why _____ (the company / reduce) the workforce last year?
4 How much _____ (the company / pay) in staff bonuses last year?
5 I like to work in a team. Can you give me some examples of how your company _____ (achieve) its goals through teamwork last year?
6 Can you explain the company culture and how this _____ (be) practised in recent years?

b Experts advised against asking three of the questions in Exercise 4a. Which do you think were the weaker questions? Why?

157

10A Module 10
Let's talk!

Writing 1 (Write essay)

Writing in the time limit
➤ EXPERT STRATEGIES page 176

To score well in *Write essay*, you need to write an essay that is well organised, with relevant content, in 20 minutes.

1a Read the essay prompt and look at the underlined words. Then discuss the questions in pairs.

> Access to <u>cable or wireless technology is essential</u> these days. Have these technologies <u>created new divisions</u> in society between those who have internet access and <u>those who do not</u>? Discuss this question, with reference to both sides.

1 Is internet access essential these days? Is it essential for everyone?
2 Who does not have internet access?
3 Are these divisions new?

➤ EXPERT WRITING pages 197–200

b Which of the four essay types that you have studied so far do you need to write for this prompt? You can read about the four essay types on pages 197–200.

2a Write a topic sentence (see page 30) for each of the paragraphs in your essay in 1–3 in the plan below. Remember that in the test you can write your notes straight onto the screen and use the *Cut*, *Copy* and *Paste* functions to move text around. Are your paragraphs in the best order (weakest to strongest arguments)?

- Introduction _____
- Para 1
  1 _____
  A _____
- Para 2
  2 _____
  B _____
- Para 3
  3 _____
  C _____
- Conclusion _____

b Start building evidence for your arguments and write them in A–C in the essay plan. Remember to write your paragraphs using the PIE method (see page 62).

3a Write your introduction (see page 94). Remember to start with the general topic and state the focus of the essay towards the end of your introduction.

b Write your conclusion (see page 126). Remember to summarise your ideas and reach a conclusion. How will you end your essay?

4 Read through your essay and think about the questions.
1 Have you addressed all the points that are underlined in the essay prompt in Exercise 1a?
2 Have you written a persuasive essay?
3 Have you written 200–300 words?

5 Turn to page 197 and complete the task. Remember that you should write your essay in 20 minutes.

➤ EXPERT WRITING page 197

➤ See **Writing 2** for more practice of this task type.

'Darling you'll be so proud of me, I've just written my first email. Now I must rush to get it in the post.'

10B Reaching the masses

Listening 2 (Highlight incorrect words)

Before you listen

1 Discuss the questions in pairs.
 1 Do you ever buy things because of adverts you see?
 2 Do you have any favourite brands?
 3 Do you trust what you hear and read in adverts? Why/Why not?

Understanding specific vocabulary

In *Highlight incorrect words* you will need to listen very closely to individual words to be able to spot errors in the transcription.

2a 🎧 127 Listen and tick (✓) the words you hear.

1	✓ brand	☐ banned	5	☐ likely	☐ unlikely
2	☐ natural	☐ liberal	6	☐ knows	☐ shows
3	☐ buy	☐ try	7	☐ jacket	☐ racket
4	☐ dissuade	☐ persuade	8	☐ worth	☐ worse

b Work in pairs. Practise saying the words in Exercise 2a to your partner. Can he/she hear the difference?

Test practice
➤ EXPERT STRATEGIES page 188

3 🎧 128 Complete the task. Remember to follow the text with your pen, underlining the words that are different.

> You will hear a recording. Below is a transcription of the recording. Some words in the transcription differ from what the speaker said. Please click on the words that are different.
>
> After targeting pet owners for years, advertisers are now going directly to the animals. One European TV ad for dog food featured a high-pitched sound, like a dog howl, that only dogs could hear, the idea being that pet dogs living in a family home would rush up to the TV and look keen. A similar idea but a year earlier: a dog food company set up a series of signboards that gave off an ultrasonic sound every ten seconds. 'Bark if you like Bonzo!' said the headline. But even if dogs are attracted to certain sounds, they're even more attracted to things that sell. Dog-food-scented ads on sidewalks were designed to persuade dogs and their owners to come over for a sniff.

Task analysis

4 Discuss the questions in pairs.
 1 Did you find this task type easier or harder than other task types?
 2 Did you lose marks for selecting words unnecessarily?

159

10B Module 10
Let's talk!

Language development 2

Reported speech

➤ EXPERT GRAMMAR page 213

1a Read the reported statements and write the speaker's exact words.

1
> The lecturer said that the purpose of adverts was to create a brand name.

> The purpose of adverts __is__ to create a brand name.

2
> She told us that advertisers had made claims about their products for decades.

> Advertisers _____ about their products for decades.

3
> She suggested that positive associations might influence more people to buy the product.

> Positive associations _____ to buy the product.

4
> She claimed that luxury clothing companies advertised to people who couldn't afford them.

> Luxury clothing companies _____ .

5
> She said that when they saw someone with a luxury item, they'd recognise it as expensive.

> _____

b Did the tense of the verbs change in the reported statements? Why/Why not?

2a Match the statements (1–6) with the people who made them (A–F). Do not complete the reported statements yet.
1 'It's been produced in a more environmentally-friendly way.'
2 'It has the ability to cure everything.'
3 'It makes you thinner.'
4 'It cures baldness.'
5 'It can prevent sore throats.'
6 'It'll give children energy until lunchtime.'

A A cereal manufacturer claimed their chocolate cereal _____ .
B A mouthwash company said their product _____ .
C Makers of a traditional medicine in the early 20th century said _____ .
D The retailer of a hat for men said that _____ .
E A petrol company claimed that their clear petrol _____ .
F A cosmetics manufacturer said their body cream _____ .

b Complete the reported statements in Exercise 2a.

3a 🎧 129 Listen to five people talking about the influence of advertising and take notes.

1 _____
2 _____
3 _____
4 _____
5 _____

b Work in pairs. Take turns to report what the people in Exercise 3a said. Use your notes to help you.

4 Find and correct five mistakes in the use of reported speech or reporting verbs and five spelling mistakes in the article.

I recently read an article about an unusual and surprising advertising campaign that took place last year. The writer explained me that earlier in the year a well-known doughnut company had created a device that produced the smell of coffee and has placed them on buses around Seoul, South Korea. She claimed that every time a spesific piece of music play on the company's ad, the device produced the smell. This seems like an extreem way to persuade customers to buy your products but the company later revealed that sales in the stores near bus stops increase by 29 percent during the campain. The writer suggested that it was successful because the customers have heard, seen and smelled the products. Perhaps multi-sensory adverts are the future?

Academic vocabulary 2 AWL ACL

Academic collocations list

1a Complete the sentences with the words in the box. Then note the collocations in *italics*.

| full | high | large | marked | well | wide |

1. Business people do a _____ *analysis* of the market before they start a new product.
2. Advertising allows companies to sell _____ *quantities* of poor quality goods.
3. Many people are _____ *aware* that adverts contain false information.
4. There is a _____ *contrast* between what we need and what we want.
5. Quality is a _____ *priority* for me.
6. There is a _____ *range* of products in the shops.

b Complete the essay with the collocations in Exercise 1a.

> **Advertising toys and games should be banned**
> For years, business professionals have carried out a ¹_____ of the effects of advertising on profits and are ²_____ of the power that marketing has. There is a ³_____ between the money spent on promoting traditional values and the advertising budgets of wealthy toy companies. Because of adverts, young people today grow up expecting ⁴_____ of presents and gifts. Even when parents cannot afford to spend money on toys, the ⁵_____ of toy dolls and cars with happy owners shown on television makes parents feel guilty for not being able to offer these things to their child. That is why I believe governments should make it a ⁶_____ to ban toy advertising.

Academic word list

2a Match the beginnings of the sentences (1–5) with the endings (A–E).
1. Shops stock too
2. Prices are cheaper when
3. Advertisers should be
4. Companies should **focus** more
5. If I'm buying a gift,

A guided by a set of **principles**.
B attractive packaging is a **definite** plus.
C on customer service than special offers.
D many **items** to choose from.
E companies sell large **volumes**.

b Write the words in bold in Exercise 2a in your vocabulary notebook with an example sentence.

Shops and advertising

3a Choose the correct options in *italics* to complete the sentences.
1. Do people enjoy *online / computer* shopping in your country?
2. Do you think that *banking / credit* cards are a good thing?
3. Are shops happy to *refund / respond* money in your country?
4. Do shops *transport / deliver* most things to your home?
5. Have you ever *saved / reserved* a new item before it's in the shops?
6. Is it common in your country for customers to try and *decrease / reduce* the price of items?
7. Do you think that the prices in the shop nearest to you are *lower / reasonable*?
8. Do you always keep *bills / receipts* after you buy things?

b Discuss the questions in Exercise 3a in pairs.

4a Complete the article with the words in the box.

advertising	brand	campaign	commercial
commission	consumer	deals	persuading
promotion	sales assistant

> **Does ¹_____ increase the cost of things?**
> Well, the answer is 'maybe'. A top actress can be paid as much as 20 million euros to become the face of a top cosmetics ²_____. Let's say a company spends six million euros on a marketing ³_____ to achieve total sales of 20 million euros. That's a third of total sales spent on ⁴_____ someone to buy the product. That figure's even higher once the ⁵_____ at the department store has been paid her ⁶_____. But that oversimplifies the issue. If a large cosmetics company has fixed costs (for their factories and staff) of 100 million euros and variable costs (for ingredients and transport) of another 100 million euros, it needs to sell ten million jars of face cream at 20 euros each just to get back their costs. If a famous actress appears in a(n) ⁷_____ which sells 20 million face creams, the fixed costs per jar go down and those savings might be passed on to the ⁸_____ in the form of price ⁹_____ or two-for-one ¹⁰_____.

b Do you think that advertising is important in society? Share your ideas with the class.

161

10B Module 10
Let's talk!

Reading 2 (Multiple-choice, choose multiple answers)

Before you read

1 Check the meaning of the words in bold in a dictionary. Then discuss the questions in pairs.
  1 Are you good at **persuading** people to do things?
  2 What **persuasion technique(s)** do you use?
  3 Have you had to **overcome** a communication problem?
  4 Does your country have a **symbol**, such as an image or an animal?
  5 What skills does a person in power need to show **leadership**?
  6 Whose head can you see on **coins** or notes in your country?

Test practice
> EXPERT STRATEGIES page 178

2 Complete the task. Remember to consider inferences in the text.

Read the text and answer the question by selecting all the correct responses. More than one response is correct.

Art has been used as a persuasion technique by people in power for centuries. As kings began to rule larger areas, they had to overcome communication issues. Darius the Great of Persia was one such man. Because very few people could read or write, he had stone sculptures created that combined artistic styles from all over the kingdom. This communicated the idea that he admired and respected his people. He also created a symbol for himself that was placed on gold coins to show his leadership.

The man who took control from Darius, Alexander the Great, took this idea one step further. To communicate his power, he used his face. He melted all of the gold coins with Darius's symbol on them and replaced them with coins showing his head. The image of a head is so influential that it still appears on coins around the world today.

Art is not just about power; it can also be used to persuade us to see things in a certain way. The earliest known use of this dates back to the Romans. Augustus asked artists to create an image of him that made people believe he was powerful but not a fighter. However, the art was a lie as he was planning to go to war.

As we can see, the leaders of the past, male and female, used paint, stone and gold. Today, we use digital images but we remain easily influenced by the persuasive power of art.

What conclusions can we make about images?

A ☐ They are not a new phenomenon.
B ☐ They can be used dishonestly.
C ☐ They are only used in certain cultures.
D ☐ They are more powerful than words.
E ☐ They can be a powerful tool for a leader.
F ☐ They encourage communication between people.
G ☐ They have been used mostly by men.

Task analysis

3 Underline the parts of the text that give the answers. Is the information stated directly or did you have to infer it?

Discussion

4 Discuss the questions in pairs.
  1 How important is art in your culture?
  2 How do people in authority use images to influence people today?

Module 10
Let's talk!   10B

Speaking 2 (Re-tell lecture)

Using notes to link ideas when re-telling a lecture

In *Re-tell lecture* you will need to quickly understand the points in your notes in order to re-tell the lecture in a logical way.

1 a You will hear a lecture. Look at the presentation slide in Exercise 3. What is the topic of the lecture?

b 🎧 130 Listen to the lecture and take notes. Were your ideas correct?

c Work in pairs. Compare your notes to the notes below. Did you organise them in the same way? Why/Why not?

> Canadians OK w. following online activity
> good news 4 cos. follow activities net/ spec ads
> 73% aware tracking
> maj happy share shopping
> 17% OK financial data
> = ppl aware ad works. X affect fin.

Sample response

2 a 🎧 131 Listen to two students re-telling the lecture. Which one interprets her notes better?

b Which of these strategies do you think the better student used? How did they help her?
1 She paid attention to the meaning of the lecture.
2 She used the ten seconds to practise what she was going to say.
3 She used the ten seconds to decide what the main point was.
4 She thought about the meaning of the lecture when she spoke.
5 She presented information in the same order as the speaker.

Test practice
➤ EXPERT STRATEGIES page 173

3 🎧 130 Complete the task in pairs. Take your own notes again, then present the information to your partner.

> ⏱ 40 sec. You will hear a lecture. After listening to the lecture, in 10 seconds, please speak into the microphone and re-tell what you have just heard from the lecture in your own words. You will have 40 seconds to give your response.

Advertising standards, Canada: report
▶ 53% happy to share location data
▶ 79% happy to share shopping data
▶ 27% happy to share financial data

Test practice
➤ EXPERT SPEAKING page 195

4 🎧 132 Turn to page 195 and complete another timed test practice.

Task analysis

5 Work in pairs. Which of the strategies in Exercise 2b did you use? How helpful were they?

163

10B Module 10
Let's talk!

Writing 2 (Write essay)

Lead-in 1 Discuss the questions in pairs.
1 What matters most to you? Number the items on the list in order of importance (1 = most important, 6 = least important).
• career • education • family • friends • health • wealth
2 Do you think work and career have become too important?

Understand the task
➤ EXPERT STRATEGIES page 176

2a Read the essay prompt and underline the key words. What kind of essay do you need to write?

> **⏱ 20 min.** You will have 20 minutes to plan, write and revise an essay about the topic below. Your response will be judged on how well you develop a position, organise your ideas, present supporting details and control the elements of standard written English. You should write 200–300 words.

> Many claim that modern society has become over-commercialised and people have lost sight of traditional values. To what extent do you agree that people's sense of identity increasingly comes from the products they buy rather than who they really are? Write with reference to one culture you know well.

➤ **HELP**
• What phrase in the second sentence explains *commercialised*?
• What is meant by *traditional values*?

b Work in pairs. Share ideas on this topic. Brainstorm as many as possible in two minutes.

To score well in *Write essay*, you need to build persuasive arguments and show clear sequencing of ideas.

Plan your essay

3a Look at the ideas from a brainstorming session. Arrange them into two paragraphs. Then decide in what order they should appear within each paragraph.
• paragraph 1: effects of commercialisation
• paragraph 2: traditional values today

Ideas
A Most people still hope for marriage and children.
B People spend money on cars for status.
C Most cars do more than transport you.
D Many adverts use traditional values (home, showing love).
E Everything is a brand these days – even toothpaste.
F Family is still the main source of support and comfort.

b Now make your essay plan. Remember that in the test you can write your notes straight onto the screen and use the *Cut*, *Copy* and *Paste* functions to move text around. Are your paragraphs in the best order (weakest to strongest arguments)?

Module 10
10B Let's talk!

Language and content

When you write in academic English, you need to build strong arguments by adding additional information.

4a Match the ideas (1–3) with the ones that logically follow them (A–C).

1 Cars do a lot more than transport people in comfort.
2 Even something as simple as toothpaste has been turned into a brand.
3 It has become harder for families to find time for each other with both mothers and fathers working these days.

A Moreover, many companies expect parents to put their work first, above the home.
B They give important information about the success of the owner, too.
C These days, there are ones which claim to be made from natural ingredients or the latest science, not to mention the claims to making you more attractive.

b Underline the linking words used to show addition in Exercise 4a and add them to the table.

Addition
and, as well, also, furthermore, or even, _____, _____, _____

c Add any other linking words you know to the table. Then think about how you can use them in your essay plan.

5a Look at the time sequencers in *italics* in the sentences and add them to the table. What tense is each often used with?

1 Prices have risen *since the 1950s*.
2 Prices will rise *next year*.
3 Prices rose *between 1988 and 2008*.
4 Prices had risen *before the start of the last century*.
5 Prices will rise *over the next few years*.
6 Prices rise *every year*.
7 Prices are rising *at the moment*.

Time sequencers	
By the year 2000 A _____	the cosmetics industry **had become** one of the top ten industries in many countries.
In 2010 B _____	only a few companies **controlled** the market.
For the last few decades C Since the 1950s	the cosmetics industry **has grown** significantly.
D _____	education **matters** more than ever.
E _____ F _____	more money **will be spent** on cosmetics than medical research.
G _____	many children **are suffering** from preventable illnesses.

b Identify places in your essay where you can use time sequencers and a better range of tenses.

Write your essay

6 Write your essay. Use your plan from Exercise 3b and the language in Exercises 4 and 5 to help you. Remember to write 200–300 words.

Check your essay

7 Check your essay using the checklist on page 196.

> EXPERT WRITING page 196

10B Module 10 Let's talk!

Review

1 Complete the article with the present perfect or past simple form of the verbs in brackets.

The development of public relations

There ¹ *have been* (be) three main phases in the development of public relations, the profession of creating and caring for the public image of companies. In the earliest phase, the Publicity Phase, one-way communication ² _____ (dominate). Most PR experts ³ _____ (build) recognition for a company or individual among the widest possible audience. In the Explanatory Phase, PR professionals ⁴ _____ (not want) to just inform but to offer explanations for the actions of companies which they ⁵ _____ (represent) so that their public would understand and then spend their money there. This approach ⁶ _____ (not be) so popular in the last few years. Organisations ⁷ _____ (find) more recently that they need to listen to the public and make adjustments to their behaviour. This is known as the Mutual Satisfaction Approach. Many still believe they can get what they want without making any changes in behaviour. Enron, for example, ⁸ _____ (claim) that they were honest and financially responsible when, clearly, they ⁹ _____ (not practise) this.

2 Read the quotes. Then complete the reported statements below.

1 'Although managing PR for companies is hard, managing celebrities will be harder.'

2 'Many celebrities are caught doing things they should not do.'

3 'It isn't a good idea to stay silent when things go wrong.'

4 'Any question is an opportunity to show your humanity and values.'

5 'If a person has demonstrated strong values over time, this will carry them forward.'

1 Daniel Spoiler, professor in PR, pointed out that although managing companies _____ hard, managing celebrities _____ harder.
2 Journalist Stephen Davis said that many celebrities _____ caught doing things they _____ .
3 One PR professional thought that it _____ a good idea to stay silent when things _____ wrong.
4 Celebrity Tanya James told readers of her blog page that any question _____ an opportunity to show your humanity and values.
5 Most people felt that if a person _____ demonstrated strong values over time, that _____ them forward.

3 Do the puzzle. What is the mystery word?

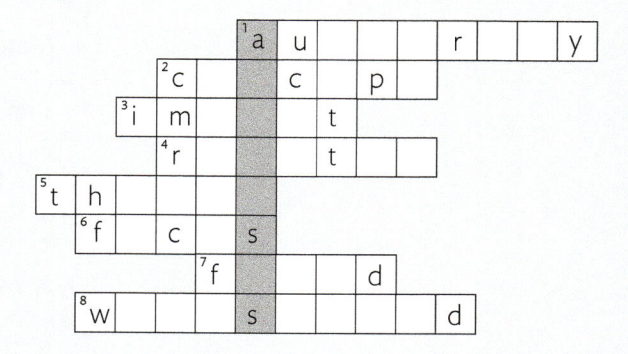

	1	a	u			r		y
2	c			c		p		
3	i	m			t			
	4	r			t			
5	t	h						
	6	f		c	s			
		7	f			d		
8	w			s			d	

1 the power someone has
2 a general idea or principle
3 an effect
4 connected
5 an idea that explains something
6 the person or subject people pay attention to
7 the subject people study or a type of work
8 happening in many places, among many people or in many situations

4 Match the beginnings of the sentences (1–8) with the endings (A–H).
1 Advertising is a high
2 It is possibly the only way to sell large
3 It is hard to get noticed among the wide
4 Associating products with qualities like 'natural' is a definite
5 Modern audiences are well
6 The best adverts connect the brand
7 Many advertising
8 There's a marked

A range of products on our shelves.
B quantities of their products.
C contrast between the methods of TV and online advertising.
D aware of the tricks of advertising.
E to certain emotions.
F priority for many companies.
G plus.
H campaigns now feature online methods of advertising.

Test reference

Test overview

In the Speaking and writing part of the test each task must be completed within the individual time limits. The recording status box or timer on screen will let you know when to start recording and when to complete your response.

You will not be able to re-record or re-write any responses.

Part 1: Speaking and writing

Section	Task type	Task description	Time allowed
Section 1	Personal introduction	After reading the instructions, you have 30 seconds to give a recorded introduction about yourself. This part is not assessed but your response is sent to institutions you choose along with your score report.	1 minute
Section 2	Read aloud	A text appears on screen. Read the text aloud.	30–35 minutes
	Repeat sentence	After listening to a sentence, repeat the sentence.	
	Describe image	An image appears on screen. Describe the image in detail.	
	Re-tell lecture	After listening to or watching a video of a lecture, re-tell the lecture in your own words.	
	Answer short question	After listening to a question, answer with a single word or a few words.	
Sections 3–4	Summarize written text	After reading a passage, write a one-sentence summary of the passage of between 5 and 75 words.	20 minutes
Section 5	Summarize written text or Write essay	Either a Summarize written text task or a Write essay task, depending on the combination of tasks in your test.	10–20 minutes
Section 6	Write essay	Write an essay of 200–300 words on a given topic.	20 minutes

Part 2: Reading

Section	Task type	Task description	Time allowed
	Multiple-choice, choose single answer	After reading a text, answer a multiple-choice question on the content or tone of the text by selecting one response.	32–41 minutes
	Multiple-choice, choose multiple answers	After reading a text, answer a multiple-choice question on the content or tone of the text by selecting more than one response.	
	Re-order paragraphs	Several text boxes appear on screen in random order. Put the text boxes in the correct order.	
	Reading: Fill in the blanks	A text appears on screen with several blanks. Drag words or phrases from the blue box to fill in the blanks.	
	Reading & writing: Fill in the blanks	A text appears on screen with several blanks. Fill in the blanks by selecting words from several drop-down lists of response options.	

Test reference

Part 3: Listening

Section	Task type	Task description	Time allowed
Section 1	Summarize spoken text	After listening to a recording, write a summary of 50–70 words.	20–30 minutes
Section 2	Multiple-choice, choose multiple answers	After listening to a recording, answer a multiple-choice question on the content or tone of the recording by selecting more than one response.	23–28 minutes
	Fill in the blanks	The transcription of a recording appears on screen with several blanks. While listening to the recording, type the missing words into the blanks.	
	Highlight correct summary	After listening to a recording, select the paragraph that best summarises the recording.	
	Multiple-choice, choose single answer	After listening to a recording, answer a multiple-choice question on the content or tone of the recording by selecting one response.	
	Select missing word	After listening to a recording, select the missing word or group of words that completes the recording.	
	Highlight incorrect words	The transcription of a recording appears on screen. While listening to the recording, identify the words in the transcription that differ from what is said.	
	Write from dictation	After listening to a recording of a sentence, type the sentence.	

Part 1 Section 1: Personal introduction

Section 1 of the Speaking and writing part of PTE Academic (Part 1) begins with a personal introduction. You will *not* be assessed on this part of the test. However, your response will be recorded and will be sent along with your score report to any institutions you select as an additional security measure and so that they have a sample of your spoken English.

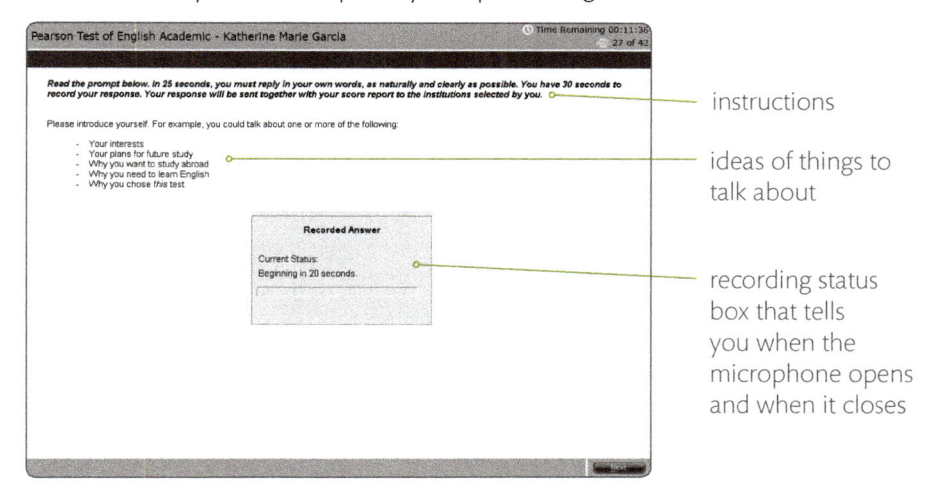

— instructions

— ideas of things to talk about

— recording status box that tells you when the microphone opens and when it closes

You will be asked to orally introduce yourself. You could talk about one or more of the following:

- your interests
- your plans for the future
- why you want to study English
- why you need to learn English
- why you chose PTE Academic

You will have 25 seconds to read the prompt and then 30 seconds to record your response.

Part 1 Section 2: Speaking

Section 2 of the Speaking and writing part of PTE Academic (Part 1) tests your ability to produce spoken English in an academic environment. The total time for Part 1 Section 2 is 30–35 minutes, depending on the combination of items in a given test. Speaking tasks are timed individually. You will need to manage your own time but can refer to the timer in the upper right-hand corner of the computer screen ('Time Remaining'), which counts down the time remaining for the speaking section.

Test reference

Read aloud

In this part of the Speaking section you will see a short text on the screen. You will be given either 30, 35 or 40 seconds to read it before the computer starts recording you. You will have the same amount of time again for the recording. When the computer starts recording, you must read the text aloud. You will do 6–7 *Read aloud* tasks.

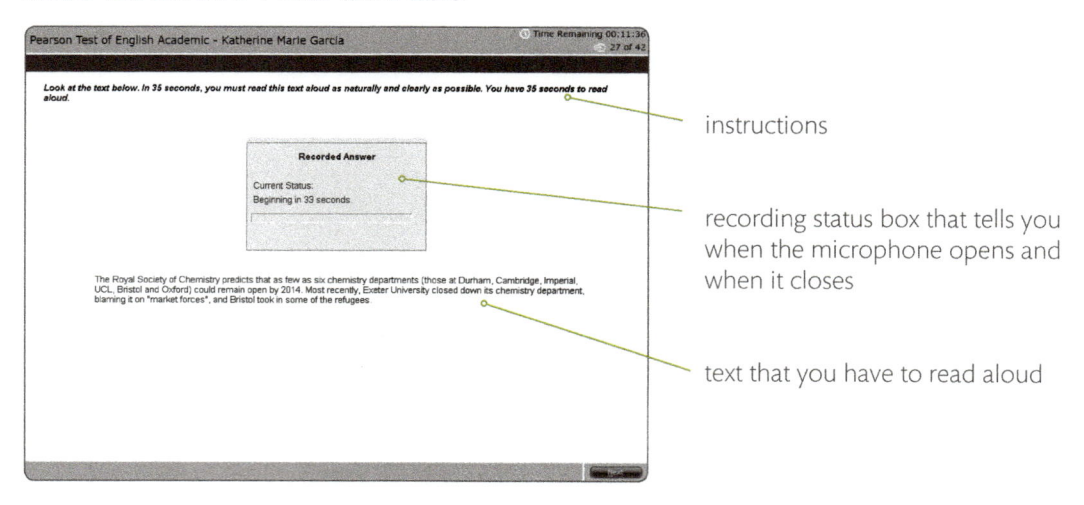

instructions

recording status box that tells you when the microphone opens and when it closes

text that you have to read aloud

EXPERT STRATEGIES

Before you speak

1 Read the text before the microphone opens. These tasks aim to test your understanding of the text. If you understand the content of the text, you'll find it easier to use stress and intonation to help express meaning.
2 Try to guess the pronunciation of any unknown words.

While you speak

3 Imagine that you are speaking to an audience. Speak clearly, at normal speed and volume. If you speak too quietly or too quickly, it might be difficult to assess your speech.
4 Use punctuation to help you identify places for brief, natural pauses. Keep your mind on meaning but pay attention to your stress and rhythm as well as pronunciation of sounds and smooth transitions between words.
5 If you make a mistake, don't go back and correct yourself. Just keep going. You will not be able to re-record anything.

> **Notes from the test developers**
> - Do not pause for more than two seconds. After three seconds, the recording stops and you cannot re-open the microphone.
> - To get a good score, your response must include all the words in the text and you must say them with good pronunciation and fluency.
> - These tasks contribute to your reading, speaking, pronunciation and oral fluency scores.

Repeat sentence

In this part of the Speaking section you will hear a sentence of between three and nine seconds in length, which you must repeat into the microphone within 15 seconds. You will do 10–12 *Repeat sentence* tasks.

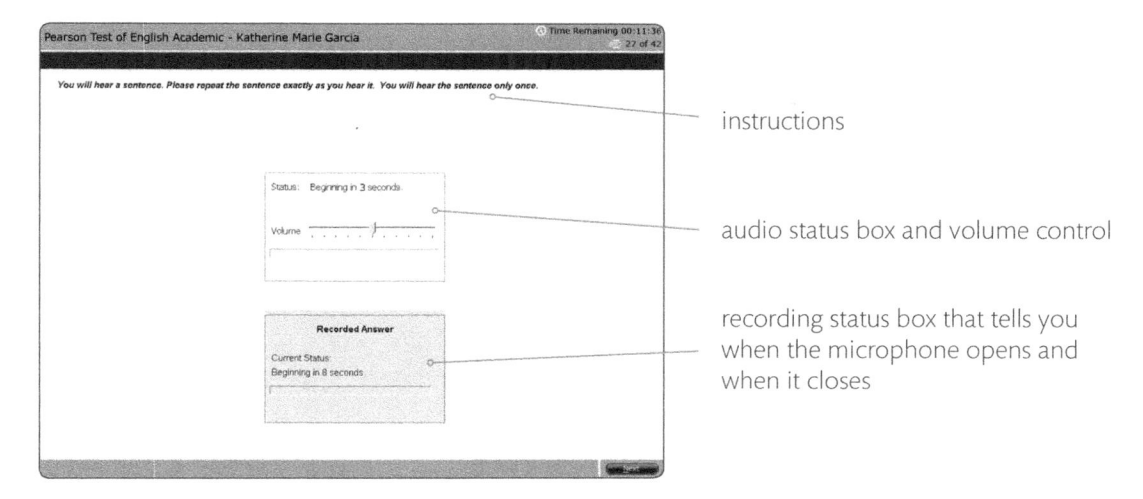

- instructions
- audio status box and volume control
- recording status box that tells you when the microphone opens and when it closes

EXPERT STRATEGIES

While you listen

1 Listen very carefully. Try to understand the meaning as this will help you to remember the words. Note down key words but only if it helps you.
2 Pay attention to the sentence stress and rhythm.

While you speak

3 Start speaking as soon as possible after the one-second pause.
4 Imagine you are speaking to another person in the room. This will help you to say the sentence clearly, naturally and at normal speed and volume. You have 15 seconds to repeat the sentence, so you do not need to speak quickly. If you speak too quietly or too quickly, it might be difficult to assess your speech.
5 Keep your mind on meaning but try to copy the sentence stress and rhythm of the speaker. However, do not try to copy their accent – use your own pronunciation of the words. Also pay attention to your pronunciation of sounds and linking between words.
6 Attempt any unknown words – you could be right!
7 If you make a mistake, don't go back and correct yourself. Just keep going. You will not be able to re-record your sentence.

> **Notes from the test developers**
> - After you hear the sentence, you will have just one second before you must repeat it.
> - Do not pause for more than two seconds. After three seconds, the recording stops and you cannot re-open the microphone.
> - To get a good score, you must repeat the words in the correct sequence and with good pronunciation and fluency.
> - These tasks contribute to your listening, speaking, pronunciation and oral fluency scores.

Test reference

Describe image

In this part of the Speaking section you will see an image such as a graph or diagram on the screen. You will have 25 seconds to look at it and try to understand it. The computer will then record you for 40 seconds as you describe the image. You will do 6–7 *Describe image* tasks.

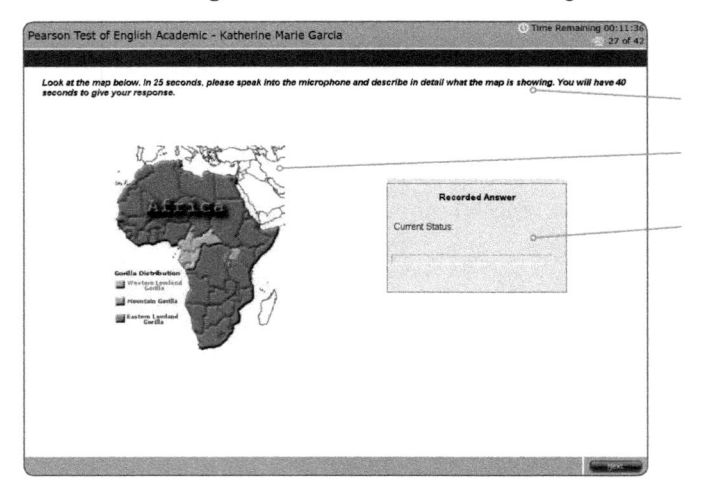

- instructions
- image that you have to describe
- recording status box that tells you when the microphone opens and when it closes

EXPERT STRATEGIES

Before you speak

1 Study the image and take short notes if you need to.
2 Check that you understand what the image shows. Read the title, sub-title and any headings or labels.
3 Make sure you know what is being measured (e.g. kilos, US$, millions, kilometres, years).
4 Consider what we can learn from the image. What is the most important information in it?

While you speak

5 Start speaking clearly, at normal speed and volume. If you speak too quietly or too quickly, it may be difficult to assess your answer.
6 Describe what the image shows, the main information, the details and then summarise your ideas.
7 Do not repeat information. Describe all the main points and support them with details (numbers, etc.). Give a conclusion or an implication.
8 Do not go back and correct yourself.
9 Try to use a range of language – show off what you can do! Also pay attention to your stress and rhythm, as well as pronunciation of sounds and smooth transitions between words.

> **Notes from the test developers**
> - Do not pause for more than two seconds. After three seconds, the recording stops and you cannot re-open the microphone.
> - To get a good score, you need to describe the key aspects of the image accurately, linking your ideas well. You also need to speak with good pronunciation and fluency.
> - These tasks contribute to your speaking, pronunciation and oral fluency scores.

Re-tell lecture

In this part of the Speaking section you are tested on both your listening and speaking skills. You will hear a lecture or watch a video on an academic subject. You will then have ten seconds to review your notes before you re-tell the key points of the lecture in 40 seconds or less. You will do 3–4 *Re-tell lecture* tasks.

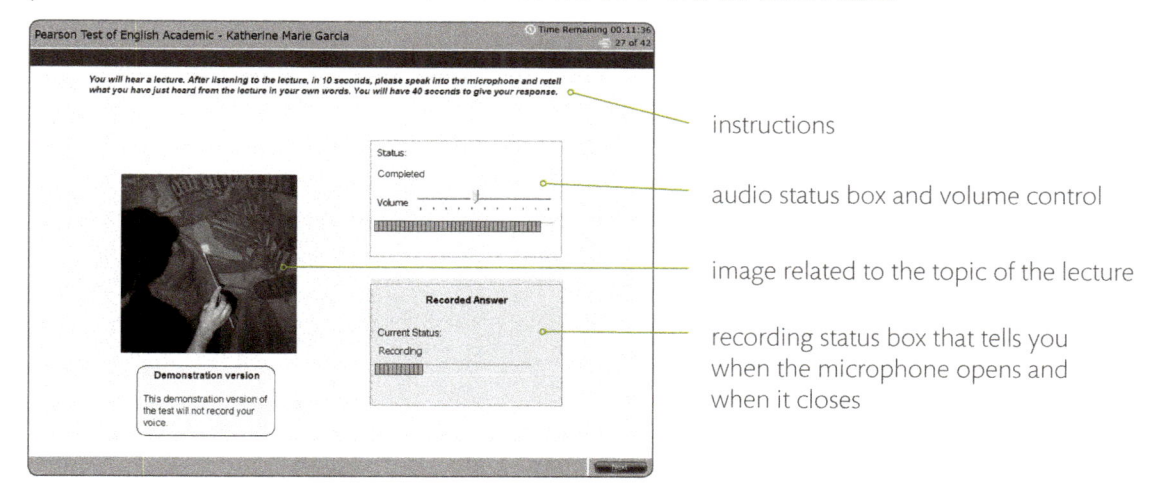

- instructions
- audio status box and volume control
- image related to the topic of the lecture
- recording status box that tells you when the microphone opens and when it closes

EXPERT STRATEGIES

While you listen

1 Listen carefully to the content of the lecture from the beginning to the end, as the speaker may repeat points or add important points.

2 Take notes on the Erasable Noteboard Booklet as you listen. Write down the key words and phrases only. Using symbols and abbreviations can help.

Before you speak

3 Use the ten seconds to review your notes and plan what you are going to say; pick out the main points.

4 Decide how to organise the information.

While you speak

5 Imagine you are speaking to a classmate to help you to speak clearly and naturally. If you speak too quietly or too quickly, it may be difficult to assess your answer.

6 Re-tell the main points using your notes. Organise this information as logically as possible. Start with a topic sentence or introductory phrase and then give supporting points. Include a conclusion or implication.

7 Avoid repeating information.

8 Keep an eye on the time remaining; try to get to all the important points before time runs out.

9 Try to use a range of language – show off what you can do! Also, pay attention to your stress and rhythm, as well as pronunciation of sounds and smooth transitions between words.

Notes from the test developers

- Do not pause for more than two seconds. After three seconds, the recording stops and you cannot re-open the microphone.
- To get a good score, you need to re-tell the main points of the lecture accurately and speak with good pronunciation and fluency.
- These tasks contribute to your listening, speaking, pronunciation and oral fluency scores.

Test reference

Answer short question

In this part of the Speaking section you will hear a question which you need to answer. The answer will be short (usually one or a very small number of words) and you will have ten seconds to answer it. You will do 10–12 *Answer short question* tasks.

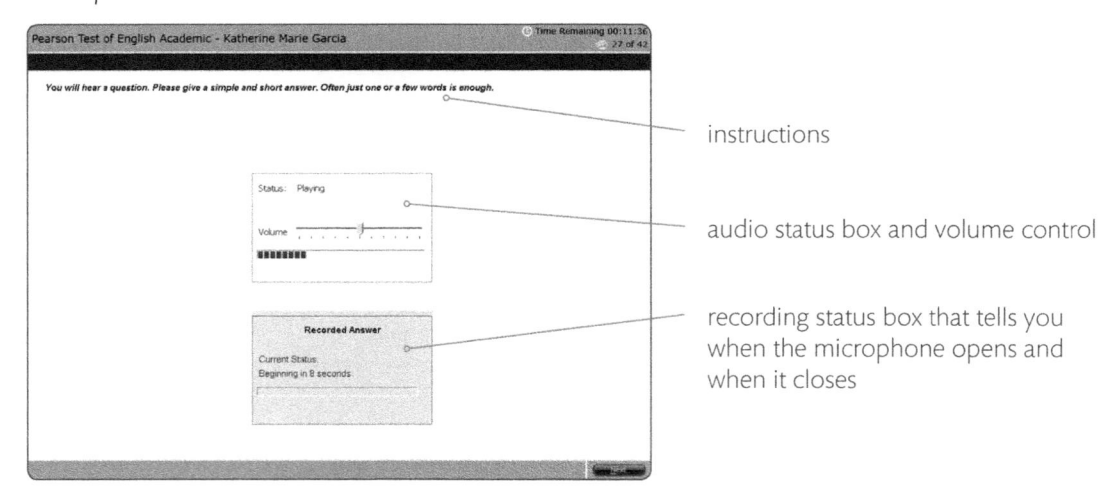

- instructions
- audio status box and volume control
- recording status box that tells you when the microphone opens and when it closes

EXPERT STRATEGIES

While you listen

1 Listen carefully to the question and decide what kind of information you need (e.g. a word to match a definition, an opposite, a phrase).

While you speak

2 Speak when the status bar changes to 'Recording'. This is not indicated by a tone.
3 Speak clearly, at normal speed and volume. If you speak too quietly or too quickly, it may be difficult to assess your answer.
4 Just give one word or one phrase as an answer. There is no need to say anything more.

Notes from the test developers

- Do not pause for more than two seconds. After three seconds, the recording stops and you cannot re-open the microphone.
- Save time on the test: once you have given an answer, click on 'Next' and move on to the next question.
- Do not waste time giving full answers. If the answer is *cat, a cat, the cat, a cat does* or *it's a cat* will all be considered correct answers and will score the same.
- You do not need any special knowledge for these questions – they test your English, not your general knowledge.
- These tasks contribute to your listening and speaking scores. Pronunciation is not scored here.

Part 1 Sections 3–6: Writing

Sections 3–6 of the Speaking and writing part of PTE Academic (Part 1) test your ability to produce written English in an academic environment.

The total time for Part 1 Sections 3–6 is 50–60 minutes, depending on the combination of items in a given test. Writing tasks are individually timed and you can refer to the timer in the upper right-hand corner of the computer screen ('Time Remaining'), which counts down the time remaining for each writing task.

Summarize written text

In this Writing section, both your reading and writing skills are tested. You will have ten minutes to read a text and summarise it in the response box in one sentence. You will do 2–3 *Summarize written text* tasks. Each text is up to 300 words long.

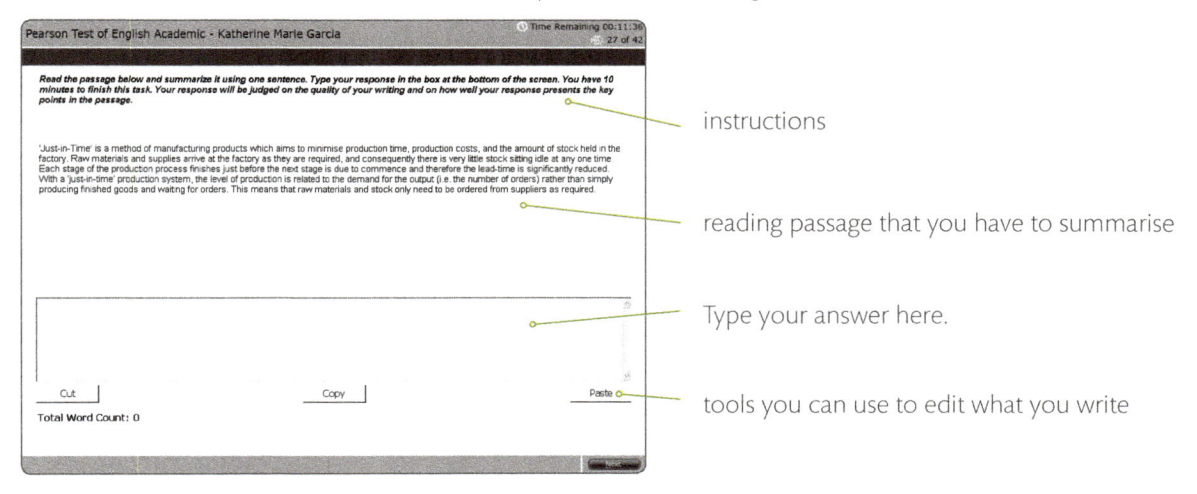

instructions

reading passage that you have to summarise

Type your answer here.

tools you can use to edit what you write

EXPERT STRATEGIES

Before you read

1. Read the instructions carefully as they will explain what you have to do.
2. Get your pen and Erasable Noteboard Booklet ready.

While you read

3. Pick out the topic sentences and take notes of the key words. Using symbols and acronyms will help you keep your notes short.

After you read

4. Review the topic sentences and/or your notes and identify the main ideas and supporting points given in the passage.
5. Type your one-sentence summary into the response box. Use the topic sentence(s) where possible, as these give the main idea, but use your own words as much as possible. Grammatical structures such as relative clauses and prepositional phrases can be very useful for fitting several ideas into one sentence.
6. Re-read your summary carefully. Check that the content covers the main points. Check your grammar, vocabulary and spelling carefully.
7. Make sure your summary is no more than one sentence long and no more than 75 words. Look at the bottom left of the response box for the word count.
8. If you find it difficult to put all the main points into one sentence, consider using two related sentences with a semi-colon between them. This is acceptable.
9. You don't get extra marks for long answers – don't use more words than necessary.

Notes from the test developers
- To get a high score, you need to include the key points of the passage and use correct grammar, vocabulary, punctuation and spelling. Do not, for example, type everything in capital letters as this will badly affect your score.
- If your summary is more than one sentence long, less than five words long or more than 75 words long, you will lose marks. Good answers are generally much shorter than 75 words.
- These tasks contribute to your reading, writing, grammar and vocabulary scores.

Write essay

In this Writing section, you are tested on your ability to write an essay on a given topic. You will have 20 minutes to plan, write and revise your essay. You MUST write between 200 and 300 words. You will do 1 or 2 *Write essay* tasks.

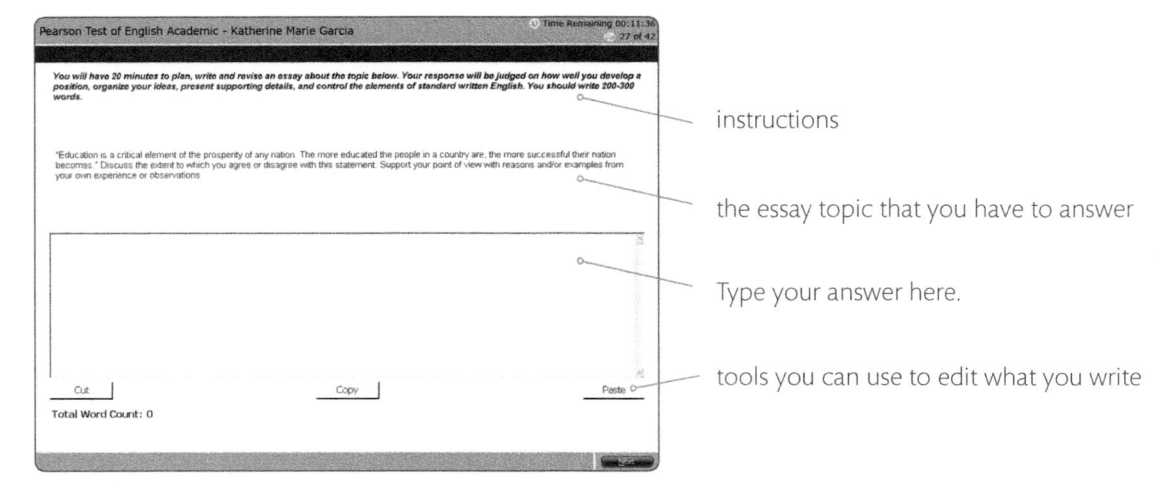

- instructions
- the essay topic that you have to answer
- Type your answer here.
- tools you can use to edit what you write

EXPERT STRATEGIES

Before you write

1. Read the essay task carefully. Make sure you understand what you have to do (e.g. agree or disagree, describe a situation, discuss advantages or disadvantages).
2. Guess the meaning of any unknown words in the task. A key idea may be restated.
3. Plan the content of your essay. Use your Erasable Noteboard Booklet to note down any helpful ideas, words or phrases, or type these straight into the response box, then plan the paragraphs and order of your ideas. Think especially about ideas that support your opinion. Check that your plan answers the question before you start to type.
4. Check the timer. Plan how much time you will need to write to be able to allow a few minutes at the end to check for errors.

While you write

5. Write quickly, watching the timer and the word count while you write. Make sure you write from your plan, to help you structure your essay well. You can write in any order – some people like to write the introduction after writing the body paragraphs.
6. Try to use a range of language – show off what you can do! Make sure the ideas in your essay are closely related to the prompt but don't copy large parts of the prompt.

After you write

7. Read your essay and check for the following: relevant content; a clear introduction; a clear conclusion; that new ideas are introduced in new paragraphs; that all ideas are developed with examples and details; that the connections between sentences and paragraphs are clear; that there is a variety of words and phrases.
8. Check the total word count, the grammar, the punctuation and the spelling, and make corrections where necessary.

Notes from the test developers

- If your essay is fewer than 200 words or more than 300 words, you will lose marks.
- To get a high score, you need to answer the question, giving details and examples to support your opinions. You will need to organise your ideas well, connect them smoothly and show a good range and control of language. Use correct grammar, vocabulary, punctuation and spelling. Do not type everything in capital letters.
- These tasks contribute to your writing, grammar, spelling, vocabulary and written discourse scores (your written discourse score comes only from *Write essay* tasks).

Part 2: Reading

Part 2: Reading of PTE Academic tests your ability to understand written English in an academic environment.

The total time for Part 2 is 32–41 minutes, depending on the combination of items in a given test. Reading items are not timed individually. You will need to manage your own time but can refer to the timer in the upper right-hand corner of the computer screen ('Time Remaining'), which counts down the time remaining for the Reading part.

Multiple-choice, choose single answer

In this reading task type you will read a text and then answer a multiple-choice question about it. There will be four options to choose from and only one is correct. You will do 2–3 *Multiple-choice, choose single answer* tasks.

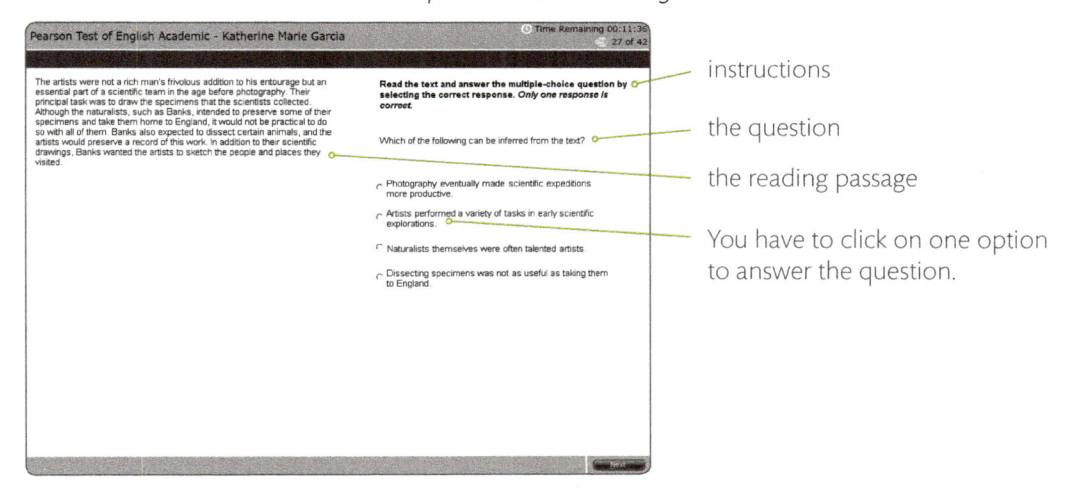

- instructions
- the question
- the reading passage
- You have to click on one option to answer the question.

EXPERT STRATEGIES

Before you read

1. Read the instructions carefully so you know how many options to choose.
2. Read the answer options quickly to give you an idea of the topic.

While you read

3. Read the text carefully. Try to understand the main point and supporting points. Think about the writer's purpose and attitude.
4. Try to guess the meaning of words you do not know by looking at the other words in the sentence – but only for words that are important to answer the question.
5. Do not choose an option just because it has words that appear in the text. Often, these options are incorrect.

After you read

6. When you think you have found the correct option, read the text again quickly to be sure you are correct.
7. Don't choose an option just because you heard some of the words in the recording. You need to make sure the whole idea is correct. Remember that ONLY ONE option will be correct.
8. If you're not sure of the answer, you can safely guess. You won't lose marks for guesses on these tasks.
9. Be mindful of the time and move on to the next task as quickly as you can.

> **Notes from the test developers**
> - This task type is scored as either correct or incorrect.
> - There is no timer for this task. When you have finished, click on 'Next' to go to the next task.
> - These tasks contribute to your reading score.

Test reference

Multiple-choice, choose multiple answers

In this reading task type, you will read a text and then answer a multiple-choice question about it. There will be between five and seven options to choose from and more than one option is correct. You will do 2-3 *Multiple-choice, choose multiple answers* tasks.

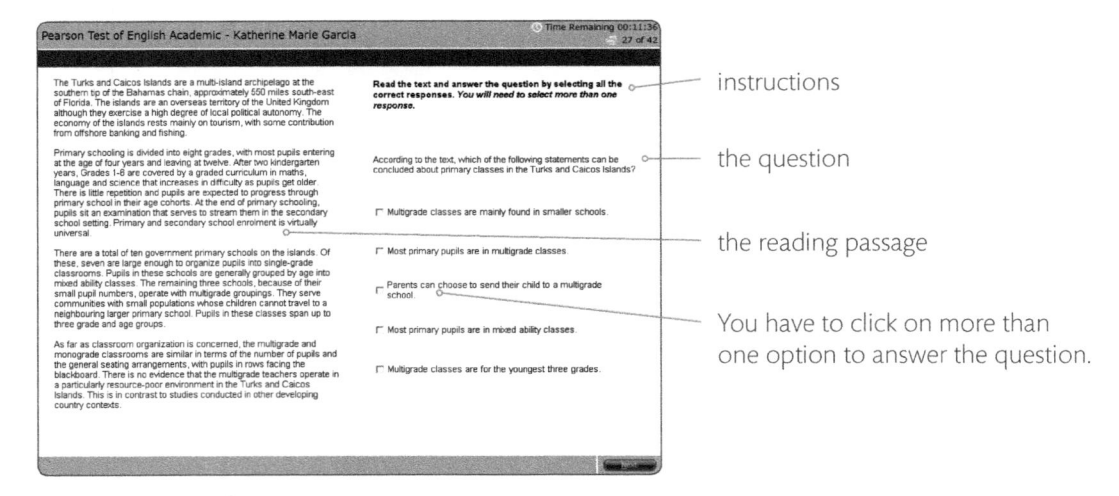

- instructions
- the question
- the reading passage
- You have to click on more than one option to answer the question.

EXPERT STRATEGIES

Before you read

1 Read the instructions carefully so you know that you should choose more than one response option.
2 Read the response options quickly. Try to decide what the question is asking for (e.g. main idea, inference, detailed information or writer's purpose).

While you read

3 Read the text carefully. Try to understand the main point and supporting points.
4 Try to guess the meaning of words you do not know by looking at the other words in the sentence – but only for words that are important to answer the question.
5 Do not choose an option just because it has words that appear in the text. Often, these options are incorrect.

After you read

6 Work through the options one by one. Try to decide whether each is correct or incorrect.
7 When you think you have found one of the correct options, read the text again quickly to be sure you are correct. You may have to read some parts of the text several times – this is normal. It can help to scan for points mentioned in the options and read in detail around this place.
8 Don't make guesses; on these tasks (unlike most) you lose a point for each incorrect answer.
9 Be mindful of the time and move on to the next task as quickly as you can.

> **Notes from the test developers**
> - You get one point for each correct response but will lose a point for each response you choose incorrectly.
> - There is no timer for this task. When you have finished, click on 'Next' to go to the next task.
> - This task contributes to your reading score.

Re-order paragraphs

In this reading task type you will see a paragraph consisting of sentences in an incorrect order. It will be divided into four or five text boxes and you must put them into the correct order. You will do 2–3 *Re-order paragraphs* tasks.

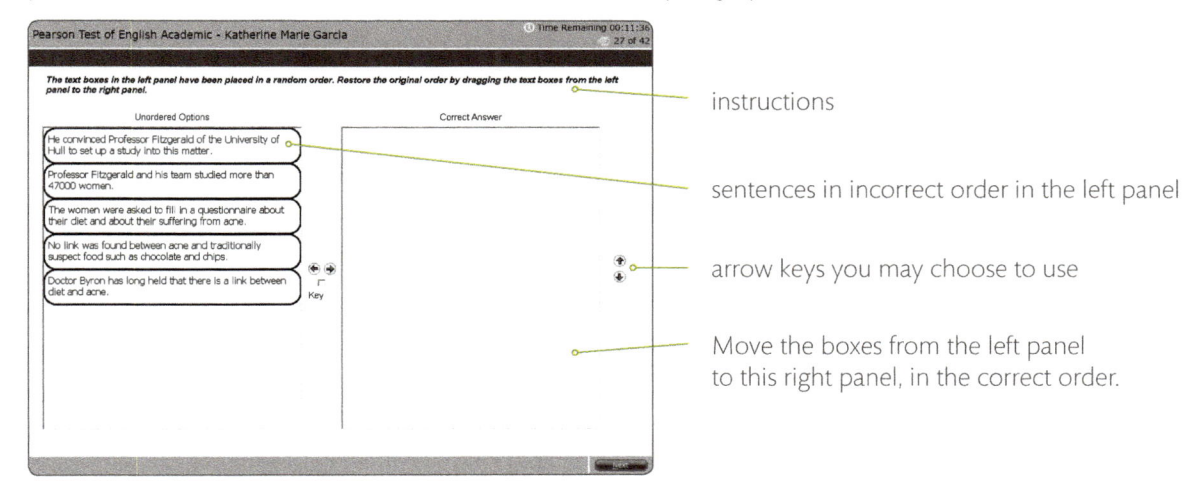

— instructions

— sentences in incorrect order in the left panel

— arrow keys you may choose to use

— Move the boxes from the left panel to this right panel, in the correct order.

EXPERT STRATEGIES

Before you read
1. Read the instructions carefully.
2. Quickly skim-read the text in the text boxes to get an idea of the topic. Look for repeated words or synonyms to help you understand the topic.

While you read
3. Read each text box carefully.
4. Look for the first sentence, which is usually the most general. This is unlikely to start with a pronoun or a linking word or phrase. It will probably be the topic sentence and will introduce the main idea.
5. Look at the pronouns in the text and think about what they refer to. This can help you to connect the sentences.
6. Look at the discourse markers, including linking words, and think about how they join the ideas in the sentences.
7. Look at the use of the definite article (*the*). If a noun is accompanied by *the*, it might not be the first time it has been introduced in the text.
8. Think about the meaning of each sentence and how the ideas fit together.

After you read
9. Drag the text boxes on the left into the correct order on the right of the screen.
10. Read the text from beginning to end carefully in your chosen order, to make sure it makes sense. You can move the paragraphs around if you change your mind, so don't be afraid to experiment.

Notes from the test developers
- In this task type you are being tested on your understanding of how texts are organised.
- To get a full score, you must re-order the text boxes correctly. If you order some of them incorrectly, you will get a partial score.
- There is no timer for this task. When you have finished, click on 'Next' to go to the next task.
- These tasks contribute to your reading score.

Test reference

Reading: Fill in the blanks

In this reading task type, you will read a text of up to 80 words in length. There will be three, four or five words missing. The missing words will sit in a blue box under the text. You will have to drag the missing words to the correct blank in the text. You will do 4–5 *Reading: Fill in the blanks* tasks.

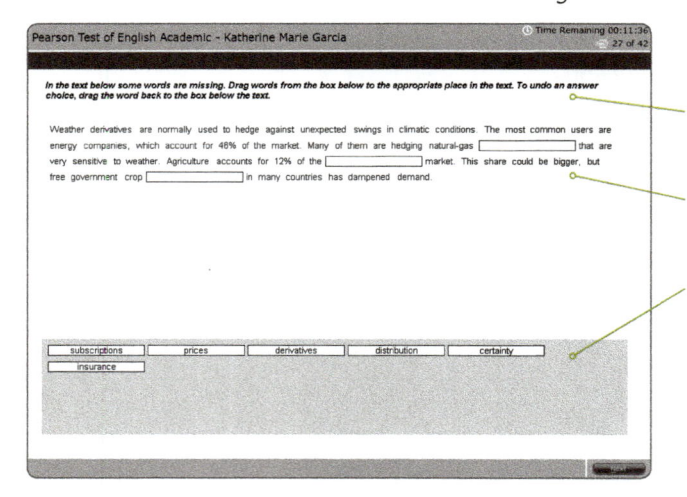

- instructions
- text with missing words
- You have to select words from this box and drag them to the blanks in the text above.

EXPERT STRATEGIES

While you read

1 Read the text quickly to understand the general topic. Ignore the blanks for now.
2 Read the text more carefully. When you arrive at each blank, try to find the missing word in the box.
3 Think carefully about the meaning of the word that is missing. For example, is it a positive word or does it have a negative meaning? Is it a linker showing the cause or effect of an action?
4 Pay attention to the type of word that is missing. For example, is it a pronoun? Is it a verb in a past tense?
5 Think about the grammar of the word. For example, is it a verb which needs a third person -s? Is it a plural noun?
6 Look at the words on both sides of the blank to find clues to help you. The missing word might be part of a collocation.

After you read

7 When you have filled all the blanks, read the text again to check that it makes sense. If not, adjust your answers.

> **Notes from the test developers**
> - There will be three words in the box that you do not need.
> - To get a full score, you must fill each blank with the correct word. If you fill just some of the blanks correctly, you will get a partial score.
> - There is no timer for this task. When you have finished, click on 'Next' to go to the next task.
> - These tasks contribute to your reading score.

Reading & writing: Fill in the blanks

In this reading task type, you will read a text of up to 300 words in length. There will be between four and five words missing. In each blank, there will be a drop-down menu with four options. You must click on the option you think fills the blank. You will do 5–6 *Reading & writing: Fill in the blanks* tasks.

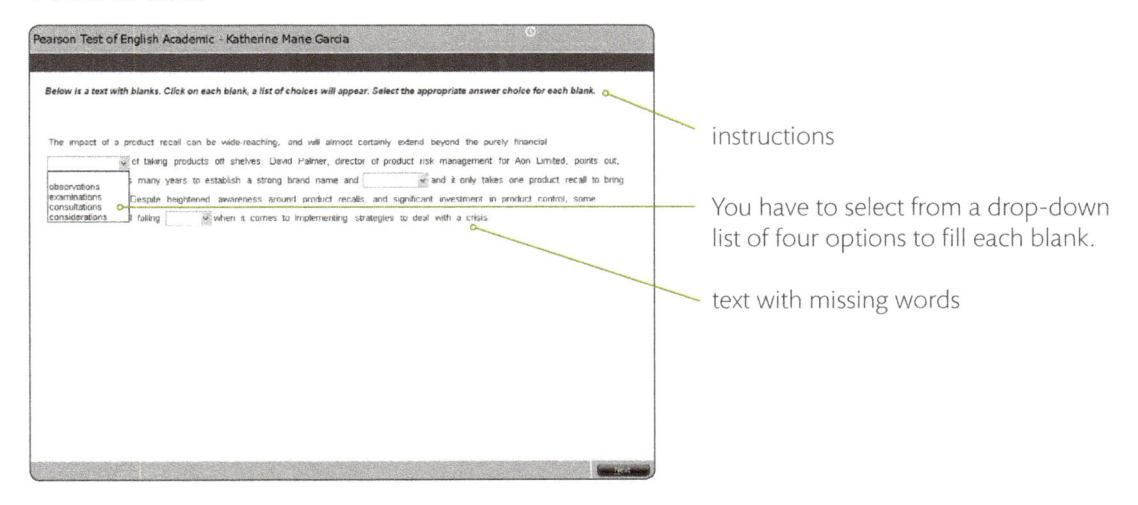

— instructions

— You have to select from a drop-down list of four options to fill each blank.

— text with missing words

EXPERT STRATEGIES

While you read

1 Read the text quickly to understand the general topic. Ignore the blanks for now.
2 Read the text more carefully. When you arrive at each blank, try to think about what word is missing. Look at the words around it and think about the meaning and grammar of the missing word. Is it positive or negative? Does it connect ideas? What type of word is it?
3 Look at the words on both sides of the blank for language clues to help you. For example, is there a preposition that fits one of the options? Does one option collocate better with the words around the blank than the others?

After you read

4 When you have chosen all of the words, read the text again to make sure it makes sense with the options you chose.

> **Notes from the test developers**
> - To get a full score, you must fill each blank with the correct word. If you fill just some of the blanks correctly, you will get a partial score.
> - There is no timer for this task. When you have finished, click on 'Next' to go to the next task.
> - These tasks contribute to your reading and writing scores.

Test reference

Part 3: Listening

Part 3: Listening of PTE Academic tests your ability to understand spoken English in an academic environment. It also tests your ability to understand a variety of accents, both native and non-native.

The total time to complete the Listening part of the test is 45–57 minutes, depending on the combination of items in a given test. Some of the items are integrated and assess both listening as well as reading and writing skills.

With the exception of *Summarize spoken text*, the listening task types are not timed individually. You will need to manage your time yourself but can refer to the timer in the upper right-hand corner of the computer screen ('Time remaining'), which counts down the amount of time remaining in the listening part.

Summarize spoken text

This task type tests both your listening and writing skills. You will have 12 seconds to read the instructions before a recording of between 60 and 90 seconds is played. You will then have ten minutes to type your summary into a response box. The summary should be between 50 and 70 words. You will do 2–3 *Summarize spoken text* tasks.

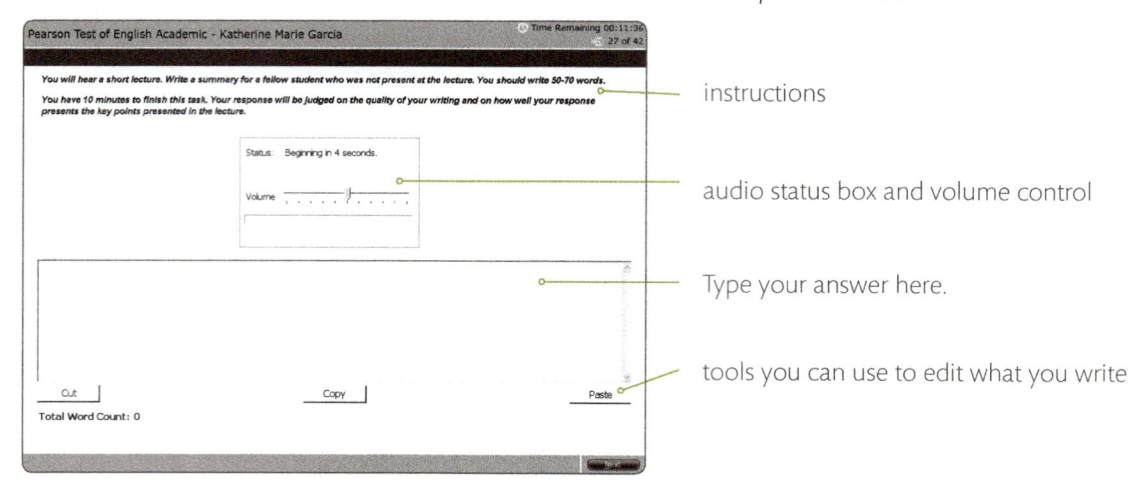

- instructions
- audio status box and volume control
- Type your answer here.
- tools you can use to edit what you write

EXPERT STRATEGIES

Before you listen
1. Read the instructions carefully.
2. Get your pen and the Erasable Noteboard Booklet ready.

While you listen
3. Listen carefully to the key points of the recording – the main idea is usually mentioned near the beginning. Often, small details stand out clearly and it's easy to get distracted by them – try to avoid this.
4. Take notes of the key words. Use symbols and abbreviations as appropriate.

After listening
5. Review your notes and identify the main ideas and supporting points given in the recording.
6. Type your summary into the response box. Start with a sentence that gives the main idea followed by two or three supporting points.
7. Re-read your summary carefully. Check that the content covers the main points. Check your grammar, vocabulary, spelling and punctuation carefully.
8. Make sure that your summary is between 50 and 70 words. Look at the bottom left of the response box for the word count.
9. Try to use a range of language.

Notes from the test developers
- The recordings are between 60 and 90 seconds.
- To score well, you need to include the key points of the recording and use correct grammar, vocabulary, punctuation and spelling. Don't type everything in capital letters.
- If your summary is less than 50 words or more than 70, you will lose marks.
- These tasks contribute to your writing, listening, grammar, spelling and vocabulary scores.

Multiple-choice, choose multiple answers

In this listening task type you will listen to a short recording or watch a short video on an academic subject and choose the correct options to a question. You must select more than one option. You will do 2–3 *Multiple-choice, choose multiple answers* tasks.

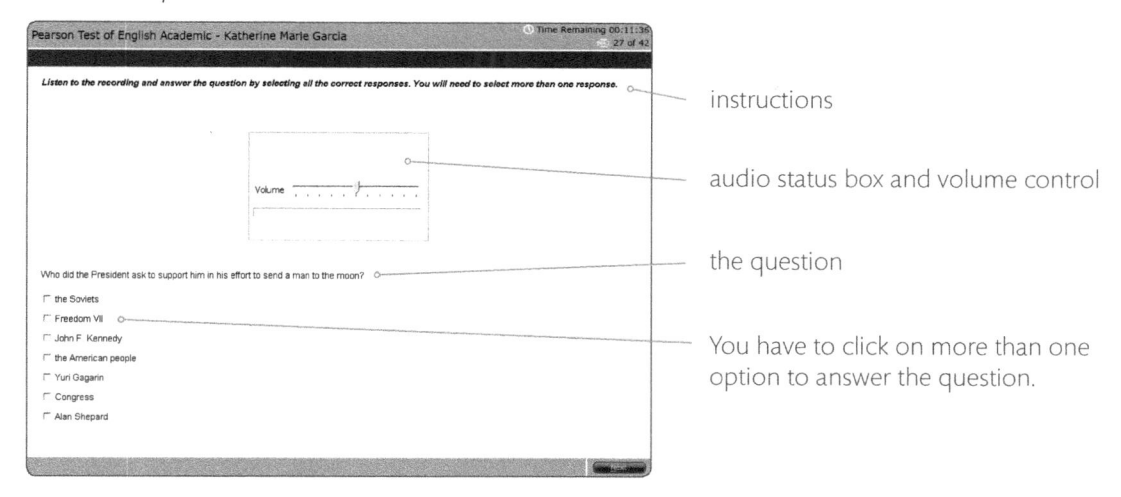

— instructions

— audio status box and volume control

— the question

— You have to click on more than one option to answer the question.

EXPERT STRATEGIES

Before you listen

1. Read the question and skim the options before the recording begins so that you know what you are listening for.
2. Get your pen and the Erasable Noteboard Booklet ready.

While you listen

3. Take notes on the Erasable Noteboard Booklet. Focus on the key words and main points. Don't try to write too much or you may miss important points. You can use symbols and abbreviations to help you take notes quickly.
4. A picture or video may be displayed while the sound is playing. This can give you additional clues about the topic.
5. Continue listening and taking notes until the end of the recording, even if you think you have the information you need. Sometimes speakers change what they say or add new information at the end.

After listening

6. Re-read the question and the options carefully.
7. Begin by deciding which answers are definitely incorrect. Then re-read the ones which remain, to see which best match the notes you have taken.
8. Don't choose an option just because you heard some of the words in the recording. You need to make sure the whole idea is correct. Remember that more than one option will be correct.
9. Don't change your first answers unless you are sure they are incorrect. Don't make guesses; on these tasks (unlike most), you lose a point for each incorrect answer.

Notes from the test developers
- You have just seven seconds to read the question before the recording starts.
- You get one point for each correct response but lose a point for each response you choose incorrectly.
- There is no timer for this task. When you have finished, click on 'Next' to go to the next task.
- These tasks contribute to your listening score.

Test reference

Fill in the blanks

In this listening task type you are tested on your ability to listen for specific words in a recording and write them correctly. You are given a short text with between four and six words missing. You listen to a recording and type the missing words into the blanks. You will do 2–3 *Fill in the blanks* tasks.

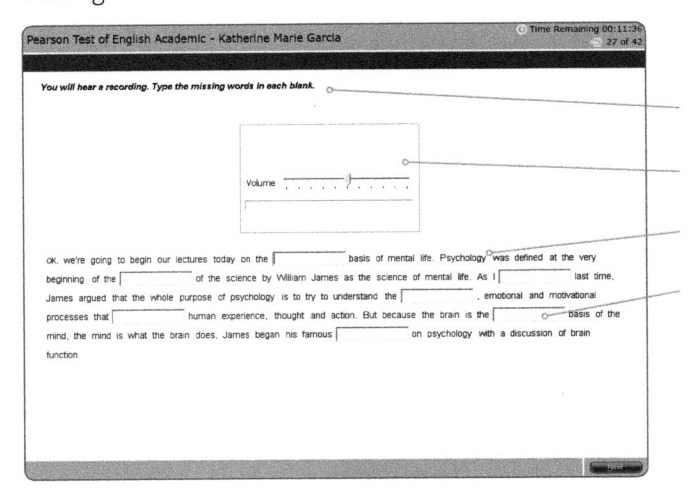

- instructions
- audio status box and volume control
- transcription of the recording with missing words
- Write the missing word you hear in each blank.

EXPERT STRATEGIES

Before you listen

1. Read the text quickly to get an idea of the topic. You won't have time to read every word at this point but try to skim to the end – or at least as far as you can.
2. Put your cursor in the first blank so you are ready to type or get your pen and Erasable Noteboard Booklet ready.

While you listen

3. Follow the text with the cursor as you listen to the recording.
4. Type the missing words into the blanks and then move your cursor to the next gap. If you are not a fast typist, write the words down on the Erasable Noteboard Booklet. Try not to take your eyes away from the text for too long if possible.

After listening

5. If you wrote the words down on the Erasable Noteboard Booklet, type them into the blanks.
6. Check you have typed the words correctly. Check the spelling and that you have used the correct form. For example, is the word singular or plural? Does the verb need an *-s* at the end? Make any necessary changes.
7. Read the whole text again to make sure that the words you chose make sense in the context.

> **Notes from the test developers**
> - You have just seven seconds to read the question before the recording starts.
> - You can take a little time to check your answers once the recording has finished but be mindful of the overall time remaining for this part of the test.
> - To get a full score, you must fill each blank with the correct word. If you fill just some blanks correctly, you will get a partial score.
> - Use the mouse to move from blank to blank: keys such as the tab key don't do this.
> - These tasks contribute to your listening and writing scores.

Highlight correct summary

In this listening task type you are tested on both your listening and reading skills. You will listen to a short recording or video on an academic subject and choose the most appropriate summary from a choice of four. You will do 2-3 *Highlight correct summary* tasks.

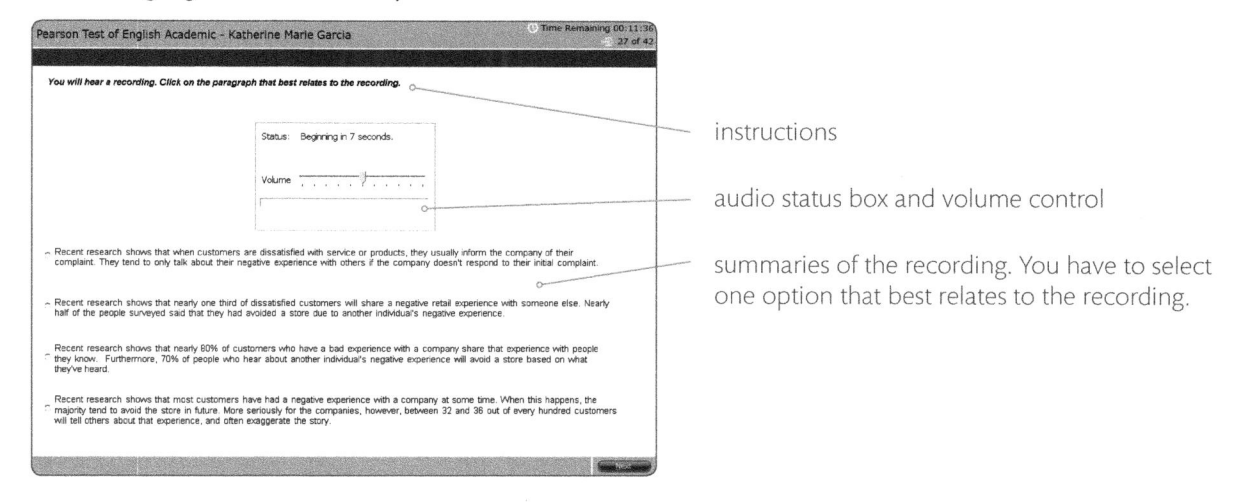

— instructions

— audio status box and volume control

— summaries of the recording. You have to select one option that best relates to the recording.

EXPERT STRATEGIES

Before you listen

1 Quickly skim the four summary options as this will give you an idea of the topic but do not read them carefully – you will not have time.

While you listen

2 Listen carefully from beginning to end as the speaker may repeat information or add new information. Think about what the main ideas are.
3 Take notes using the Erasable Noteboard Booklet. Note down the key words or phrases. Use abbreviations and symbols if they help you.

After listening

4 Read each summary and think about the differences between them.
5 Use your notes to help you to choose the option that best summarises what you heard. Rule out summaries which include incorrect information or information that was not included in the talk. Also rule out any summary which focuses on information that you heard but was not the main point of the talk.
6 If you are not sure, make a guess – you may be right!

> **Notes from the test developers**
> - You have ten seconds to read the question before the recording starts.
> - This task type is scored as correct or incorrect only.
> - There is no timer for this task. When you have finished, click on 'Next' to go to the next task.
> - These tasks contribute to your listening and reading scores.

Test reference

Multiple-choice, choose single answer

In this listening task type you will listen to a short recording or watch a short video on an academic subject and choose ONE correct answer to a question from a choice of four options. You will do 2–3 *Multiple-choice, choose single answer* tasks.

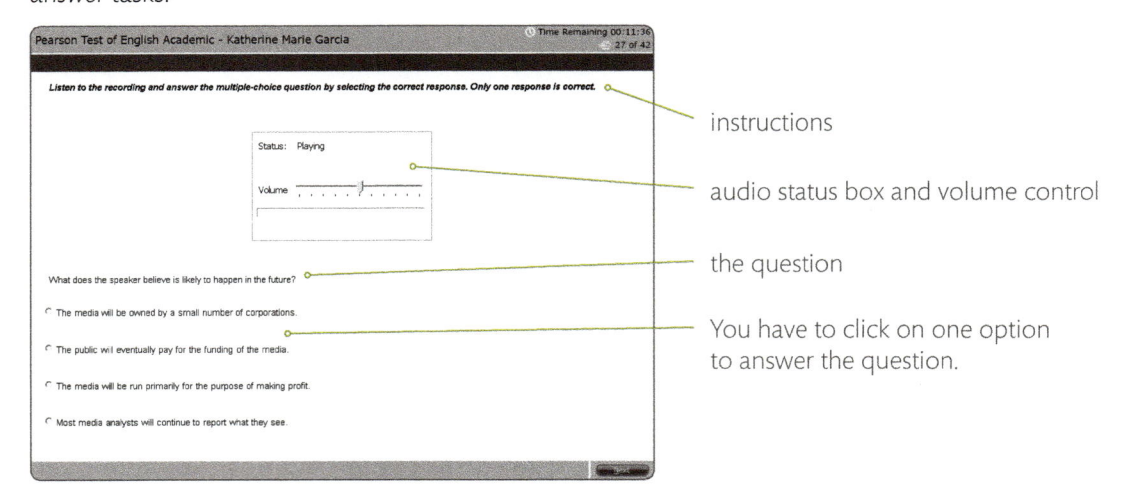

- instructions
- audio status box and volume control
- the question
- You have to click on one option to answer the question.

EXPERT STRATEGIES

Before you listen
1 Read the prompt carefully so that you know what you are listening for.

While you listen
2 Take notes on the Erasable Noteboard Booklet. Focus on the key words and main points. Don't try to write too much or you may miss important points.
3 A picture or video may be displayed while the sound is playing. This can give you additional clues about the topic.
4 Continue listening and taking notes until the end of the recording, even if you think you have the information you need. Sometimes speakers change what they say or add new information at the end.

After listening
5 Re-read the question and the options carefully.
6 Begin by deciding which answers are definitely incorrect. Then re-read the ones which remain to see which best match your notes.
7 Don't choose an option just because you heard some of the words in the recording. You need to make sure the whole idea is correct. Remember that ONLY ONE option will be correct.
8 Don't change your first answer unless you are sure that it is incorrect. If you're not sure of the answer, you can safely guess. You won't lose marks for guesses on these tasks.

> **Notes from the test developers**
> - You have just five seconds to read the question before the recording starts.
> - This task type is scored as correct or incorrect only.
> - There is no timer for this task. When you have finished, click on 'Next' to go to the next task.
> - These tasks contribute to your listening score.

Select missing word

In this listening task type you will listen to a short recording or watch a short video on an academic subject. At the end of the final sentence, there will be a missing word or phrase that is replaced by a beep. You will select the missing word or phrase from a choice of three to five options. You will do 2-3 *Select missing word* tasks. These tasks test your ability to infer the final words from the points that the lecturer makes.

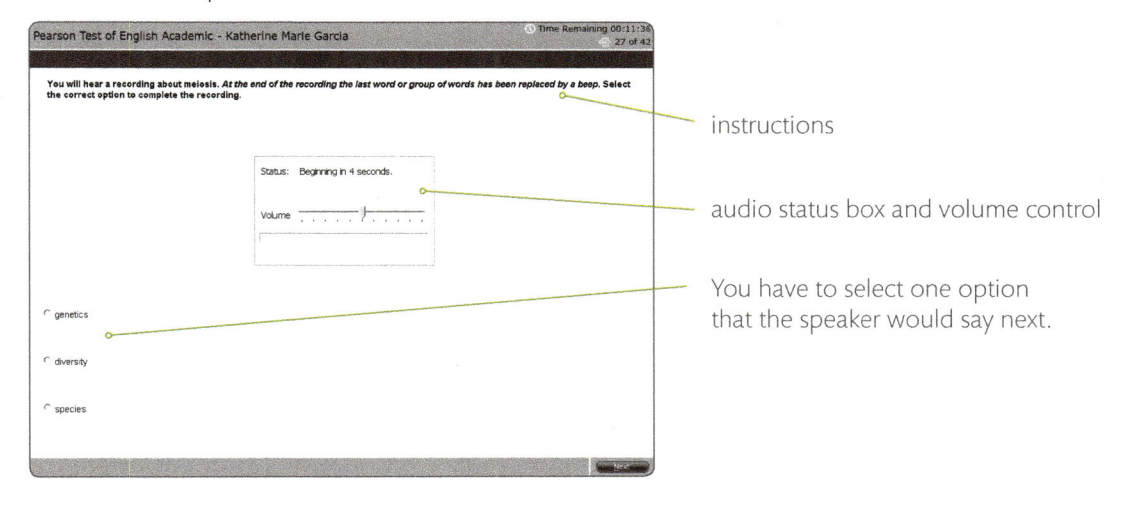

- instructions
- audio status box and volume control
- You have to select one option that the speaker would say next.

EXPERT STRATEGIES

Before you listen

1 The instructions tell you what general topic the speaker is going to talk about. Read the topic, then quickly skim-read the options as these will give you further clues.

While you listen

2 Listen carefully to the speaker and follow his or her ideas. Make sure you listen from the beginning to the end of the talk or you may miss the final sentence. Do not spend time worrying about words you have not understood. Try to understand the general idea and the main points, and try to follow the relationships between ideas.

3 While listening, try to decide which options are more or less likely.

4 Look at the timer on the screen as this will help you to know when the talk is going to end.

After listening

5 Read the options – there will be between three and five. If there is one that matches your idea, this could be the correct answer.

6 Once you have chosen your answer, make sure that it fits the meaning of the sentence and talk.

7 If you are not sure of the answer, make a guess from amongst the most likely options – you could be right!

> **Notes from the test developers**
> - You have just seven seconds to read the topic in the question and the options before the recording starts.
> - This task type is scored as correct or incorrect only. There is no penalty for guessing.
> - There is no timer for this task. When you have finished, click on 'Next' to go to the next task.
> - This task contributes to your listening score.

Highlight incorrect words

In this listening task type you are tested on your ability to listen to and read a text at the same time. As you read and listen, you must highlight up to seven words which are different from the recording. You will do 2–3 *Highlight incorrect words* tasks.

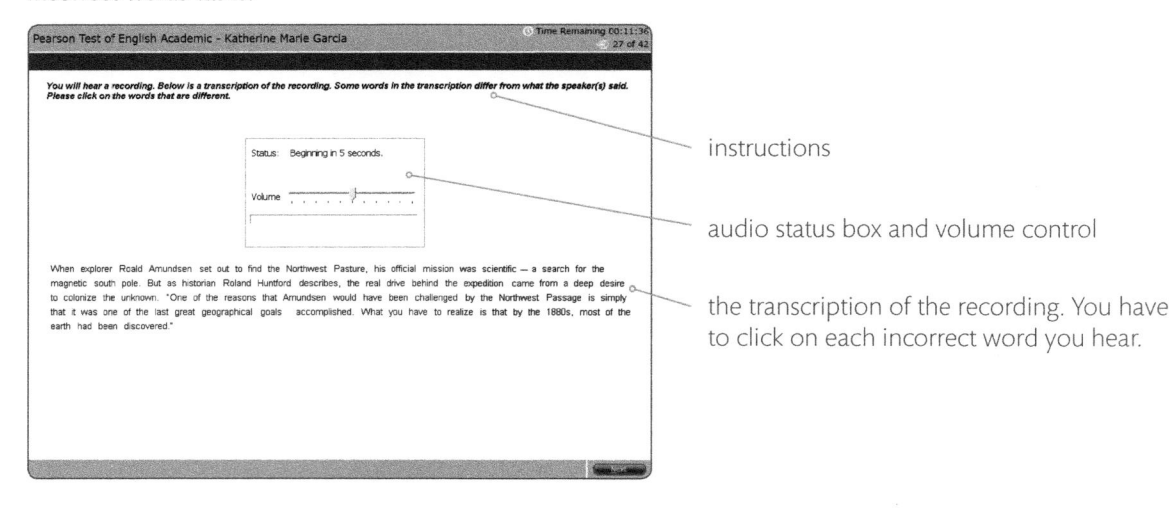

- instructions
- audio status box and volume control
- the transcription of the recording. You have to click on each incorrect word you hear.

EXPERT STRATEGIES

Before you listen

1 Skim-read as much of the text as you can in the ten seconds before the recording starts to get an idea of the topic.
2 Put your cursor over the first word but do not click on it.

While you listen

3 Follow the words in the text as you hear them, moving the cursor along as you listen.
4 If a word in the recording is different to a word in the text, click on it.
5 Listen carefully as some words will sound very similar but are not exactly the same.
6 Only click on those words that you are sure are different. If you click on a word by accident, click on it again to undo the highlight.
7 Don't guess – incorrect answers will lose marks on these tasks. For the same reason, only change an answer if you are sure it was incorrect.

> **Notes from the test developers**
> - You have ten seconds to read the question before the recording starts.
> - To get a full score, you must select all the incorrect words. If you choose just some of the incorrect words, you will get a point for each. You will lose a point for each word you select that is actually correct.
> - There is no timer for this task. When you have finished, click on 'Next' to go to the next task.
> - This task contributes to your listening and reading scores.

Write from dictation

In this listening task type you are tested on your ability to listen and write what you hear. You will hear a sentence which you must then type into the box on the screen exactly as you heard it. You will do 3-4 *Write from dictation* tasks.

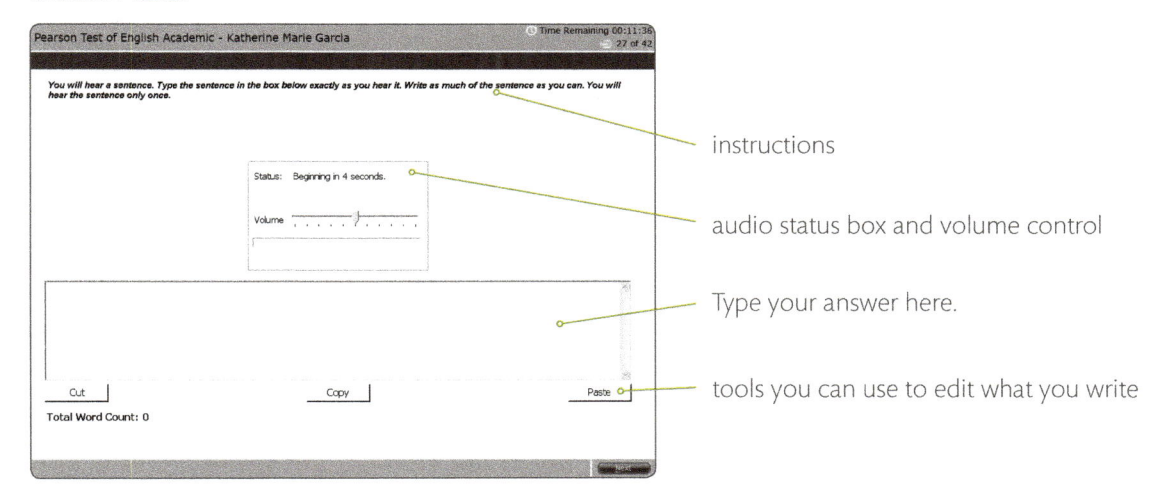

— instructions

— audio status box and volume control

— Type your answer here.

— tools you can use to edit what you write

EXPERT STRATEGIES

Before you listen

1 Put your cursor in the response box so you are ready to type or get your pen and the Erasable Noteboard Booklet ready.

While you listen

2 Listen carefully to the sentence. Focus on the meaning as this will help you to remember it. You will hear the sentence only once.

After listening

3 Keep saying the sentence in your head and type it into the box; or write it on the Erasable Noteboard Booklet and then type it into the box.

4 Check what you have written. Have you written the same words? Does your sentence have the same meaning as the sentence you heard? Are the words spelt correctly? If you are unsure of or forget a word, try to work out what it is from the other words in the sentence, using your knowledge of grammar and collocation.

Notes from the test developers
- You have just seven seconds to read the question before the recording starts.
- To get a full score, you must type all of the words and spell them correctly.
- There is no timer for this task. When you have finished, click on 'Next' to go to the next task.
- These tasks contribute to your listening and writing scores.

Expert speaking

General speaking guidelines/Checklist

Describe image

Did you:	
use an introductory phrase?	☐
describe the most significant information?	☐
emphasise the point that's most important (only if one stands out above the others)?	☐
(if applicable) give figures and use the language of approximation if figures are not exact?	☐
give an implication or a conclusion?	☐

Re-tell lecture

Did you:	
use an introductory expression?	☐
mention key points, not minor details?	☐
only give information from the talk, not your own ideas?	☐
organise ideas logically, using discourse markers?	☐
avoid repeating information?	☐
give an implication or a conclusion?	☐
speak smoothly, without many hesitations?	☐

Describe image

Module 1

Speaking 2, page 19, Exercise 5

Complete the task in pairs. Take turns to describe the chart.

40 sec. *Look at the chart below. In 25 seconds, please speak into the microphone and describe in detail what the chart is showing. You will have 40 seconds to give your response.*

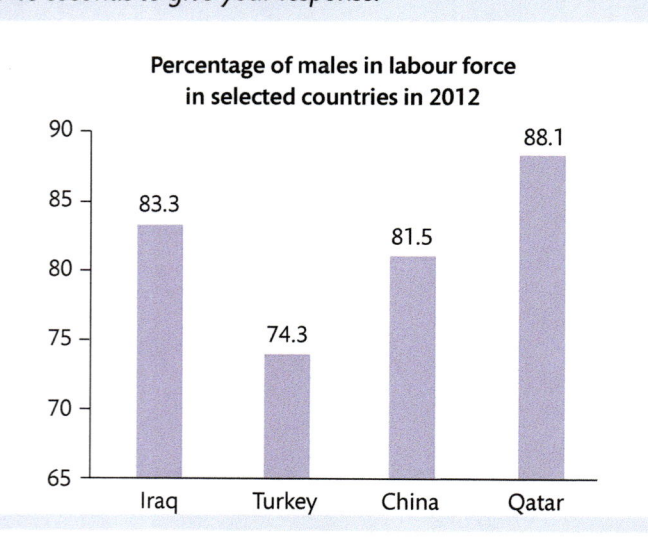

Percentage of males in labour force in selected countries in 2012

- Iraq: 83.3
- Turkey: 74.3
- China: 81.5
- Qatar: 88.1

> HELP

- Look at the title. What's the key difference between this chart and the one you just described?
- Look at the numbers in the chart. Where do they start and end?

Expert speaking

Module 3

Speaking 2, page 51, Exercise 5

Complete the task in pairs. Take turns to describe the diagram.

40 sec. *Look at the diagram below. In 25 seconds, please speak into the microphone and describe in detail what the diagram is showing. You will have 40 seconds to give your response.*

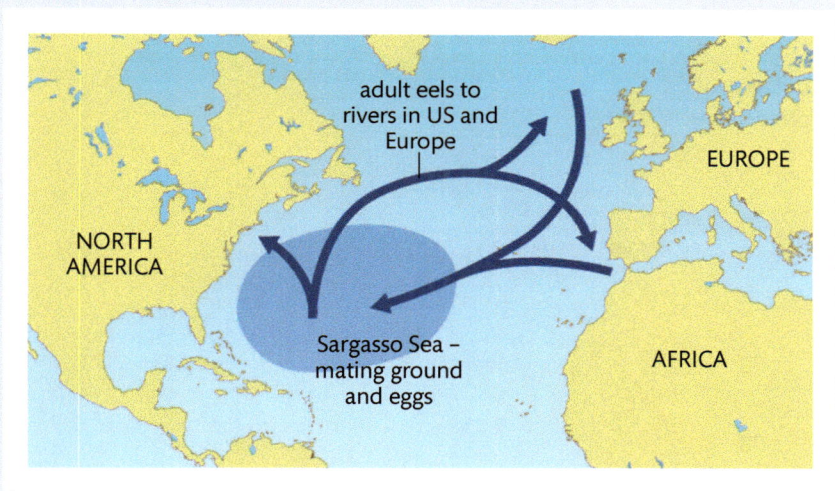

[Map showing: NORTH AMERICA, EUROPE, AFRICA; adult eels to rivers in US and Europe; Sargasso Sea – mating ground and eggs]

➤ HELP

- What is the best place to start your description?
- What happens in the Sargasso Sea?
- Do all the eels move to Europe?

Module 5

Speaking 2, page 83, Exercise 6

Complete the task in pairs. Take turns to describe the charts. Record your answers.

40 sec. *Look at the charts below. In 25 seconds, please speak into the microphone and describe in detail what the charts are showing. You will have 40 seconds to give your response.*

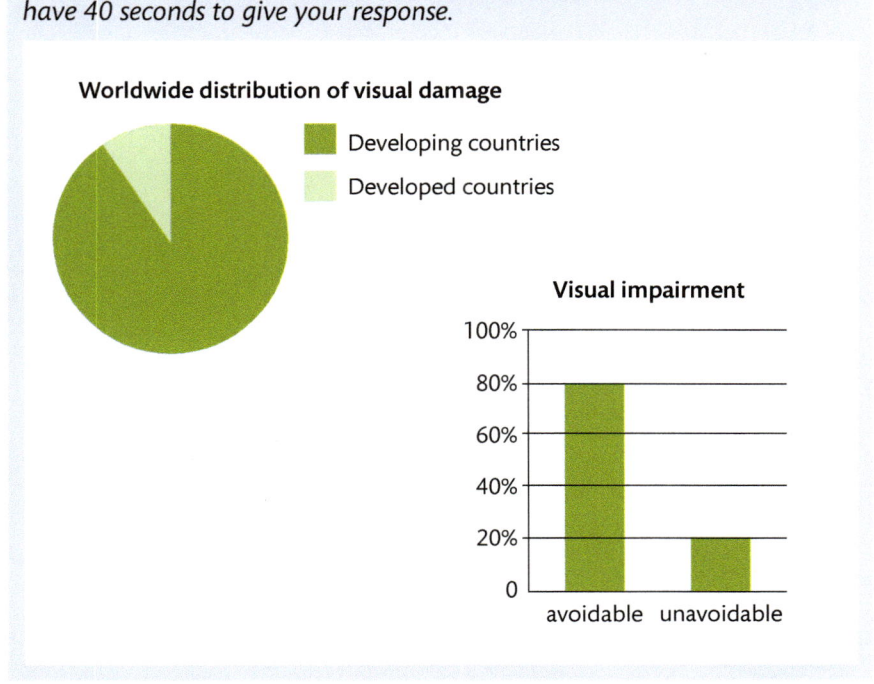

Worldwide distribution of visual damage
- Developing countries
- Developed countries

Visual impairment
- avoidable: 80%
- unavoidable: 20%

Expert speaking

Module 7

Speaking 2, page 115, Exercise 4

Complete the task in pairs. Take turns to describe the diagram.

40 sec. *Look at the diagram below. In 25 seconds, please speak into the microphone and describe in detail what the diagram is showing. You will have 40 seconds to give your response.*

The relationship between the stages of production and the value of coffee beans

- sold to customers — $4.00
- sold on the international stock exchange
- farming and harvesting — $0.28

Module 9

Speaking 2, page 147, Exercise 4

Complete the task in pairs. Take turns to describe the charts.

40 sec. *Look at the charts below. In 25 seconds, please speak into the microphone and describe in detail what the charts are showing. You will have 40 seconds to give your response.*

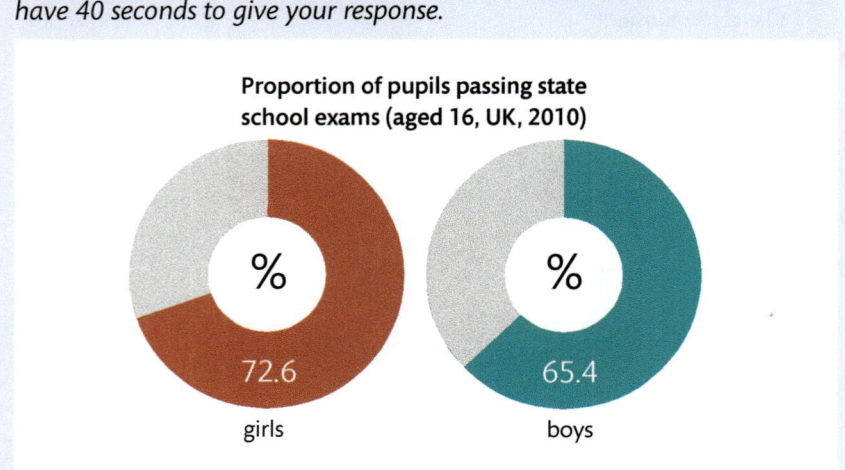

Proportion of pupils passing state school exams (aged 16, UK, 2010)

- girls: 72.6%
- boys: 65.4%

Expert speaking

Re-tell lecture

Module 2

Speaking 2, page 35, Exercise 4

🎧 22 Complete the task in pairs. Take notes, then present the information to your partner.

⏱ 40 sec. *You will hear a lecture. After listening to the lecture, in 10 seconds, please speak into the microphone and re-tell what you have just heard from the lecture in your own words. You will have 40 seconds to give your response.*

➤ HELP

- Look at the photo. What's the topic of the lecture? What vocabulary do you think you might hear?
- According to the speaker, what are the benefits of smiling to the smiler and to other people?

Module 4

Speaking 2, page 67, Exercise 4

🎧 54 Complete the task in pairs. Take notes, then present the information to your partner.

⏱ 40 sec. *You will hear a lecture. After listening to the lecture, in 10 seconds, please speak into the microphone and re-tell what you have just heard from the lecture in your own words. You will have 40 seconds to give your response.*

Esperanto
- 'one who hopes'
- 10,000 fluent speakers
- 1 million students

➤ HELP

- You do not need to remember Dr Zamenhof's name. You can say *One academic believed …*
- How can the information on the presentation slide help you?

Expert speaking

Module 6

Speaking 2, page 99, Exercise 5

🎧 78 Complete the task in pairs. Take notes, then present the information to your partner.

> ⏱ 40 sec. *You will hear a lecture. After listening to the lecture, in 10 seconds, please speak into the microphone and re-tell what you have just heard from the lecture in your own words. You will have 40 seconds to give your response.*
>
> **Homes: 300 years of change**
> - materials
> - indoor heating
> - technology
> - family size

> ➤ HELP
>
> - Look at the presentation slide. What do you learn about the topic?
> - According to the speaker, how have homes changed in the last 300 years?

Module 8

Speaking 2, page 131, Exercise 5

🎧 105 Complete the task in pairs. Take notes, then present the information to your partner.

> ⏱ 40 sec. *You will hear a lecture. After listening to the lecture, in 10 seconds, please speak into the microphone and re-tell what you have just heard from the lecture in your own words. You will have 40 seconds to give your response.*

Expert speaking

Module 10

Speaking 2, page 163, Exercise 4

🎧 132 Complete the task in pairs. Take notes, then present the information to your partner.

> ▶ 40 sec. You will hear a lecture. After listening to the lecture, in 10 seconds, please speak into the microphone and re-tell what you have just heard from the lecture in your own words. You will have 40 seconds to give your response.

Expert writing

Editing checklists

Write essay

Essay checklist	
Does the introduction have a general statement, an opinion and a preview, as appropriate?	☐
Does each body paragraph have a clear topic sentence?	☐
Does each body paragraph make only one main point?	☐
Does the conclusion effectively summarise the ideas in the body paragraphs?	☐
Do the ideas flow logically from the introduction to the body paragraphs to the conclusion?	☐
Is there good cohesion between sentences and paragraphs?	☐
Is there a good variety of vocabulary?	☐
Are there 200–300 words?	☐
Have you checked the grammar, punctuation and spelling, making sure that you've used only UK, US, Australian or Canadian spelling?	☐

Summarize written text

Summary sentence checklist	
Are all the important ideas included?	☐
Are minor ideas missed out?	☐
Are all the points from the text, not your own knowledge?	☐
Is there a mixture of words from the text and their synonyms?	☐
Is there one sentence only, of 5–75 words?	☐
Have you checked the grammar, punctuation and spelling, making sure that you've used only UK, US, Australian or Canadian spelling?	☐

Summarize spoken text

Summary checklist	
Does your summary have a clear overview, giving the main topic?	☐
Are all the important ideas included?	☐
Are minor ideas missed out?	☐
Are all the points from the text, not your own knowledge?	☐
Is there a mixture of words from the recording and their synonyms?	☐
Are there 50–70 words?	☐
Have you checked the grammar, punctuation and spelling, making sure that you've used only UK, US, Australian or Canadian spelling?	☐

Write essay: Argumentative essay

An argument essay requires you to give both sides of an argument and then reach a conclusion.

Task

20 min. *You will have 20 minutes to plan, write and revise an essay about the topic below. Your response will be judged on how well you develop a position, organise your ideas, present supporting details and control the elements of standard written English. You should write 200–300 words.*

> 'To meet the demands of a modern society, schools should stop teaching arts and humanities such as music and history and focus on science and technology, which are more useful in the modern age.' To what extent do you agree with this view?

Model answer

Start your introduction generally. Then move to the main point of the essay.

Students today need to learn different things from their parents' generation. Since the invention of computers and the internet, business has never been the same. However, there are still benefits to keeping subjects such as arts in schools.

PIE: Make a Point, Illustrate it, then Explain why this information is important.

Computers have changed the world these days, and science has become more and more important. To add computer science to the school timetable, schools have had to reduce the time that they spend on other subjects. It is true that all jobs these days need computer skills, whereas few people find art and history useful after they leave school, which is perhaps the strongest argument against teaching these subjects.

Use academic vocabulary.

Link ideas between paragraphs.

However, many people do work in the arts. The music and fashion industries are worth billions to the economy and offer employment to many people directly, not to mention the people who work indirectly, such as through advertising fashion products in the media. The humanities are also important. For example, a knowledge of mistakes which people made in earlier times is necessary for politicians.

Use cohesive devices and grammatical links.

These subjects have an important impact on students and learning, too. A variety of lessons will always be more interesting, particularly at a very young age. For primary school children, art may be an opportunity to relax. Studies suggest that having this time to think improves learning in general, and it would be wrong to take away these opportunities.

Use academic collocations.

Conclude by stating your position.

So in conclusion, it has been necessary to move some more traditional subjects, such as cooking and woodwork, out of the school timetable to make space for computer science and technology. However, in my opinion, it would be a mistake to make students study just academic subjects from a young age.

197

Expert writing

Write essay: Persuasive essay

A persuasive essay is an essay used to persuade someone that a particular idea is good. It requires you to give one side of an argument, although a good essay will show some concession.

Task

⏱ 20 min. You will have 20 minutes to plan, write and revise an essay about the topic below. Your response will be judged on how well you develop a position, organise your ideas, present supporting details and control the elements of standard written English.

> 'Qualifications benefit individuals, therefore governments should make individuals meet the full costs of their education.' Do you agree or disagree with this statement?

Model answer

Start your introduction generally. Then say which side of the argument you are going to argue.

There is no doubt that individuals benefit from education. Many jobs require qualifications and, generally, people who have attended university earn more than people who have not. Not only that, they also usually enjoy more interesting jobs. However, modern nations need a well-educated population and for that reason, I believe governments should help pay some of the costs.

Everyone in society benefits from excellent doctors, engineers and experts in business. These people offer health, homes and jobs to the rest of the population. It is also important that the most intelligent, hard-working and talented people work in these professions. The best people may not be from families who can afford to pay for education and will need government help.

PIE: Make a Point, then Illustrate it and Explain why this reason is important.

Link ideas between paragraphs.

Use academic collocations.

However, all countries need to look internationally these days and need to sell their products and services abroad. A strong economy can improve living standards for everyone. Japan and South Korea are good examples of what a government can do for economic growth. In the middle of the last century both nations paid for young people to travel abroad to learn from other countries. When those young people returned, they were able to build strong economies. An individual cannot make this kind of change. Only governments can.

Use academic vocabulary.

Conclude by restating your main point.

So, in conclusion, although an individual does benefit from their own education, the benefits go much further. For that reason, I believe that governments should offer financial help to able, well-qualified children to complete their education so that they can take the country into the future.

Use cohesive devices and grammatical links.

Write essay: Problem-solution essay

A problem-solution essay requires you to analyse a problem and one or more possible solutions. You will normally need to recommend a solution in the conclusion.

Task

20 min. *You will have 20 minutes to plan, write and revise an essay about the topic below. Your response will be judged on how well you develop a position, organise your ideas, present supporting details and control the elements of standard written English. You should write 200–300 words.*

> 'Given the fact that smoking-related illnesses cost the economy millions each year, governments should introduce a complete ban on cigarettes.' To what extent do you agree with this solution?

Model answer

- Start your introduction stating the problem and reasons why it is important.
- Offer a solution and give advantages and disadvantages of that solution.
- Use cohesive devices and grammatical links.
- Offer another solution and give advantages and disadvantages of that solution.
- Conclude by recommending one of the solutions or a combination of more than one.

Research suggests that the financial and human cost of smoking-related illness is high. Thousands die an early death each year. In fact, many people, particularly non-smokers, see no benefits to continuing to allow people to sell and buy cigarettes. However, this essay will argue that a complete ban would have too many negative consequences.

It is true that a ban on smoking would force people to give up. However, cigarettes are addictive and some smokers will find it impossible. It is also highly likely that organised crime groups will begin to sell tobacco illegally as soon as the ban is in place. If this happens, the police will need to spend a considerable amount of time on this instead of other crimes. In addition, the cigarette industry gives jobs to a large number of people. In particular, the poor farmers who grow tobacco and their families would suffer. It takes a lot of time to change a farm and start growing a different crop.

- Use academic vocabulary.
- Use academic collocations.

Because of these problems, many countries have chosen to control the number of people smoking by introducing laws gradually. Although this solution will not stop smoking as quickly as a complete ban, very high taxes on cigarettes can make them too expensive for many people. A ban on smoking in public places such as public transport, cafés and offices can persuade people to stop smoking over time.

In conclusion, the evidence suggests that a complete ban is likely to have many negative consequences. However, there are strong arguments in favour of making it much harder for individuals to smoke.

Expert writing

Write essay: Case study essay

A case study essay requires you to consider a problem or argument by analysing a particular situation, such as a particular company, government or city.

Task

> **⏱ 20 min.** You will have 20 minutes to plan, write and revise an essay about the topic below. Your response will be judged on how well you develop a position, organise your ideas, present supporting details and control the elements of standard written English. You should write 200–300 words.

> What are the benefits of living in cities rather than in rural areas? Write with reference to a city that you are familiar with.

Model answer

Start your introduction generally. Then say which 'case' you will consider in your answer.

At the beginning of this century, for the first time ever, more people chose to live in urban areas rather than in the countryside. This suggests that there are many benefits to city living in modern life. I intend to discuss these benefits with reference to the city of Bogota.

PIE: Make a Point, then Illustrate it with reference to your 'case' and Explain what this can teach you about wider society.

The main attraction of Bogota is work opportunities. Although there may be factories, shops and other jobs available in villages, these jobs have low wages. Management jobs and professional opportunities are generally only found in the city, particularly the capital city. Because of the large number of opportunities, young people can get promoted more quickly there, too. Of course, not everyone who moves to the city finds work. There is still a lot of unemployment but unless you go there, your opportunities are very limited.

Use cohesive devices and grammatical links.

Use academic vocabulary.

Link ideas between paragraphs.

Cities also offer better entertainment, particularly for sports and music. There are no big stadiums for concerts in the countryside and young people get bored. When they watch television or read magazines, they see images of Bogota and the news is full of events which happen there. This is also clearly important in encouraging people to move to the city. Now that almost everyone has friends or relatives in Bogota already, it is also relatively easy to move there.

Use academic collocations.

Conclude by stating your position.

For these reasons, cities in my country, particularly the capital city, Bogota, are growing very quickly every year. Of course, this causes problems of congestion and unemployment but life in the city is still better than in the country.

Expert writing

Summarize written text

Summarize written text requires you to identify the main points in a text and summarise it in one sentence.

Task

> **10 min.** Read the passage below and summarize it using one sentence. Type your response in the box at the bottom of the screen. You have 10 minutes to finish this task. Your response will be judged on the quality of your writing and on how well your response presents the key points in the passage.

Identify the topic sentence(s).

Underline the key words in the text to help you understand the main idea.

Despite many people believing that face-to-face lessons are most beneficial, online learning can provide a much more effective learning experience for some people because it provides a more equal platform for discussion. In the classroom, it is impossible for all students to offer opinions at the same time, which means it is the confident, quick-thinking students who are able to talk and present their ideas. While they benefit from being able to receive immediate feedback from the teacher on these comments, not everyone is so lucky. Online learning allows some students to take their time to think about the topic and contribute to the discussion.

In addition to this, learners are much more able to take control of their own learning. They can decide when to learn, where to learn and how to learn. This is beneficial because every person learns differently and not all of us can learn in a specific place at a specific time of the day. Learners can plan their own timetable and work on particular areas in the way that helps them. They can also do other activities such as a part-time job or voluntary work and still continue to study. It is this flexibility which can allow different learners to learn effectively.

Model answer

Use the topic sentences in the text to help you write your summary. Focus on the main point(s).

Online learning can provide an effective learning experience for some people because it offers a more equal platform for discussion and learners are much more able to take control of their own learning because they can decide when, where and how to learn.

Don't write more than one sentence. Make sure you write no more than 75 words.

Include no more than three clauses. Link them with appropriate linkers.

Add in a supporting point, but only if you can include it in the sentence.

201

Expert writing

Summarize spoken text

🎧 133 *Summarize spoken text* requires you to listen to a lecture, an interview or watch a video and write a summary which identifies the main points.

Task

> Read the instructions carefully to check whether you are going to hear a lecture, an interview or watch a video.

> ⏱ **10 min.** You will hear a short lecture. Write a summary for a fellow student who was not present at the lecture. You should write 50–70 words.
>
> You will have 10 minutes to finish this task. Your response will be judged on the quality of your writing and on how well your response presents the key points presented in the lecture.

> Listen carefully and take notes on the main point and supporting points.

Model answer

> Use the topic sentence to summarise the main point of the recording.

> Follow the topic sentence with some supporting points but remember you won't be able to include everything.

> People do not always know what they will want in the future and can be poor at predicting what will make them happy. In an experiment, two groups of people chose sandwiches, one group on the day and one group in advance. The former group often chose the same sandwich each day and were reasonably happy. The latter group chose different sandwiches but were less happy with their choice.

> Link your ideas with appropriate linkers.

> Make sure you write between 50 and 70 words.

Expert grammar

1

Parts of speech (page 13)

A Main parts of speech

1 Important parts of speech are nouns, verbs, adjectives, adverbs, prepositions, articles, pronouns and conjunctions.
I've just dropped my folder on the floor but it's fine.

nouns = *folder, floor*
verbs = *'ve, dropped, 's*
adjective = *fine*
adverb = *just*
preposition = *on*
pronouns = *I, my, it*
conjunction = *but*
article = *the*

2 A noun describes an object, person, thing, place or idea.
*The **professor's lecture** is about **motivation**.*
*The **students** discussed their **beliefs** in the dining room.*

3 A verb describes an action or a state.
*They **worked** hard all day.* (action)
*He **felt** satisfied with his test results.* (state)

4 An adjective describes a noun. It tells us 'what kind' or 'how many'.
*People are **interested** in achieving new goals.*
***Challenging** goals motivate people.*

5 An adverb gives us information about how, where and when.
*Some students travel **abroad** to study.*
*Student numbers are increasing **slowly**.*

6 A preposition gives us information about time and place.
*I'm going **to** university later.*
*The meeting's **at** six.*

7 A pronoun can replace a noun and includes words such as *she, they, them, ours, him, this, these*.
*He set **us** some homework this morning.*
***This** annoyed all of **us**.*

8 A conjunction links words, phrases and clauses.
*The test will take place in room B **because** room A is out of use.*
***Although** you can use a dictionary in class, you cannot use it in the test.*

9 An article (*a, an* or *the*) is a word which sits with a noun.
*This is **a** useful book.*
*There's **an** interesting article on happiness here.*
***The** lecture's in room D at 3 p.m.*

B Word formation

1 There are many words in the English language that can be found in noun, verb, adjective and adverb form. Words are formed by adding prefixes or suffixes.

Verb	Noun	Adjective	Adverb
agree	agreement	agreeable	agreeably

2 Prefixes are letters which are added to the beginning of a word. They change the meaning of the word but the form usually stays the same. Prefixes can make a word negative.
*They are **un**happy about the changes.*
Some prefixes carry a meaning, such as *re-* (= again), *over-* (= more than is needed) or *ex-* (= before).
*I need to **re**view my notes.*
*Many parts of the area are considered to be **over**crowded.*
*The **ex**-president of the company is coming to the dinner.*

3 Suffixes are letters which are added to the end of a word. The purpose of a suffix is usually to change the form of the word, but not the meaning. These suffixes include *-ment, -sion, -tion, -y*.
*Scientists believe argu**ments** are an important part of communication.*
*That was an interesting discus**sion**.*
*Nois**y** places can be stressful.*

Some suffixes give the word a different form and meaning, e.g. *-ful* (= full of), *-less* (= not having), *-able* (= can).
*Students should be care**ful** not to copy others' material.*
*Care**less** work will not be graded highly.*
*This work is not accept**able**.*

Present tenses (page 16)

A Present simple

1 We use the present simple when we are talking about regular repeated actions, routines and habits.
*Students **take** exams every month in my country.*
*Lecturers **don't teach** on Wednesday afternoons.*

2 We also use the present simple when we are talking about permanent situations.
*The president **lives** in the capital city.*
*Most coffee **comes** from Brazil.*

3 To form the present simple we use the base form of the verb. *He/She/It* forms are different.
Positive
*I/You/We/They **like** academic life.*
*He/She/It **likes** academic life.*
Negative
*I/You/We/They **don't like** academic life.*
*He/She/It **doesn't like** academic life.*

203

Expert grammar

Question

We use the auxiliary verb *do* to make present simple questions.
Do *I/you/we/they* **like** *academic life?*
Yes, I/you/we/they **do**./*No, I/you/we/they* **don't**.
Does *he/she/it* **like** *academic life?*
Yes, he/she/it **does**. *No, he/she/it* **doesn't**.

B Present continuous

1 We use the present continuous when we are talking about actions happening now.
The government **are looking** *at the situation.*

2 We also use the present continuous when we are talking about temporary situations.
Dr Brown's **visiting** *the US this summer.*

3 To form the present continuous we use *be + -ing* form.
Positive
I'm/You're/He's/She's/It's/We're/They're **work**ing.
Negative
I'm not/You aren't/He isn't/She isn't/It isn't/We aren't/They aren't **working.**
Question
The subject and verb *be* are inverted.
Are *you* **working** *at the moment?*
Is *he* **finishing** *his homework?*

C State verbs

Some verbs describe states and are not normally used in a continuous form. State verbs often:

1 describe emotions or mental states (e.g. *agree, like, hate, prefer, want, need, mind, understand, disagree, promise, seem*).
2 describe the senses (e.g. *hear, see, smell, sound, taste*).
3 describe owning things (e.g. *belong to, have, own*).

D Subject and object questions

1 When a question asks for information about the object, we use the auxiliary verb in the sentence, and the order of the subject and auxiliary verb changes.

Question word/phrase	Auxiliary verb	Subject	Main verb + rest of sentence
What	did	I	miss in the last lesson?
Where	do	you	go after class?
How long	does	this course	last?
Where	did	Da Vinci	live and work?

2 When a question asks for information about the subject, we don't use the auxiliary and we don't change the order of the subject and verb.

Question word/phrase	Main verb	Rest of sentence
Who	missed	yesterday's class?
	met	you at the station?
What	fell	down?
	made	that noise?

Compare:
Who saw *the documentary last night?* (question about the subject)
What makes *people happy?* (question about the subject)
with:
Who did you see *in the documentary last night?* (question about the object)
What did you make *for dinner last night?* (question about the object)

2

Relative clauses (page 29)

A Defining relative clauses

1 We use defining relative clauses to identify or classify a noun/pronoun.
Fear is an emotion **which causes stress**. (= Fear is an emotion. **It causes stress**.)

B Relative pronouns

1 We use a relative pronoun as the subject of a relative clause.
Fear is an emotion **which** *causes stress.* (= Fear is an emotion. **It causes stress**.)
We do not use a subject pronoun (*he, she, it,* etc.) after a subject relative pronoun.
A person **who** *is frightened* **he** *goes white.*

2 We can use a relative pronoun as the object of a relative clause.
Surprise is a feeling **that** *people can enjoy.* (= Surprise is a feeling. People can enjoy **it**.)
We can omit the relative pronoun if it is the object.
Happiness is a feeling **that** *we all want to experience.*

3 We use these pronouns in relative clauses:
which/that for things
who/that for people
whose for possessions
where for place
when for time
Individuals **whose** *suggestions or ideas have been rejected will feel disappointed.*
Places **where** *people feel fear are usually dark.*
A time **when** *people may get a surprise is on their birthday.*

204

Note
We can use *that* instead of *which* and *who* in defining relative clauses. In more formal texts, *which* and *who* are more common.

Sentence structure and prepositional phrases (page 32)

Although there are some other possibilities, the basic word order in an English sentence that is not a question or a command is usually:

Subject/ Subject group	Verb/ Verb group	Object/ Object group	Manner (adverb or prepositional phrase)	Place	Time
I	walk	my dog		around the park	every day.
The man	spoke to	me	calmly.		
The scientists	looked at	a large number	*of* people	*in* their study.	
Over 90 percent of people in the UK	enjoyed watching	television			every week in 2013.

A Subjects and subject groups

A subject is normally a noun, pronoun or noun phrase. It usually goes before the verb.
Dr Brown *carried out the study.*
There *were a large number of differences.*
The number of bicycles in London *increased in 2000.*

B Objects and object groups

An object is normally a noun, pronoun or noun group. It usually goes after the verb in active sentences.
They looked at **the homework** *together.*
The scientists found **it** *too late.*
The students gave **good answers to the questions**.

C Manner, place and time expressions

Manner, place and time expressions are often either prepositional phrases or relative clauses.
The scientists *wanted answers.* (subject)
The scientists from LSE *wanted answers.* (subject + prepositional phrase)
The scientists in the computer department at LSE in the 1980s *wanted answers.* (subject + prepositional phrases of manner, place and time)

The researchers looked at **the problem**. (object)
The researchers looked at **the problem in a new way.** (object + prepositional phrase of manner)
The researchers looked **at the problem of low wages among the factory workers over a period of time.** (object + prepositional phrases of manner and time)
The researchers looked at **the problem which had beaten scientists for years.** (object + relative clause with prepositional phrase of time)

D Adding more than one prepositional phrase

Long subject or object groups are common in academic English. To add more than one prepositional phrase, follow the same order (noun, manner, place, time).
The man spoke **English**.
The man spoke **English to me in a perfect accent at the meeting last week.**
The expert gave **his opinion**.
The expert gave **his opinion on the rise in crime in the city over the last five years.**

3

Future forms (page 45)

A *will* and *going to*

1 We use *will* + infinitive to make predictions based on our thoughts or beliefs.
   I believe that people **will do** *more to help the environment in future.*
   Scientists **will find** *a solution to global warming.*

2 We use *be* + *going to* + infinitive for predictions based on present evidence and for intentions.
   The storm **is going to get** *much worse tomorrow.* (present evidence = satellite photos)
   The team **is going to do** *more underwater exploration in the next two or three years.* (intention)

B Present continuous

1 We use the present continuous for arrangements and planned events.
   Experts **are meeting** *on Tuesday to discuss the problem.*
   The newspaper **is printing** *a story about the ocean floor tomorrow.*

2 An arrangement is something that has been organised and agreed, e.g. an event that is in your diary. An intention is a plan but nothing has been organised or agreed yet.
   The Chinese Space Agency **is sending** *a shuttle into space next month.* (arrangement)
   NASA **is going to find out** *more about Mars in future.* (intention, but no arrangement)

Expert grammar

C definitely, probably, possibly

1. We use *definitely* when we are very sure that something is true. We use *probably* when we are quite sure that something is true. We use *possibly* when we are not sure that something is true.
   Things are **definitely** going to improve.
   The population of the city will **probably** increase next year.
   The development of technology will **possibly** start to slow down soon.

2. We use *definitely*, *probably* and *possibly*:
   between *will* (*not*) and the infinitive.
   The changes **will definitely not happen** soon.
   between *be* and *going to*.
   Environmentalists **are probably going to** try and stop the government building a new airport.

D likely/unlikely

We can also use *be likely/unlikely* + *to*-infinitive to say that we are quite sure that something will/won't happen in the future. The meaning is similar to *probably*.
Developing countries **are likely to get** richer in future.
Developed countries **are unlikely to be** as powerful as they were.

Zero and first conditionals (page 48)

A Zero conditional

We use the zero conditional to talk about rules, things that are true or things that always happen. The form is:
if/when + subject + present simple (*if* clause), subject + present simple (main clause).
If you warm water to 100 degrees, **it boils**.
Animals soon experience problems **when** plants die out.

B First conditional

We use the first conditional to talk about things that might happen in the future, i.e. for future possibility. The form is: *if* + subject + present simple (*if* clause), subject + *will* + infinitive (main clause).
If the project **is** successful, thousands of people **will benefit**.
If you **don't practise** hard, you **won't improve**.

C Punctuation in conditionals

When the *if* clause comes in the first half of the sentence, we use a comma (,) between the two clauses. When it comes in the second half, no comma is needed.
If the group get enough money, they will be able to finish their work.
The group will be able to finish their work **if** they get enough money.

D Words to introduce conditionals

There are several words we can use instead of *if* but they often have more limitations.

1. *when*

   We use *when* to describe things that happen all the time. We use *when* in zero conditional sentences only.
   The science class is cancelled **when** the teacher is sick.
   When scientists begin new projects, they usually have clear aims.

2. *provided that*

   We use *provided that* to say that something good, i.e. with a positive outcome, will happen, only if another thing happens. We only use *provided that* with things that we want to happen. We use *provided that* in zero and first conditional sentences.
   Provided that the new drug passes all the tests, it will be available soon.

3. *even if*

   We use *even if* to emphasise that something will still be true if another thing happens. We can use *even if* in any conditional form.
   The project will work **even if** they don't get enough sunshine.
   Even if the project failed, the research wouldn't be wasted.

4. *unless*

   We use *unless* to mean *if not*. However, *unless* is stronger than *if not* and is often used to make a warning sound stronger. We use *unless* in zero and first conditional sentences.
   If we **don't do** something soon, there will be no planet left to protect.
   Unless we **do** something soon, there will be no planet left to protect.
   The species will soon die out **if** its habitat **is not protected**.
   The species will soon die out **unless** its habitat **is protected**.

4

Past tenses (page 61)

A Past simple

1. We use the past simple when we are talking about an action that started and finished in the past.
   The researcher **took** a photo.
   I **finished** my essay.

2. We also use the past simple when we are talking about a general situation in the past.
   I **studied** maths for ten years.
   The professor **was** really happy with the result.

3. Time expressions commonly used with the past simple are *ago*, *at* (*six o'clock*), *before* (*2000*), *in* (*2008*), *last month*, *yesterday*.

4. We form the past simple as follows:
   Positive: subject + verb + -ed (for regular verbs)
   I **worked** there five years ago.

Note that there are many irregular verbs, which don't take -ed in the past simple.
They **left** at half past eight.
Negative: subject + *didn't* + infinitive
I **didn't see** him.
Question: *did* + subject + infinitive
Did you **finish** the project?

B used to

1 We use *used to* when we are talking about past habits and states that don't occur now or no longer exist.
This town **used to have** a public swimming pool but it doesn't now.
There **didn't use to be** so many cars on the road.
John **used to study** on this course but he changed.

2 The form is:
Positive: *used to* + infinitive
I **used to know** him.
Negative: *didn't use to* + infinitive
I **didn't use to study** there.
Question: *did* + subject + *use to* + infinitive
Did you **use to visit** your grandparents often?

C Past continuous

1 We use the past continuous when we are talking about an action that was in progress when another past action happened. This action may have stopped.
The water **was boiling** when the pan fell over.
The scientist **was heating** the liquid when it exploded.

2 We use the past continuous when we are talking about two past actions in progress at the same time.
He **was mixing** the chemicals while the water **was heating**.
We **were planning** the next stage while the builders **were working** on the first stage.

3 We use the past continuous when we are talking about a past temporary action.
I **was working** in a shop during the summer holidays.
He **was visiting** the university for the summer.

4 The form is:
Positive: subject + *was/were* + *-ing*
I **was taking** notes all lesson.
Negative: subject + *wasn't/weren't* + *-ing*
They **weren't studying** in that class.
Question: *was/were* + subject + *-ing*
Were you **watching** that experiment?

D Past perfect simple

1 We use the past perfect simple when we are talking about a past action that happened before another past action.
I applied for this course because I**'d enjoyed** studying history at school.

2 We often use the past perfect simple in time expressions with *by*, *before* and *after*.
By 2004, the numbers **had risen** to over 100.
Before they built the new centre, they**'d spent** six months planning.
The law changed after they**'d seen** the report.

3 We form the past perfect simple as follows:
Positive: subject + *had* + past participle
I **had** already **seen** the new project.
Negative: subject + *hadn't* + past participle
They **hadn't finished** by the end of the talk.
Question: *had* + subject + past participle
Had they already **seen** the new building?

Second conditional (page 64)

A Use and form
We use the second conditional to talk about the result of unreal, unlikely or imagined present situations. The form is: *if* + subject + past simple (*if* clause), *would* + infinitive.
If I **were** a faster learner, I**'d study** several languages. (unreal: I'm not a faster learner).
If everyone **spoke** the same language, global communication **would be** simpler. (imagined, unlikely)
If I **became** president, I**'d make** a better life for everyone. (unlikely)

B was/were

We can use both *was* and *were* in the first person. Many people believe that *were* is the correct form but in today's English *was* is also very common and considered to be correct.
If I **were** given the option, I would choose to study in further education.
If I **was** able to learn a third language, I would choose Chinese.

C Clause order and punctuation

We can start a second conditional sentence with the *if* clause or with the main clause without changing the meaning. When the *if* clause comes in the first half of the sentence, we use a comma (,) between the two clauses. When it comes in the second half, no comma is needed.
If there was an airport, the economy would grow faster.
Communication would be better **if** there were more phone lines.

Expert grammar

5

Expressing quantity (page 77)

A Countable/Uncountable nouns

1 Nouns are countable when we can count them (e.g. *person, film, song, artist, gallery*). They have a singular form and a plural form.
   The *film was* very educational.
   Fewer Hollywood *films appear* at the cinema nowadays.

2 Nouns are uncountable when we cannot count them (e.g. *art, music, entertainment, happiness, depression*). There is just one form which is used with a singular verb.
   Popcorn is a popular food purchased at cinemas.
   Information comes in various forms.

3 Some nouns can be both countable and uncountable depending on how you use them.
   Shall we have some **coffee** and some **chocolate**?
   Shall we have a **coffee** and a **chocolate**? (= a cup of coffee and one chocolate from a box)
   People should drink around eight **glasses** of water a day. (= container)
   Glass makes up two-thirds of the building. (= material)

4 Some nouns always appear in a plural form with a plural verb, even though we are talking about just one item.
   Trousers were not generally worn by women until the 20th century.
   Scissors for left-handed people **are** available.

B Quantifiers

1 With countable nouns, we can use *some, any, many, a few, few* and *a lot of*. We use *some, many, a few, few* and *a lot of* with positive verbs. We use *any, many* and *a lot of* with negative verbs.
   Cinemas **show some films** in 3D.
   There **aren't many** new galleries opening these days.

2 With uncountable nouns, we can use *some, any, much, a little, little* and *a lot of*. We use *some, a little, little* and *a lot of* with positive verbs. We use *any, much* and *a lot of* with negative verbs.
   There **is a lot of unemployment** these days.
   There **is not much chance** of it happening in future.

3 We use *a few* and *a little* when the meaning of the sentence is positive. We use *few* and *little* when the meaning of the sentence is negative.
   There are **a few jobs** available for graphic designers. (= There aren't many but I think there are enough.)
   There are **few opportunities** in the arts industry. (= I don't think there are enough.)
   Young people can enjoy **a little** entertainment in the area. (= some but not much)
   There is **little** good music played on the radio these days. (= not enough)

4 In academic and formal English, it is common to use *many* and *much* in positive sentences but in everyday spoken English a *lot of/lots* of are more likely to be used.
   Many people disagree. (= academic)
   Lots of people disagree. (= everyday spoken)
   There is **much** discussion about it. (= academic)
   There's **a lot of** discussion about it. (= everyday spoken)

C too/enough

1 We use *too many/too much* when we want to say that there is more than we want. We use *too many* with countable nouns and *too much* with uncountable nouns.
   Too many people are ignoring books these days.
   Too much television is bad for children.

2 We use *too few/too little/not enough* when we want to say that there is less than we want. We use *too few* with countable nouns and *too little* with uncountable nouns. We use *not enough* with both countable and uncountable nouns.
   There are **too few educational programmes** on TV these days.
   Too little sport can be bad for your health.
   There are **not enough facilities** for young people in the area.
   There **is not enough entertainment** for people over 65.

D Describing graphs

1 We can use percentages to describe quantity.
   Thirty-six percent of people prefer reading to watching the film.
   Just under 50% of the student body rides a bicycle to class.

2 We can use fractions to describe quantity.
   Over half of the people enjoy going to the cinema.
   Nearly two-thirds of the class watched a film last night.
   Two in five adults take a walk at the weekend.
   One in three children does regular sport.

3 We use certain verbs + prepositions to describe graphs.
   The percentage of people who can draw **stands at** 34 percent.
   The number of adults who have a hobby **fell by** 6 percent in 2012, from 18 percent to 12 percent.
   The amount of downloaded music **increased to** 45 percent of the market last year.
   The number of hours spent watching TV **decreased from** four **to** three per day.

Comparatives and superlatives (page 80)

A Comparative and superlative forms of adjectives and adverbs

1 One-syllable adjectives and adverbs
   We add *-er* and *-est* to form the comparative and superlative with one-syllable adjectives.
   The new park was **bigger than** the old one.
   It's the **fastest** method of travelling.

We double the consonant before adding -er and -est to form the comparative and superlative with one-syllable adjectives that end in one vowel + consonant.
big – bigger – biggest
sad – sadder – saddest
We add -r and -st to form the comparative of words ending in -e.
safe – safer – safest
With adjectives ending in consonant + -y, we replace the -y with -i.
dry – drier – driest

2 **Two-syllable adjectives and adverbs**
We use *more* and *most* with some two-syllable adjectives.
*He was **more famous** than his sister.*

3 **Three-syllable adjectives and adverbs**
Use *more* and *most* with three-syllable adjectives or adverbs.
*He spoke **more confidently** than before.*
*Prof Hawkins is the **most important** physicist in the UK.*

4 **Irregular comparative and superlative adjectives**
These are the most common irregular forms:
good – better – best
bad – worse – worst
far – further – furthest

B Using comparatives with multiples

1 With *twice* or *half*, we use *twice/half* + *as* + adj + *as*.
*Swimming was **twice as popular as** playing tennis.*
*White rhinos are **half as common as** black rhinos.*

Note
We do not say *twice more* or *half more*.

2 With *three* times or *more* we can use either *three times* + adj + *-er* or *three times* + *as* + adj + *as*.
*Sales online were **ten times higher than** sales in stores.*
*Sales online were **ten times as high as** sales in stores.*

6

Verb patterns (page 93)

A -ing forms

We can use the *-ing* form of a verb like a noun. We use it in the following situations:

1 **as subject or object**

We can use an *-ing* form as the subject or object of a sentence. We are usually talking about the action in a general way.
***Cycling** is more popular than **running**.*
***Planning** is the most important stage of essay **writing**.*

2 **after prepositions**
We use *-ing* forms after prepositions.
*I'm not happy **about working** late.*
*Brian's nervous **about taking** his test.*

3 **after certain verbs**
We use *-ing* forms after certain verbs. These include *avoid, prevent, consider, finish, give up, imagine, involve, mind, practise, recommend, suggest, understand.*
*The researchers **suggested introducing** higher tax.*
*The project **involved building** a new centre for the homeless.*

B Infinitives

An infinitive is the base form of the verb. It is usually preceded by *to* (*to*-infinitive) but sometimes it is used without it (bare infinitive). We use the *to*-infinitive in the following situations:

1 **after adjectives**

We use the *to*-infinitive after many adjectives.
*It is **difficult to identify** the main causes.*
*It was **hard to meet** all the objectives.*

2 **after certain verbs**

We use the *to*-infinitive after certain verbs. These include *afford, agree, appear, arrange, ask, choose, decide, expect, hope, learn, manage, offer, plan, refuse, want.*
*The researchers **agreed to disagree**.*
*The results **appeared to show** a difference in the two groups.*

3 **to express purpose**

We use the *to*-infinitive to show purpose.
*The researchers separated the two groups **to compare** the results later.*
*The results were checked **to make** sure they were correct.*

C -ing forms and infinitives

1 Some verbs can be followed by an *-ing* form or an infinitive without a change in meaning. The most common ones are *begin, start, continue.*
*The professor started **talking**.*
*The professor started **to talk**.*

2 Sometimes there is a small difference in meaning between the *-ing* form and the infinitive. The most common verbs are *remember, forget, stop.*
*The students **stopped discussing** their test results and went home.* (The action they stopped was 'discussing their test results'.)
*The students **stopped to discuss** their test results.* (They stopped another action, e.g. doing their homework, so they could discuss their test results.)
*He **forgot reading** the book when he was a teenager.* (He read the book when he was a teenager and he has forgotten that fact.)
*He **forgot to read** the instructions and didn't know what he had to do.*
(He forgot that he needed to read the instructions.)

Expert grammar

Expressing probability (page 96)

A Expressing present probability

Probability is regularly expressed in academic English as is is often necessary to say whether we think something is or will be true and why.

1 We use *must* + infinitive when we are sure that something is true.
   *City life **must be** more exciting than life in the country.*

2 We use *can't/cannot* + infinitive when we are sure that something is not possible.
   *Living in a tent **cannot be** comfortable for most people.*

3 We use *might/may/could* + infinitive when we think that something is possible but we are not sure.
   *Today's air pollution **might be** caused by an increase in the number of cars on the road.*
   *Traffic jams **may be** a result of a poor road system.*

B Expressing future probability

1 We can use the following modal verbs to express probability in the future:
   will definitely (*not*) + infinitive (= I'm sure.)
   will probably (*not*) + infinitive (= I'm quite sure.)
   will possibly (*not*) + infinitive (= It's possible but I'm not sure.)
   might (*not*) / *may* (*not*) + infinitive (= It's possible but I'm not sure.)

   *Technology **will definitely change** our home lives even further.*
   *Our homes **may not be** so different in 2030.*
   *Robots **will probably not run** our households.*

2 We can also use other structures to express future probability. These are particularly common in academic texts because they are more formal in style.
   There is a small chance that our road system will be completely different. (= small possibility)
   There is a strong possibility that there will not be enough city housing for everyone. (= strong possibility)
   It is quite likely that more people will move to cities. (= weak probability)
   It is highly likely that cities will become wetter with global warming. (= strong probability)
   *Many cities **are likely to** become more multicultural.* (= probability)

7

The passive (page 109)

A Use

We use the passive:

1 when the agent is unknown.
   *The fruit **was imported**.*

2 when the agent is obvious or not important.
   *The fruit **is picked** during the autumn.*

3 when we do not want to say who the agent is.
   *Something **should be done** about this situation.*

B Present passive

1 We use *am/is/are* + past participle to form the present simple passive.
   *Trucks **are used** to transport the goods.*

2 We use *am/is/are being* + past participle to form the present continuous passive.
   *People **are being given** access to food from around the world.*

C Past passive

1 We use *was/were* + past participle to form the past simple passive.
   *The items **were placed** carefully into boxes.*

2 We use *was/were being* + past participle to form the past continuous passive.
   *Products **were being moved** to another warehouse when the accident happened.*

3 We use *had been* + past participle to form the past perfect passive.
   *The meat **had been stored** for several weeks before it arrived at the supermarket.*

D Future passive

1 We use *will be* + past participle to form the passive with *will*.
   *The food **will be consumed** before the end of the week.*

2 We use *am/is/are going to be* + past participle to form the passive with *going to*.
   *The crops **are going to be gathered** next week.*

E Modal verbs and the passive

The passive can be used with modal verbs using the following pattern: modal verb + *be* + past participle.
*Fertilizer **can be used** to protect crops.*
*Rules **must be followed** when transporting goods.*

Expert grammar

Reduced relative clauses (page 112)

A Reduced relative clauses with active verbs

1. The present participle of a verb (e.g. *being, involving, containing*) can be used in place of defining relative clauses if the verb is in the active form. We use reduced relative clauses to be able to write more ideas in a smaller space and it is particularly common in academic writing.

2. In active sentences, delete the relative pronoun and change the verb to the *-ing* form. Note that it does not need to be a verb in the present tense.
   The group ~~who are~~ **studying** tigers have reported an increase in numbers.
   The group **studying** tigers have reported an increase in numbers.
   The number of people ~~who smoked~~ went down.
   The number of people **smoking** went down.

B Past participle

1. The past participle (*involved, eaten, given*) can be used in place of defining relative clauses if the verb is in the passive form.

2. In passive sentences, delete the relative pronoun and the verb *be*.
   The system ~~which was~~ **used** in this company was very inefficient.
   The system **used** in this company was very inefficient.
   The cover was made from a plastic ~~which is~~ **based** on a type of sugar.
   The cover was made from a plastic **based** on a type of sugar.

8

Expressing obligation and permission
(page 125)

A Present obligation

1. We use *must/must not* when:
   we decide *for* ourselves that something is necessary, obligatory or prohibited.
   I **must send** this email now.
   Children **must spend** less time in front of a computer screen.
   we express strong opinions.
   You **must do something** about this terrible problem.
   we give instructions, especially in writing:
   Assignments **must be completed** by Friday.

2. We use *have to* for an obligation placed on us by someone else.
   I **have to do** my homework tonight. (My tutor told me.)
   She **has to finish** the project before tomorrow. (Her manager told her.)

3. We use *should* to express mild obligation. This is advice rather than a strong obligation.
   He **should speak** to his tutor if he has a problem.

4. We use *do not have to* to say there is no obligation.
   You **don't have to read** the article but you can if you want to.
   We **don't have to be** polite but it makes life more pleasant.

B Past obligation

1. We use *had to* to talk about an obligation in the past. This is the past form of both *have to* and *must*.
   I **had to stay up** late last night to finish my work.

2. We use *did not have to* to say there was no past obligation.
   We **didn't have to hand in** our essays this morning but I did it anyway.

C Future obligation

1. We use *will have to* to talk about future obligation.
   The company **will have to reduce** their costs next year.

2. We use *won't/will not have to* + infinitive to say there is no future obligation.
   Science students **will not have to attend** the meeting.

D Formal ways to express obligation and permission

1. We can use *it is/was necessary (for sb)* when we talk about an obligation in the present or past.
   It **is necessary for all staff to report** to reception.

2. We can use *it is/was not necessary (for sb)* when we talk about no obligation in the present or past.
   It **was not necessary for people to say** thank you but many of them did.

3. We use *be allowed to* when we talk about permission in the present or past.
   I **was not allowed to spend** time watching TV when I was a child.
   They **are not allowed to talk** in class.

4. We can use *not be allowed to/be prohibited from* when we talk about no permission in the past or present.
   Many members **were not allowed to express** their true opinions.
   Students **are prohibited from entering** the staff room.

Academic language (page 128)

There are five key features of academic English.

1. Use speculative language (e.g. *may, might, could, suggest, some*) instead of definite language (e.g. *is, are, will be, says, all*).
   The results ~~show~~ that watching television ~~is~~ bad for ~~all~~ children.
   The results **suggest** that watching television **may** be bad for **some** children.

211

Expert grammar

2 Join ideas with noun phrases.
Sales rose ~~because~~ *the population* ~~has got~~ *richer* ~~and has~~ *more money to spend.*
Sales rose **as a result of** *a richer population with more money to spend.*

3 Use the passive.
~~Somebody transports~~ *the coffee beans to the roasting room.*
The coffee beans **are transported** *to the roasting room.*

4 Use reduced relative clauses.
They introduced a new advert, ~~which was~~ *shown at key times.*
They introduced a new advert shown at key times.

5 Use vocabulary from the Academic Word List and Academic Collocations List.
People ~~really liked~~ *the product* ~~because it~~ ~~was exactly what they wanted.~~
The product was **widely accepted as** *it* **met all their expectations**.

9

Articles (page 141)

A *a/an*

1 We use *a/an* before a single, countable noun that we talk about for the first time. The speaker and listener do not share any knowledge of this noun.
There's **a** *football match on tonight.*
Is there **an** *event on at the social club next week?*

2 We use *a/an* before a noun that describes something which is just one of many in a group.
There is **a** *theory about humans and their ability to run.*
A scientist has carried out **an** *interesting experiment.*

B *the*

1 We use *the* before a single, countable noun that we have mentioned before.
There's **a** *football match on tonight. It's* **the** *match between the two Manchester clubs.*
Is there **an** *event on at the social club next week?* **The** *events there are usually fun.*

2 We use *the* before uncountable nouns or plural nouns that refer to a specific thing. In this situation, the two people speaking have a shared knowledge of the thing. Compare:
The professor's giving **a** *lecture next Thursday.* (The listener does not know about this lecture. It is new information.)
The professor's giving **the** *lecture next Thursday.* (The listener knows about the lecture. The new information is the date.)

C No article

1 We use no article before uncountable and abstract nouns when we are talking about something in general, not something specific.
Money *in sport is far too high.*
Sports people need **power** *and* **determination** *to succeed.*

2 We use no article before plural countable nouns when we make a generalisation.
Marathon runners *are fitter than most* **footballers**.
Sports coaches *are necessary to create* **winners**.

3 We use no article before countries, cities, towns, continents, languages and names.
Alex *has moved to* **Venice** *in* **Italy** *because he wants to learn* **Italian**.

Note
We use *the* before a small number of countries including *the USA, the UK* and *the UAE*.

Grammatical linkers (page 144)

We use *this, these, that, those* and *so* to link ideas.

A *this/these*

1 We use *this* to replace a singular noun.
There was an **increase** *in sales of umbrellas.* **This** *was largely due to the weather.*

2 We use *this* + synonym to repeat an idea.
Organisers **decided** *to hold the competition every two years, rather than every year.* **This change** *was made to give competitors more time to prepare.*

3 We use *these* to replace a plural noun.
There were a lot of **complaints** *after the competition. Most of* **these** *related to the decision to cancel the final race.*

4 We use *these* + synonym to repeat an idea.
The number of **teenagers** *in the city who regularly did sports decreased. The closure of the main sports centre was the main reason reported by* **these young people**.

B *that/those*

We use *that* to replace a singular noun and *those* to replace a plural noun only if:

they are very distant in time or space.
The closest star to our system is **Proxima Centauri**, *which is 4.2 light years away.* **That star** *will not always be the closest, though.*
Agriculture began **in prehistoric times**. *At* **that time**, *farming was only practised in parts of India and Egypt.*

they follow a comparison form or *the same as*.
Nurses' **salaries** *increased more slowly than* **those** *in other employment groups.*
The **statistics** *for women in their 60s were the same as for* **those** *in their 20s.*

C *those who*

We use *those who* to replace *people who*.
Many **people** were happy with the results. **Those who** were not were largely from coastal areas.
Over 10,000 **women** agreed to take part in the survey. They were separated into **those who** were in full-time work and **those who** were not.

D *so*

We use *do so* in place of *do it*.
A large number of people **chose to stay**. Those who **did so** listed worries about the security of their home as the main reason.
The researchers **decided to study** a much smaller group. By **doing so**, they were able to collect much more detailed information about those individuals.

E Other structures to link ideas grammatically

1 *There was a large amount of flooding in the capital city. However,* **similar situations** *were reported across the country.* (introduces similar results in another place)

2 *The research gave evidence of* **what** *many people already thought: the stomach is strongly affected by emotions.* (introduces an idea about something that was not known or not certain)

3 *They built the transport system in 1980. Since* **then***, the population has increased considerably.* (to refer to a time you have mentioned)

4 *They could either make the older building larger or take it down and create a completely new building. Of the two solutions,* **the former** *seems more practical than* **the latter***.* (*the former* = the first of two people or things you have mentioned; *the latter* = the second of two people or things you have mentioned)

10

Present perfect and past simple (page 157)

A Past simple

See page 205 for the general rules for the past simple.

B Present perfect

1 We use the present perfect to talk about an action that started and finished in the past but the time is indefinite (unknown or not important). When we use the present perfect in this way, we are usually talking about an action that happened at some time in our lives.
Have you ever **taken** an evening course?
I'**ve read** this article.

2 We use the present perfect to talk about an action that started in the past but is not finished and is continuing now. We usually use *for* or *since*. *For* describes the length of the action. *Since* describes the starting point of the action.
We'**ve known** each other **since** 2010.
This course **has been available for** six months.

3 We use the present perfect to talk about repeated actions which have continued from a past time to the present time.
The Centre **has carried out** several studies.
I'**ve read** this page twice and I still don't understand it.

4 Time expressions commonly used with the present perfect are *already, ever, just, not yet, recently, so far, until now, up to now, yet*.

5 We form the present perfect as follows:
Positive: subject + *have/has* + past participle
Negative: subject + *haven't/hasn't* + past participle
Question: *have/has* + subject + past participle

Reported speech (page 160)

When we report what someone else said, we make changes to the verb tenses, pronouns and references to time and place, in order to be clear.

A Tense changes

1 We change the tenses by 'backshifting' one step further back in the past.
'Advertising **will change** *considerably in the future.'*
The speaker said that advertising **would change** *considerably in the future.*

The tenses change as follows:

Direct speech	Reported speech
present simple	past simple
past simple	past perfect
present perfect	past perfect
will	would
can	could
might	might

He said, 'It's an important exam.'
He said it **was** *an important exam.*

She said, 'I **read** *an interesting article on commercials.'*
*She told us that she'***d read** *an interesting article on commercials.*

2 We do not backshift:
when the reporting verb is in the present:
'Direct advertising to children **is** *wrong.'*
She **says** *that direct advertising to children* **is** *wrong.*

Expert grammar

with the past perfect and modal verbs:
'We **had done** a lot of research before we **launched** the product.'
They said they **had done** a lot of research before they **launched** the product.

'Companies **must not tell** lies in adverts.'
She said companies **must not tell** lies in adverts.

3 We can choose whether to backshift or not if the present and future events are still true.
'Our medicine **will make** you feel better.'
They said their medicine **will make** you feel better.

B Changes in pronouns and adverbs

When we report what someone else said in a different time and place, we have to change the pronouns and adverbs to be clear.

'Advertising companies are following my online spending habits **now**.'
He said that advertising companies were following his online spending habits **then**.

'The meeting will be in **this** room **tomorrow**.'
She said the meeting would be in **that** room **the next day**.

C Using reporting verbs

We can report what people say by using different reporting verbs. Reporting verbs follow different patterns.

1 **verb + *that* clause**
   e.g. *admit, agree, announce, argue, claim, complain, explain, hope, mention, recommend, report, request, suggest, warn*
   'We are going to launch our new product next week.'
   They **announced that** they were going to launch their new product **the following week.**

2 **verb + *to*-infinitive**
   e.g. *agree, ask, decide, expect, hope, intend, refuse*
   They **agreed to allow** us to use their facilities.
   We **decided to hold** the lecture another day.

3 **verb + object + *to*-infinitive**
   e.g. *advise, ask, expect, persuade, tell*
   She **told us to pay** no attention to the advert.
   He **advised them to study** harder.

4 **verb + *-ing* form**
   e.g. *admit, deny, mention, report, suggest*
   He **suggested reading** a particular book on the subject.
   They **admitted making** a mistake.

214

Pearson Education Limited
Edinburgh Gate
Harlow
Essex CM20 2JE
England
and Associated Companies throughout the world.

www.pearsonELT.com

© Pearson Education Limited 2014

The right of Clare Walsh and Lindsay Warwick to be identified as authors of this Work has been asserted by them in accordance with the Copyright, Designs and Patents Act 1988.

All rights reserved; no part of this publication may be reproduced, stored in a retrieval system, or transmitted in any form or by any means, electronic, mechanical, photocopying, recording, or otherwise without the prior written permission of the Publishers

First published 2014

ISBN: 978-1-4479-7500-7

Set in Mundo Sans
Printed and bound by CPI Group (UK) Ltd

Acknowledgements
The publishers and authors would like to thank the following people and institutions for their feedback and comments during the development of the material: Fiona Aish, Steve Baxter, Victoria McKay and staff (Kaplan), Dorothy Adams Metaxopoulou, Zhang (Jamie) Min

Author Acknowledgements
The authors would like to thank all the team at Pearson for their hard work and dedication, and Cesar, Elliot and Alex for their continued love and understanding. They would like to give special thanks to their parents Howard and Evelyn Walsh, and Mal and David Warwick for their kind support while writing this book and for the many years prior to that.

We are grateful to the following for permission to reproduce copyright material:

Figures
Figure on page 147 from http://www.guardian.co.uk/education/2010/aug/24/gcse-results-2010-coursework Guardian, Jeevan Vasagar, 24 August 2010, Guardian News and Media Ltd

Text
Extract on page 8 adapted from http://www.education.com/reference/article/motivation-affects-learning-behaviour/, Education.com / Excerpt from Educational Psychology Developing Learners, by J.E. Ormrod, 2008 edition, Pearson pp384–386, ORMROD JEANNE ELLIS, EDUCATIONAL PSYCHOLOGY: DEVELOPING LEARNERS, 6th Ed., ©2008, pp.384–386. Reprinted and Electronically reproduced by permission of Pearson Education, Inc., Upper Saddle River, New Jersey.; Extract on page 9 adapted from http://www.buzzle.com/articles/homeschooling-statistics.html, Kundan Pandey / Buzzle.com; Article on page 14 adapted from http://bits.blogs.nytimes.com/2009/08/19/study-finds-that-online-education-beats-the-classroom/, NY Times, Steve Lohr, August 19 2009; Article on page 16 adapted from http://knowledge.wharton.upenn.edu/article.cfm?articleid=1531, The Wharton School University of Pennsylvania 28 July, 2006; Extract on page 15 adapted from http://www.youtube.com/watch?v=uLG9jwgAios, WorldatWorkTV 5 September 2012, WorldatWork ; Box on page 18 adapted from http://www.newstatesman.com/martha-gill/2012/11/why-brain-teasers-dont-work, New Statesman 5th November 2012; Article on page 28 adapted from http://www.istc.cnr.it/question/why-do-we-feel-surprise, Institute of Cognitive Sciences and Technologies, Cristiano Castelfranchi,; Article on page 38 adapted from Permissions: http://hbr.org/2012/01/the-science-behind-the-smile/ar/1, From 'The Science Behind the Smile' by Daniel Gilbert and Gardiner Morse. Harvard Business Review, January 2012; Article on pages 24-25 adapted from http://scienceline.org/2006/10/ask-driscoll-tears/ Accessed 13 August 2012, Emily V Driscoll / Scienceline; Article on page 35 adapted from http://bigthink.com/ideas/16660, Big Think, Tal Ben-Shahar, Accessed 2 October 2012, Dr Tal Ben-Shahar; Article on page 41 adapted from http://io9.com/5950271/could-artificial-trees-solve-the-global-warming-crisis, Goldsmith's University of London, December 11th 2011, George Dvorsky; Article on page 50 adapted from http://www.nypost.com/p/news/opinion/opedcolumnists/why_we_love_our_pets_too_much_rOY6LJROEKBQ09XkTwkjFl, New York Post, Hal Herzog, 5 September 2010; Quote on page 55 from http://www.brainyquote.com/quotes/quotes/j/jackwelch163678.html#MUyp87Vw5hFX0Jbg.99, Jack Welch, Jack F Welch Former CEO General Electric; Article on page 73 adapted from http://www.psychologytoday.com/articles/201204/emotion-what-does-disgust-sound, Psychologytoday.com, Becca Weinstein ,30 April 2012; Article on page 82 adapted from http://www.health24.com/news/Eye_vision/1-909,75830.asp, Health First ,August 1 2012, Robert Perkins / USC University; Article on page 111 adapted from http://www-psych.stanford.edu/~lera/psych115s/notes/lecture11/, Professor Lera Boroditsky; Article on page 134 adapted from http://www.guardian.co.uk/science/2013/jan/27/20-human-body-facts-science, The Guardian, Guardian News and Media Ltd 2013; Article on page 129 adapted from *Sociology ISBN-13: 978-0745643588*, sixth, Polity Press (Giddens, A) p.391, Polity Press; Article on page 150 adapted from Why Failure Drives Innovation, *STANFORD GRADUATE SCHOOL OF BUSINESS* (Shivon), https://www.gsb.stanford.edu/news/research/ShivonFailureandInnovation.html, With kind permission of Professor Baba Shiv; Quote on page 135 from Michael Jordan http://www.brainyquote.com/quotes/authors/m/michael_jordan.html Brainyquotes.com, Accessed 15 December 2012, Michael Jordan. (n.d.). BrainyQuote.com. Retrieved December 15, 2012, from BrainyQuote.com Web site: http://www.brainyquote.com/quotes/quotes/m/michaeljor127660.html ; Article on page 154 adapted from http://www.clearlycultural.com/geert-hofstede-cultural-dimensions/power-distance-index/, Clearly Cultural,21 April 2009; Extract on page 157 adapted from http://www.thetimes.co.uk/tto/science/psychology/article3688772.ece; Article on page 162 adapted from http://www.miletbaker.com/2011/06/13/notes-on-how-art-made-the-world-art-of-persuasion/#.UM8qR-Rg-So, 13th June 2011 Jon Baker, Jon Milet Baker

In some instances we have been unable to trace the owners of copyright material and we would appreciate any information that would enable us to do so.

Picture Credits
The publisher would like to thank the following for their kind permission to reproduce their photographs:

(Key: b-bottom; c-centre; l-left; r-right; t-top)

akg-images Ltd: 97, De Agostini Pict.Lib. 193, Jim West 57; **Alamy Images:** Anatolii Babii 151br, Best View Stock 39br, Blend Images 148, Caro 66, Disability Images 121, i love images / business office 21, Image Source 27, Image Source Plus 7l, Johner Images 111, Juniors Bildarchiv GmbH 52, Marcus Quartly 44, Studio-FI Creative 15, Kiyoshi Takahase Segundo 79, Tetra Images 69, VisualJapan 108, Kevin Wheal 130, David White 47; **Bridgeman Art Library Ltd:** Museo Archeologico Nazionale, Naples, Italy / Giraudon 162, The Art Institute of Chicago, IL, USA 82; **Corbis:** 146t, Hal Beral 40, Demetrio Carrasco / JAI 39tr, Frantzesco Kangaris / epa 55c, Rainer Holz 95, Hamad I Mohammed / Reuters 194, Imaginechina 119l, JLP / Jose Luis Pelaez 8, Juice Images 164, Evertt Kennedy Brown / epa 124t, KidStock / Blend Images 30, KidStock / Blend Images 30, Oliver Lucanus / Foto Natura / Minden Pictures 51, Peter M. Fisher 20, Leo Mason 135r, Lucy Nicholson / Reuters 93, Ocean 36r, George Steinmetz 119r, 131, Topic Photo Agency 88l; **DK Images:** Demetrio Carrasco 91, StockTrek. Photodisc 98, Christine Webb 87r; **FLPA Images of Nature:** Neil Bowman 62, Rinie Van Meurs / FN / Minden 39bl; **Fotolia.com:** Africa Studio 103tl, Aaron Amat 78, diego cervo 65, crimson 104l, Eisenhans 113, Elnur 17, Petro Feketa 35, lassedesignen 71b, leungchopan 87l, Dudarev Mikhail 103b, Sergey Nivens 36l, pharadorn 114, Photobank kiev 46, pitakire 43, Daniel Prudek 49, sakkmesterke 151t, U.P.images 75, Vitas 92, Guido Vrola 71tl, Monika Wisniewska 104r, yanlev 136, Mara Zemgaliete 116; **Getty Images:** AFP 56, 137, Daniel Allan 60, Robert Churchill 55l, Jon Feingersh 12, FilmMagic 28, Hulton Archive 72t, Jeff J Mitchell 139, Adam Jacobs 72b, Sungjin Kim 89, Andersen Ross 99, Justin Sullivan 88r, TommL 155; **John Foxx Images:** Imagestate 23tc; **PhotoDisc:** Alan D. Carey 48; **Photoshot Holdings Limited:** Oceans Image 39tc, Adam Pacitti 151bl, Xinhua 39tl; **Press Association Images:** Bikas Das / AP 135c, Ton Koene / DPA 55r, Santiago Lyon / AP 24, Khin Maung Win / AP 135l; **Reuters:** Mike Hutchings 90, Kim Kyung-Hoon 123, Stringer China 59, Chris Wattie 142; **Rex Features:** Paul Brown 94, Masatoshi Okauchi 124b, Solent News 159; **Shutterstock.com:** bonga1965 191bl, Franck Boston 107, Jacek Chabraszewski 138, Andrew Chin 71tr, Sarah Clark 105, Creativa 143, Chepko Danil Vitalevich 25, Emelyanov 14, Olesya Feketa 117, glenda 23tr, gosphotodesign 146b, Nikola Kikovic 23bl, lavitrei 154, Lightspring 127, Maridav 140, Mmaxer 100, Tyler Olson 192, Julia Pivovarova 34, ra2studio 126, Federico Rostagno 110, Tursunbaev Ruslan 134, Igor Stevanovic 84, Jason Stitt 23tl, 23bc, Andrey Tiyk 54, Twonix Studio 191c, Valua Vitaly 132, vvoe 191tr, Bogdan Wankowicz 103r, YanLev 23br; **SuperStock:** TAO Images 63; **The Kobal Collection:** United Artists 76; **TopFoto:** Topham Picturepoint 11; **www.CartoonStock.com:** Ferdie Aberin / fabn16 156, Aaron Bacall / aban1702 7r, Gary Cook / gckn310 158, Ralph Hagen / rhan977 18, Royston-Robertson / rron816 129, Bradford Veley / bven368 31

All other images © Pearson Education

Every effort has been made to trace the copyright holders and we apologise in advance for any unintentional omissions. We would be pleased to insert the appropriate acknowledgement in any subsequent edition of this publication.

Illustrated by David Semple